W. K. Clifford and "The E

W. K. Clifford and "The Ethics of Belief"

By

Timothy J. Madigan

CAMBRIDGE
SCHOLARS
PUBLISHING

W. K. Clifford and "The Ethics of Belief", by Timothy J. Madigan

This book first published 2009. The present binding first published 2010.

Cambridge Scholars Publishing

12 Back Chapman Street, Newcastle upon Tyne, NE6 2XX, UK

British Library Cataloguing in Publication Data
A catalogue record for this book is available from the British Library

Copyright © 2010 by Timothy J. Madigan

All rights for this book reserved. No part of this book may be reproduced, stored in a retrieval system, or transmitted, in any form or by any means, electronic, mechanical, photocopying, recording or otherwise, without the prior permission of the copyright owner.

ISBN (10): 1-4438-1648-5, ISBN (13): 978-1-4438-1648-9

To Joe and Barbara Levee and Dick and Lois Siggelkow, for their constant encouragement and moral support. They believed beyond all evidence that I would complete this!

TABLE OF CONTENTS

Acknowledgements ix

Introduction 1

Chapter One 7
The Ethics of Belief and the Victorian Crisis of Faith

Chapter Two 27
W. K. Clifford: Life and Philosophy

Chapter Three 73
An Analysis of "The Ethics of Belief"

Chapter Four 85
Clifford's Contemporary Critics

Chapter Five 133
Clifford's Modern Critics

Chapter Six 165
The Virtues of "The Ethics of Belief"

Bibliography 187

Index 199

ACKNOWLEDGEMENTS

This work began as a doctoral dissertation at the State University of New York at Buffalo, written under the guidance of Peter H. Hare, John Corcoran, and Kenneth Barber. My outside reader was Richard Taylor, from the University of Rochester, with whom I enjoyed many fascinating discussions before his untimely death. I am indebted to all of these fine philosophers, but most especially to Professor Hare, who chaired the dissertation committee and who first suggested to me that I consider writing a monograph on W. K. Clifford's seminal essay "The Ethics of Belief." Professor Hare was an inspiration to me, and I was looking forward to giving him a copy of this book. Sadly, he died during the very week that I sent it to the publisher.

I would also like to thank my good friends Lois and Richard Siggelkow and Barbara and Joseph Levee for their encouragement and support during the years that I was engaged in researching, writing and revising this work. Their belief in me most definitely at times went well beyond the evidence, but I think even Clifford would have found this a moral rather than immoral state of affairs. Thanks are also due to Norman Bacrac, Monty Chisholm, Tim Delaney, David Hestenes, Robert Holmes, Jennifer Jeynes, Paul Kurtz, Rick Lewis, Sherrie Lyons, Ken and Molleen Matsumura, Warren Allen Smith, Anja Steinbauer, Tim Wilder, the late Paul Edwards and all the many other individuals in the United States and the United Kingdom with whom I have discussed Clifford's life and work these past few years. I would particularly like to thank my colleagues in the Department of Philosophy at St. John Fisher College for the excellent discussions I have had with them on the never-ending topic of the Ethics of Belief: Robert Brimlow, Joseph Lanzalaco, Barb Lowe, Charles Natoli and David White.

Finally, I would like to give thanks to the memory of W. K. Clifford himself. I was delighted to learn that that are still many people interested in both his mathematical and his philosophical writings. Thanks to his rare abilities to make abstruse concepts accessible and his daring speculations on all manner of topics, he continues to live on in the only way imaginable for such a hardcore materialist – through his influence.

Introduction

William Kingdon Clifford's essay "The Ethics of Belief" was originally delivered on April 11, 1876, to the learned debate organization the Metaphysical Society. It has never since ceased to be a focal point of discussion for individuals interested in the overlap between the fields of epistemology and ethics.

The following study will examine "The Ethics of Belief" and its continuing relevance to epistemological and ethical discussions. First, the essay will be placed in its historical context, focusing on the origins of the "ethics of belief" discussion in the English empirical tradition. The so-called Victorian Crisis of Faith, and the origins of the Metaphysical Society, will also be discussed. Second, the life and philosophical teachings of W. K. Clifford himself will be summarized. Third, a detailed analysis of his essay "The Ethics of Belief" will be given. The fourth chapter will present a representative perspective on the ways in which several of Clifford's contemporaries responded to its chief points. The ways in which modern-day philosophers have continued to refer to, and critique, Clifford's evidentialism will then be examined in chapter five. Finally, chapter six will present a defense of "The Ethics of Belief" from a virtue-theory approach which utilizes an "as if" methodology to encourage intellectual inquiry and communal harmony. A synopsis of each chapter follows.

Chapter One: The Ethics of Belief and the Victorian Crisis of Faith

The first part of this chapter will focus on the influences of Locke, Hume, and Mill on "the Ethics of Belief" debate in general, and on Clifford in particular.

The so-called Victorian Crisis of Faith will be discussed in the second part of this chapter. Clifford most definitely underwent such a crisis. The Metaphysical Society, which he joined as an active participant, was founded in 1869 by Sir James Knowles because of his concern that a growing sense of disbelief among the educated elite would have a deleterious impact on the morals of general society. Most of the members of the Society, whatever their personal metaphysical views, shared this concern, and the discussions tended to address the main challenges to traditional beliefs found in physics, biology, mathematics, and logic. It is within such a context that Clifford presented his talk "The Ethics of Belief".

Chapter Two: W. K. Clifford: Life and Philosophy

This chapter will trace Clifford's intellectual development. He shared many of the virtues of the Victorian era: a strong sense of duty, a melioristic attitude, and an emphasis on hard work.

Clifford was one of the first persons to discuss the ethical implications of Darwin's work, and as a mathematician he was among the first to appreciate the work being done by Lobachevski and Riemann in non-Euclidean geometry. He was also impressed by the systematic philosophy of Herbert Spencer, although he found it to be overly speculative. It was Clifford's expressed desire to develop a new system of ethics, combining the exactness of utilitarianism with the evolutionary perspective of Darwinism. He had hoped to arrange all of his ethical writings in a systematic treatise, but unfortunately he died before completing this project. His friends Leslie Stephen and Frederick Pollock arranged for the posthumous publication of his various lectures and essays, including "The Ethics of Belief". A knowledge of Clifford's other writings offers a better understanding of "The Ethics of Belief". Like that essay, most of these were originally delivered as public lectures, or published in learned journals meant to reach a nonacademic audience. They demonstrate his urgent desire to promulgate an ethics that is in harmony with the latest scientific findings of his time.

The influence which Clifford had on such areas as mathematics, psychology, and the social sciences in general will also be examined, to show the connection all of these had with his philosophical writings, most particularly "The Ethics of Belief".

Chapter Three: An Analysis of "The Ethics of Belief"

Clifford begins his essay with a description of a shipowner who allows a vessel which was badly in need of repairs to go out to sea. He dismisses from his mind any doubts as to the ship's seaworthiness. The ship, laden with passengers, goes down in mid-ocean, killing all aboard. Clifford holds that the owner is culpable for their deaths, because he had no right to believe on such evidence as was before him that the ship could make the journey. He adds that even if the ship *had* made it safely to shore, the owner would still be guilty. This might lead one to assume that Clifford's argument for evidentialism is essentially deontological - one has a duty to apportion one's belief to the evidence, regardless of the consequences. However, later in the essay, he pursues a more teleological line of argument. He declares that believing is not a private matter. Believing for unworthy reasons not only weakens a person's powers of self-control, it also adversely affects one's community of inquirers. If this were to continue, then humankind itself would sink back into savagery.

Another element explored is the religious language of the essay. This is not wholly ironic. Clifford recognized that such language would resonate with his readers, who had been raised in religious environments. In a sense, he sought to use traditional language as a means of getting people to accept untraditional, even iconoclastic, ideas.

Chapter Four: Clifford's Contemporary Critics

This chapter will summarize the immediate reaction to "The Ethics of Belief" from such Metaphysical Society members as R. H. Hutton, T. H. Huxley, Leslie Stephen and W. G. Ward, and from nonmembers such as Matthew Arnold. The views toward "The Ethics of Belief" of two great philosophical contemporaries - William James and Charles S. Peirce - will then be examined in detail.

Although they were unaware of each other's writings, there are many similarities between the writings of Clifford and Friedrich Nietzsche. These will be looked at in the following section.

Karl Pearson was Clifford's successor as professor of applied mathematics at University College, London, and was in many ways his intellectual successor. This chapter will discuss how Pearson was influenced by Clifford's writings.

The final figure to be discussed was not technically a contemporary of Clifford's, for he was only five years old at the time of Clifford's death. Nonetheless, he shared many of his values, and Clifford was an influence on his own decision to become a mathematician and philosopher. Bertrand Russell (1872-1970) can be considered to be the Last Victorian. He continued to espouse a Cliffordian ethical view well into the twentieth century.

Chapter Five: Clifford's Modern Critics

A brief overview will be given of the ways in which such modern figures as C. S. Lewis, Walter Kaufmann, J. L. Mackie, and Richard Double have continued to explore the Clifford/James debate.

In recent years, the focus of attention has tended to shift to Clifford's epistemic views. The second part of this chapter will therefore examine how this has been addressed by such philosophers as Michael Martin, Peter van Inwagen, and Alvin Plantinga.

Other philosophers have addressed Clifford's ethical views. A brief examination of the writings of Richard Gale and Richard Rorty on this aspect of Clifford will follow.

This chapter will end with a look at three philosophers who have examined the interconnection between Clifford's epistemic and ethical arguments: Susan Haack, Anthony Quinton, and Lorraine Code.

Chapter Six: The Virtues of "The Ethics of Belief"

In the final chapter, I will discuss my own views on the relevance of Clifford's "Ethics of Belief", and attempt to defend it from a virtue ethics perspective. The concluding chapter will propose that Clifford's own ethics of belief can be viewed as an "as if" position for moral betterment and epistemic perfection.

I will argue that Clifford's evidentialism is a type of creative fiction. Even if Clifford did not actually believe that all people, regardless of their station, could live up to the ideal he set, he felt that by *assuming* they could do so one showed them respect, and could help to motivate them to fulfill whatever intellectual capacities they did in fact possess. Clifford, particularly in his discussions of metaphysics, was willing to use an "as if" approach when it came to issues like the uniformity of nature, and it is not inconsistent to think that this approach could also pertain to his ethical writings.

The "as if" attitude can best explain why "The Ethics of Belief" is still relevant, and still worth discussing, even if its ethical and epistemological assumptions are no longer tenable. Such an approach is in accord with a virtue ethics. Clifford not only hoped to combat the growth of nihilism which he felt might spring from the growing dissatisfaction with theologically grounded ethics, but also welcomed the challenge. He hoped to foster a new, more scientifically grounded ethics which could unify all humankind. Without taking this aspiration into account, it is difficult to understand what Clifford was attempting to achieve in "The Ethics of Belief".

CHAPTER ONE

THE ETHICS OF BELIEF
AND THE VICTORIAN CRISIS OF FAITH

I. Introduction

"It is wrong always, everywhere, and for any one, to believe anything upon insufficient evidence."[1] So wrote William Kingdon Clifford (1845-1879) in his 1876 essay, "The Ethics of Belief". Clifford was 31 years old when he delivered his lecture to the exclusive debating group called the Metaphysical Society, the members of which met in London nine times a year to discuss issues pertaining to philosophical ideas and religious beliefs. He was at the time Professor of Applied Mathematics at University College, London.

Clifford, who found attending the Society's meetings and participating in its often heated discussions to be one of the chief pleasures of his life, delivered a total of three papers before the Society, whose members included such notables as future English Prime Minister Arthur James Balfour, current English Prime Minister William Gladstone, biologist Thomas Henry Huxley, theologian F. D. Maurice, Catholic Archbishop Henry Edward Manning and Alfred Lord Tennyson, the Poet Laureate. But it is "The Ethics of Belief" which generated the most controversy of all his three talks, and it remains his best known work. Even today, the essay is often reprinted in philosophy of religion and introduction to philosophy textbooks.

Unfortunately, such textbooks give little if any background information on Clifford which would help to enlighten the reader as to why he might have held such a strong position regarding the duty to apportion one's beliefs to sufficient evidence. Clifford's position is, at times, set up as a "straw man" argument. For instance, William Gale writes: ". . . Clifford

---

1 W. K. Clifford, "The Ethics of Belief" in *Lectures and Essays, Vol. II.* (London: Macmillan, 1879), 186.

has greatly exaggerated the deleterious consequences of allowing ourselves even a single epistemically unwarranted belief, however trivial and disconnected from the workaday world."[2] Anthologies which reprint "The Ethics of Belief" quite often couple it with William James' "The Will to Believe" (1897), which was written in part to respond to (using James' own description of him) Clifford's "robustious" evidentialism.

And yet, this *"enfant terrible"*, as James affectionately referred to him, still has relevance to the present day. Even those who strongly disagree with his epistemological views often express admiration for him. In his 1996 book *Metaphilosophy and Free Will,* the philosopher Richard Double writes: "For me, the persona of W. K. Clifford I derived from reading 'The Ethics of Belief' was very moving, although I think Clifford's argument is hyperbolic and philosophically weak."[3] George Levine, Professor of English at Rutgers University, goes so far as to make allowances for Clifford's hyperbole, and that of such other members of the Metaphysical Society as Thomas Huxley and Leslie Stephen, stating that "the naturalists' pugnacity was not unreasonable in a society that was only slowly and reluctantly allowing them serious professional status . . ."[4] Intellectuals in those days were still expected to accept, and indeed to publicly profess belief in, the tenets of the Anglican faith if they expected to be gainfully employed in any academic position. Criticizing religious dogmas was not simply a matter of demonstrating one's own personal convictions – it was also a political maneuver done in an attempt to get the Church to relinquish its hold on the scientific professions.

Placing "The Ethics of Belief", then, in its historical context, and attempting to understand just what it was that the naturalists themselves were advocating, will help us to see why Clifford engaged in such hyperbole, and why a distinguished mathematician and logician made assertions which he himself must have known to be exaggerations.

In his own study of the Victorian time period, the Swedish intellectual historian Stefan Andersson asserts: "Although Clifford is briefly discussed in studies on agnosticism and histories of mathematics, no monographs, as far as I have been able to find out, have been written about him as a critic

---

2 William Gale, *On the Nature and Existence of God* (New York: Cambridge University Press, 1993), 356.
3 Richard Double, *Metaphilosophy and Free Will* (New York: Oxford University Press, 1996), 54.
4 George Levine, "Scientific Discourse as an Alternative to Faith" in *Victorian Faith in Crisis*, edited by Richard J. Helmstadter and Bernard Lightman (Stanford, California: Stanford University Press, 1990), 231.

of religion and ethics, as a philosopher of science and as a mathematician."[5] It is interesting to note that, like many of his fellow Victorians, Clifford engaged in numerous personal activities, all done to enlighten his fellow citizens to the many exciting intellectual revolutions occurring in such fields as biblical history, biology, geometry, and politics (Clifford, for instance, was an ardent admirer of the Italian revolutionary Giuseppe Mazzini, who helped to unify the Italian states by challenging the temporal holdings of the Catholic Church). He was somehow able to balance his meticulous work in mathematics with an almost full-time career as a polemicist against what he felt to be the pernicious influence of sloppy thinking.

II. The Roots of the Victorian Crisis of Faith

To best grasp why such a careful scholar as Clifford would deliver such a pugnacious address as "The Ethics of Belief", one needs to place him within the context of his time. One of the reasons Clifford's essay had such power is due to its use of biblical and religious language - for instance, his assertion that to purposefully avoid examining one's beliefs constitutes one long "sin" against humankind. It seems rather strange that a forthright opponent of organized religion in general, and Christianity in particular, would use such terminology. However, if one looks at the audience to whom he was addressing "The Ethics of Belief", this becomes less paradoxical. "The Ethics of Belief" is in many ways a secular sermon, delivered to exhort individuals to live up to their highest epistemic abilities. It was Clifford's fear that a growing societal dissatisfaction with traditional theological arguments might lead to increasing laxity toward ethical obligations. This was a fear he shared with most of the members of the Metaphysical Society, who - regardless of their own worldviews - all tended to have experienced what has been called the Victorian Crisis of Faith. This was a growing feeling that the tried-and-true teachings of the Anglican religion, or indeed of any Christian religion, were no longer relevant to the contemporary world. There was a sense that the scientific perspective and traditional religious faith were becoming increasingly incompatible. Such a rift might well have consequences for the moral realm. How were people to live if they were no longer satisfied with the teachings of religion? What, if anything, could replace such time-honored views?

---

5 Stefan Andersson, *In Quest of Certainty* (Stockholm, Sweden: Almqvist & Wiksell International, 1994), 33.

Although these questions became of prime interest during the Victorian period, they were by no means new. They can in fact be traced to the earlier period of the English Civil war (1640-1660), when religious differences had great political repercussions. John Locke (1632-1704) was the first philosopher to issue what might be called an "evidentialist" challenge to religious believers, although as Nicholas Wolterstorff rightly points out, he did so "as a Christian who thought that he could meet the challenge."[6] Locke was critical of those he called *enthusiasts* - individuals who claimed to have received private revelations from God but who could offer no evidence other than their own claims to support these. He was not only troubled by the seeming irrationality of such claims; he also held that enthusiasm in this regard was anti-social. "Who can reasonably expect arguments and conviction from him in dealing with others," Locke wrote, "whose understanding is not accustomed to them in his dealing with himself?"[7] Locke held that only religious beliefs that could be supported by evidence were worthy of being held. He was confident that the doctrines of Christianity could be so supported - a view which Clifford would later strongly oppose.

Gerald McCarthy, in his introduction to the 1986 book *The Ethics of Belief Debate,* writes that a prime motivator in this quest for intellectual integrity was the new research program inaugurated by Francis Bacon in works such as *The Great Instauration,* the *Novum Organon,* and *The Advancement of Learning.* These books argued that human intellectual progress had been stymied for centuries by adherence to superstition, bad reasoning, and credulity. Experimental logic, properly used, would free the mind from its shackles and bring about an era of unprecedented progress. In this program, McCarthy argues, one can see the roots of the cognitive-ethical formula (namely, intellectual error begets moral evil) which would find further development in Locke's writings: "Such arguments for the connection between meliorism and scientific procedure recur frequently in the centuries that follow and . . . find their most explicit statement in Clifford's essay ['The Ethics of Belief']".[8]

---

6 Nicholas Wolterstorff, "The Migration of the Theistic Arguments: From Natural Theology to Evidentialist Apologetics," in *Rationality, Religious Belief, and Moral Commitment: New Essays in the Philosophy of Religion,* edited by Robert Audi and William J. Wainwright (Ithaca, New York: Cornell University Press, 1986), 39.
7 John Locke, *An Essay Concerning Human Understanding,* edited by Peter H. Nidditch (Oxford: Clarendon Press, 1975), 698.
8 Ibid., 5.

Another factor motivating Locke was the savage religious conflict which had followed from the Protestant Reformation, splitting most of Europe into warring camps. The rise of religious sects basing their beliefs primarily upon the fervency of their emotions was particularly evident in England after its Civil War. Locke was interested in finding a means to bind people together rather than seeing them further divide due to baseless enthusiasms.

"Thus," McCarthy writes, "Locke's attack on 'Enthusiasm' in the course of which he formulated the description of the 'lover of truth' that was to be so influential in the subsequent discussion of the 'Ethics of Belief' was not motivated exclusively by epistemological concerns."[9]

One key issue which arose in this discussion was whether or not it is possible to actually choose one's beliefs, or alter them at will. Unlike Locke, David Hume (1711-1776) raised serious questions about humans' ability to actually control their own beliefs. Most people, he argued, simply accept what they are told without much examination of whether these views can be supported by objective evidence. It is only a tiny minority which can even evaluate the reasonableness of such beliefs, let alone consciously alter them. Locke had given the following definition of belief: "The admitting or receiving [of] any proposition for true, upon arguments or proofs that are found to persuade us to receive it as true, without certain knowledge that it is so" (*Essay,* IV, xv, 3). John Passmore, in his 1976 essay "Hume and the Ethics of Belief", writes:

> Hume would object to this definition on three grounds: the first, that vague phrases like 'the admitting', 'the receiving' conceal the fact that we are not told in what *believing* consists as a psychological phenomenon; the second, that to define belief as admitting or receiving a proposition as true upon *arguments* or *proofs* wrongly suggests that our beliefs are all of them the conclusions of arguments; the third, that the phrase 'admitting or receiving' – 'receiving' has here the same force as in 'the Ambassador received the guests' – makes it appear that we believe as we do only after scrutiny, whereas in fact our beliefs are automatic responses to particular forms of experience.[10]

But Hume also had his own "ethics of belief." He made a distinction between the vulgar masses, who in general do not examine their beliefs,

---

9 Ibid., 8.
10 John A. Passmore, "Hume and the Ethics of Belief" in *David Hume - Bicentenary Papers,* edited by G. Morice (Edinburgh: Edinburgh University Press, 1977), 89.

and the wise, who as a result of experience have formed the habit of developing their critical faculties. Clifford would make no such distinction. For him, the duty to examine one's beliefs is the same for the intellectual in the ivory tower as it is for the simple tradesman drinking a beer in the alehouse. "No simplicity of mind," he was to write in "The Ethics of Belief", "no obscurity of station, can escape the universal duty of questioning all that we believe."[11] McCarthy notes that: "Interestingly, Hume's arguments influenced both sides of the 'Ethics of Belief' debate" in Victorian England.[12]

III. Mill

In his book *A History of Atheism in Great Britain,* David Berman claims that it was John Stuart Mill (1806-1873) who could be said to "inaugurate the ethics of belief - a merging of logic and morality."[13] Mill had argued that the onus of proof had passed from the unbeliever to the believer regarding the truths of religion. While Clifford shared this aspect of Mill's philosophy, he would nonetheless disagree with Mill's further assertion, in the latter's posthumously published *Three Essays on Religion,* that from the standpoint of rationality, the belief in an eternal life and the belief that there is no eternal life are on the same level, since each lacks sufficient evidence. Indeed, D. C. Somervell, in *English Thought in the Nineteenth Century,* writes the following about Mill's *Three Essays on Religion*:

> . . . when they were posthumously published they met with much disapproval among most of those who had accounted themselves his disciples; and indeed it is not hard to imagine what Bentham and James Mill would have thought of them. Not only does the apostle of rationalism recognize the "Utility of Religion" but he holds in the last essay (though not in its predecessor) that the best religion is one involving a Personal God.[14]

In addition, Mill argued that a hopeful disposition - believing something when there is insufficient evidence either for it or against it -

---

11 Clifford, Ibid., 181.
12 McCarthy, 12.
13 David Berman, *A History of Atheism in Britain: From Hobbes to Russell* (London: Routledge, 1988), 235.
14 D. C. Somervell, *English Thought in the Nineteenth Century* (New York: David McKay Company, 1965), 97.

can have a positive effect upon one's life. These were issues that William James would return to, in his own criticism of Clifford's ethics of belief.

Yet Somervell also points out the tremendous *personal* influence which Mill had on the times. "He did as much as any freethinker to persuade simple-minded religious people that it is possible to be both an atheist and a good man, and he did this more by his life than by his writings."[15] In his autobiography (which was also published posthumously), Mill described his unique upbringing. His father James Mill, a friend of the utilitarian philosopher Jeremy Bentham, decided to educate his son as soon after birth as possible, and to prepare him to become a public servant. Mill was raised without any indoctrination in religious belief, writing that "I looked upon the modern exactly as I did upon the ancient religion, as something which in no way concerned me."[16] Mill argued that those without religion had a moral obligation to make known the irrational bases of such religious beliefs:

> On religion in particular the time appears to me to have come, when it is the duty of all who being qualified in point of knowledge, have on mature consideration satisfied themselves that the current opinions are not only false but hurtful, to make their dissent known; at least, if they are among those whose station, or reputation, gives their opinion a chance of being attended to. Such an avowal would put an end, at once and for ever, to the vulgar prejudice, that what is called, very improperly, unbelief, is connected with any bad qualities either of mind or heart. The world would be astonished if it knew how great a proportion of its brightest ornaments – of those most distinguished even in popular estimation for wisdom and virtue – are complete sceptics in religion; many of them refraining from avowal, less from personal considerations, than from a conscientious, though now in my opinion a most mistaken apprehension lest by speaking out what would tend to weaken existing beliefs, and by consequence (as they suppose) existing restraints, they should do harm instead of good.[17]

In addition, Mill points out in his "Utility of Religion" (1874) that the very notion of religion having a pragmatic justification would not have even arisen if the arguments for its *truth* had not first been found wanting. Utility is an inferior ground of defense, and for unbelievers in particular it means advocating a well-meant hypocrisy. He calls this a kind of moral bribery, in which those who find the evidence for religious beliefs to be

---

15 Ibid.
16 John Stuart Mill, *Autobiography,* edited by Jack Stillinger (Boston: Houghton Mifflin, 1969), 28.
17 Ibid., 28-29.

less than sufficient are urged to quiet their doubts so as to avoid doing irreparable damage to humankind. Mill wonders whether humankind might not be more damaged by such suppression of doubts – a theme which Clifford would explore in great detail in "The Ethics of Belief".

Yet Mill allowed that religion could be morally useful even if intellectually unsustainable, and that to deny this would be itself a form of prejudice. It is here that he comes closest to the later arguments of William James and other advocates of the "Will to Believe". Interestingly enough, Mill did not consider himself to be an atheist, and had qualms about those who made it their personal task to show the flaws in religious arguments in-and-of-themselves. He therefore distanced himself from the freethought community of his time, and such champions of aggressive agnosticism as Clifford.

Mill was a prominent figure in the so-called Victorian Crisis of Faith, although he was one of the few figures who did not personally seem to have experienced such a crisis. As Richard Taylor writes in his introduction to Mill's last work, *Theism* (1874):

> John Stuart Mill (1806-1873) was virtually unique in his generation, and would be hardly less so in ours, in having passed to maturity with no deliberately inculcated religious influences, the remarkable education he received from his father simply omitting both religious and anti-religious instruction altogether. He thus, unlike many distinguished men of his day, never lost his religion, simply because he had none to lose, and he was able, in his writings, to view the Christianity of his contemporaries in much the same detached way in which we consider the religious and moral concepts of antiquity, with a disposition neither to defend nor to attack them, but simply to consider them on their own merits, in the light of such knowledge as we have from experience, science and philosophy, and without any pretensions to special revelations from the Almighty.[18]

It is this lack of deep feeling toward metaphysics of any sort which perhaps led to Mill's "a plague on both your houses" attitude toward religionists and freethinkers, and which led him to refuse membership in the Metaphysical Society upon its formation in 1869.

---

18 Richard Taylor, editor's introduction, John Stuart Mill, *Theism* (New York: Bobbs-Merrill, 1957), vii.

IV. Evolution and the Crisis of Faith

By the middle of the nineteenth century, the most cherished Christian beliefs regarding the origin of humankind, the authenticity of the Bible, and the nature of God, had been called into question. As James C. Livingston writes in *The Ethics of Belief: An Essay on the Victorian Religious Conscience*: "The Victorian Era was an age of faith. It was also the time when that faith underwent a series of severe crises . . . The Victorian conscience was torn between two moral commitments: viz., to a scrupulous intellectual honesty and the demand for a forthright assent to the creeds and formularies of the Church of England."[19] Clifford, as we shall see, most definitely underwent such a crisis of faith.

The certainties that had shored up the social, economic and political – as well as the religious – foundations of society were being called into question. In *The Victorian Frame of Mind,* Walter E. Houghton describes the radical changes that were occurring:

> The fact is, while moral values were firm until about 1870, all intellectual theories, including those of morality, were insecure. . . . It was not only in religion that one faced a series of alternatives: is there a God or is there not, and if so, is he a person or an impersonal force? Is there a heaven and a hell? Or a heaven but no hell? or neither? If there *is* a true religion, is it Theism or Christianity? And what is Christianity? Roman Catholicism or Protestantism? Is it Church or Chapel? High Church? Broad Church? Low Church? Similar questions, if not so pressing or so widespread, invaded ethical theory and the conception of man: have we free-will or are we human automatons? And if we have the power of moral choice, what is its basis? A God-given voice of conscience? Or a rational calculation deciding which of two actions will promote the greatest happiness of the greatest number? Is man a man or simply a higher ape?[20]

Houghton adds: "Most of the time the Victorian mind contained beliefs and not doubts – but the beliefs were shaky. What *is* constantly present . . . is the fear or suspicion, or simply the vague uneasy feeling, that one was not sure he believed what he believed."[21]

The Victorian Crisis of Faith involved more than just personal struggles of conscience. There was also a struggle to reform the existing

---

19 James C. Livingston, *The Ethics of Belief: An Essay on the Victorian Religious Conscience* (Tallahassee, Florida: American Academy of Religion, 1974), 1.
20 Walter E. Houghton, *The Victorian Frame of Mind* (New Haven: Yale University Press, 1969), 11-12.
21 Ibid., 21.

educational institutions. One of the most active in this movement was Thomas Huxley (1825-1895). As Frank Miller Turner writes in *Between Science and Religion: The Reaction to Scientific Naturalism in Late Victorian England,* Huxley had boasted of "a New Nature created by science", which needed to be defended against those who continued to interpret the natural world in a theistic framework. In Turner's words:

> Huxley and others believed the New Nature and the scientific theories associated with it sufficient for the expression, explanation, and guidance of human life. A wholly secular culture seemed altogether possible. Nevertheless, Huxley realized that before the complete physical and moral benefits of the New Nature could be enjoyed, two tasks must be accomplished. First, the ordinary Englishman must be persuaded to look toward rational, scientific, and secular ideas to solve his problems and to interpret his experiences rather than toward Christian, metaphysical, or other prescientific modes of thought. Second, scientifically trained and scientifically oriented men must supplant clergymen and Christian laymen as educators and leaders of English culture.[22]

The defense of the scientific endeavor had become a sort of crusade. Houghton writes: "Perhaps the most important development in nineteenth-century intellectual history was the extension of scientific assumptions and methods from the physical world to the whole life of man."[23] Nowhere was this more evident than in the heated debates arising from the contemporary writings of Charles Darwin (1809-1882) on evolution, with Thomas Huxley and Ernst Haeckel being the most famous defenders of the scientific theory of organic evolution.

Darwin himself was careful to avoid getting into polemical debates over the implications of evolution, allowing Huxley and other defenders to take the field in his name. Darwin studiously avoided references to *human* evolution in his major work *On the Origin of Species* (1859), with the exception of a brief remark that "Much light will be shed on the nature of man and his history."[24] He added references to God in the last four editions of the work, to counter the criticism that his scientific theory was irreligious. Huxley, though, was not loathe to draw out the meaning of

---

[22] Frank Miller Turner, *Between Science and Religion: The Reaction to Scientific Naturalism in Late Victorian England* (New Haven: Yale University Press, 1974), 9.
[23] Houghton, 33.
[24] Charles Darwin, *The Origin of Species,* sixth and final edition of 1872 (New York: Modern Library, 1936), 373.

evolution for the human species, addressing this in countless public lectures and his own work *Evidence as to Man's Place in Nature* (1863).

In 1871, Darwin published his *The Descent of Man*, which did directly address the role that evolution had played in the origin and history of the human species. Of particular interest was his discussion of the role of morality in distinguishing our species from other members of the animal kingdom. Although the difference between the human animal and the ape is admittedly immense, he even speculated that the moral sense was not necessarily unique to humans:

> The following proposition seems to me in a high degree probable – namely, that any animal whatever, endowed with well-marked social instincts, the parental and filial affections being here included, would inevitably acquire a moral sense or conscience, as soon as its intellectual powers had become as well, or nearly as well developed, as in man.[25]

Although he kept his views on religion to himself, it is clear from his posthumously published autobiography that Darwin had long ceased to be a believing Christian. He accepted the classification that Huxley would coin – "agnostic". Darwin wrote: "The mystery of the beginning of all things is insoluble by us; and I for one must be content to remain an Agnostic."[26] He remained content to let Huxley and other evolutionists draw out the metaphysical implications and theological ramifications of this all-important theory in science.

There was no denying that evolution had caused a great degree of excitement in the mid-Victorian era. In Houghton's words: "After Darwin had made the greatest 'discovery' of the period in 1859, the imagination of young liberals was fired by the vision of a life spent in contributing, no matter how little, to the great revelation of all knowledge."[27] Concomitant with an understanding of the meaning of this theory for human society was a desire for the reconstruction of such society on a scientific and rational basis. Leaders of this movement, including Darwin's cousin Francis Galton, argued that the new knowledge meant a new ethical outlook. Houghton describes their aspirations thusly: "To improve the physical conditions of life, especially in the new towns, through the

---

25 Charles Darwin, *The Descent of Man*, second edition, 1874 (Amherst, New York: Prometheus Books, 1998), 101. Refer to the introduction by H. James Birx, *ix– xxvii*.
26 Charles Darwin, *The Autobiography of Charles Darwin* (New York: W. W. Norton, 1969), 48.
27 Ibid., 34.

alliance of legislation and science, was to improve not only health but moral habits as well."[28] Yet to do so, it would be necessary to directly challenge the moral authority, as well as the political and social powers, of the dominant religious institutions.

V. The Metaphysical Society

During the Victorian era, many religious leaders and intellectuals became concerned that a growing sense of disbelief among the educated elite would have a deleterious impact on the morals of general society. One such individual was the influential editor of the *Contemporary Review,* James Knowles. In the autumn of 1868, he had as dinner guests Alfred Lord Tennyson, the Poet Laureate, and the Reverend Charles Pritchard, the noted astronomer. During their discussion, the idea came to them to found a Theological Society, in which individuals interested in such topics could gather together to explore the issues. Knowles volunteered to found such a Society, with the provision that Tennyson and Pritchard would promise to belong to it. Although Tennyson was to later joke that Knowles could not differentiate a "concept" from a "hippopotamus", he and Pritchard agreed to join.

Knowles was known for his organizing skills. He immediately contacted other notables with whom he was familiar, such as Archbishop Manning, the Reverend James Martineau, and his fellow editors, William Ward of the *Dublin Review* and R. H. Hutton of the *Spectator,* all of whom consented to become founding members. One of Knowles' closest friends was the liberal theologian Arthur Stanley, Dean of Westminster, who not only became a member but helped to shape the structure of the Society, suggesting that it open the membership to those who were *opposed* to theology. As Alan Willard Brown describes it:

> Dean Stanley was one of Knowles's best friends and as one of the first to be asked was in a position to offer advice. To him and to his wife, Lady Augusta Stanley, the plan for a Theological Society seemed narrow and unwise. All that such a society could do would be to widen the breach between the religious and scientific points of view. *Rapprochement,* Stanley felt, would help more than organized resistance. Martineau, too, refused to join a society of believers to fight unbelievers. Knowles himself, with his own theological uncertainty, his eclecticism of mind, his breadth of social and conversational sympathy, now found himself in hearty sympathy with Stanley's attitude. All finally agreed, with an English love

---

28 Ibid., 41.

of fair play, that it was only just that their opponents be allowed to state their case. So, apparently at the suggestion of Lady Augusta Stanley, the name of the Society was changed from "Theological" to "Metaphysical," and plans were laid for a tactful ensnaring of the scientific and materialist opposition.[29]

Mill was invited to become a member, but begged off due to ill health. His lack of interest in metaphysics was another reason he remained aloof from the organization. Another much sought after potential member was Herbert Spencer (1820-1903). Even though the subject of the very first meeting was his own philosophical writings on ethics, Spencer, who was famous for his reclusiveness, never became a member. Nor did the prominent convert to Catholicism John Newman. But many other well-known figures of the time eagerly accepted the invitation to join.

Sir Frederick Pollock, who was elected to the Society near its end, had a long acquaintance with Knowles. In his autobiography, Pollock wrote that Knowles "did believe in the simplest good faith that if a number of students of philosophy and natural science, representing every kind of school and opinion, could only be brought together to discuss the nature of things freely and at large on a neutral ground, the ultimate truth, or a sure cure to it, would somehow emerge."[30] He went on to add: "The Metaphysical Society was the oddest mixture of philosophers and persons otherwise more or less eminent who did not even know where metaphysics began, and did not understand the most elementary philosophical terms."[31]

The best capsule description of the Society comes from Alan Willard Brown:

> There is little question that the Metaphysical Society attracted the most distinguished and representative Englishmen of the seventies, with the exception of Matthew Arnold, G. H. Lewes, and the aged Carlyle, besides Browning, Mill, Newman, Spencer, and Bain, who were asked but refused to join. There were statesmen: Gladstone, Robert Lowe, Lord Selborne, and the Duke of Argyll; powerful ecclesiastical figures: Archbishop Manning, Thomson, Archbishop of York, and Magee, Bishop of Peterborough; politicians and men of the world: Grant Duff and Lord Arthur Russell; lawyers: Fitzjames Stephen and Frederick Pollock. There were

---

29 Alan Willard Brown, *The Metaphysical Society: Victorian Minds in Crisis, 1869-1880* (New York: Octagon Books, 1973), 21-22.
30 Frederick Pollock, *Remembrances of an Ancient Victorian* (London: John Murray, 1933), 93.
31 Ibid., 95.

others whose primary concern was with the life of the heart and the intellect; theologians: Martineau, Maurice, Mozley, Ward, and Dalgairns; scholars: Bishop Ellicott and F. Gasquet; professional philosophers: Sidgwick, A. C. Fraser, Hodgson, and C. B. Upton; amateur philosophers and philosophical critics: James Hinton, Roden Noel, Matthew Boulton, Balfour, and Barratt. There were historians: Thirlwall, Froude, Seeley, Stanley, Church, Grove, and Pattison; important editors and critics; R. H. Hutton, Alford, Leslie Stephen, Morley, Knowles, Bagehot, W. R. Greg, Frederic Harrison, and Ruskin. There were great physiologists: W. B. Carpenter, Huxley, and Mivart, as well as the latter's friend Robert Clarke; an astronomer, Pritchard; a physicist, Tyndall; an anthropologist, Lubbock. There were the psychologists G. Croom Robinson and James Sully; a famous mathematician, Sylvester; and a philosophical mathematician, Clifford. There were academic leaders from great universities: Alfred Barry, E. Lushington, Sir Alexander Grant. And there were the distinguished representatives of the profession of medicine: Dr. Henry Acland, Dr. J. C. Bucknill, Sir William Gull, and Dr. Andrew Clark. And aloof from them all, symbolizing the virtues as well as the weaknesses of that brilliant and tortured age, Tennyson, the Poet Laureate.[32]

It was indeed a unique collection of individuals, but it would be wrong to say, as Pollock did, that none of the members were learned in metaphysics. Indeed, several were professional theologians, and even the professional scientists involved had either written or lectured on speculative topics pertaining to the origins of the universe and the place of humankind within it.

Perhaps the two members who were most active, as well as most opinionated, throughout the Society's history were the agnostic Huxley and the ultra-conservative Catholic W. G. Ward. Their differences were expressed at one of the earliest of the Society's meetings. Houston Peterson, in his biography of Huxley, gives the following amusing anecdote, which nicely captures the sharp differences as well as the mutual respect the members had for one another:

> Someone had suggested that all moral approbation should be avoided during the debates and Ward interrupted: "While acquiescing in this condition as a general rule, I think it cannot be expected that Christian thinkers should give no sign of the horror with which they would view the spread of such extreme opinions as those advocated by Mr. Huxley." Thereupon Huxley retorted: "As Dr. Ward has spoken, I must in fairness say that it will be very difficult for me to conceal my feeling as to the intellectual degradation which would come of the general acceptance of

---

[32] Brown, 165-166.

such views as Dr. Ward holds." Henceforward, Ward and Huxley clashed in discussion, but there was no friction. Personalities were avoided almost too completely, and the society finally died of too much love, as someone said.[33]

That someone was Huxley himself. As we shall see, the actual cause of the Society's death was due in no small part to Clifford's address "The Ethics of Belief", which furthered the philosophical differences between the various members. The pugnacious tone of Clifford's essay was responded to in kind by Ward and other religious believers. Rather than too much love, the Society ended when its members could no longer agree upon a common ground for reasoned discussion.

In his book *Apes, Angels, and Victorians,* William Irvine adds some colorful descriptions of those two polar opposites, Ward and Huxley:

> Quite apart from the vital questions of correct tone, the exchange between Ward and Huxley was prophetic. From the brilliant, disorganized Homeric warfare of the early debates, these two men stood out as the opposing champions. Tall, dark, and intense, Huxley looked rather like a talkative mystic; and Ward, jovial, round, and rosy, looked very much like an equally talkative country squire. Both were clear-headed and quick-tongued. More the dialectician Ward tended toward the subtle and self-conscious, combining great openness of mind and readiness for logical adventure with lighthearted assurance in the certainty of Catholic truth and the paradoxical freshness of extreme conservatism rationally defended. Questioned about Catholic doctrine on a point of conduct, he replied, "There are two views, of which I, as usual, take the more bigoted."[34]

As will be seen in chapter four, Ward was one of the first and strongest critics of Clifford's "The Ethics of Belief", while Huxley was one of its most vocal defenders.

VI. Agnosticism

It was his participation in the Metaphysical Society that led Thomas Huxley to coin the word "Agnostic". This word, whose meaning was then and continues to be much debated, was thereafter used to describe the views of not only Huxley himself, but his intellectual allies and fellow

---

33 Houston Peterson, *Huxley: Prophet of Science* (London: Longmans, Green, 1932), 171-172.
34 William Irvine, *Apes, Angels, and Victorians* (New York: Time Incorporated, 1963), 309.

Metaphysical Society members Leslie Stephen and W. K. Clifford. As Huxley describes it in his 1889 essay entitled "Agnosticism":

> When I reached intellectual maturity and began to ask myself whether I was an atheist, a theist, or a pantheist; a materialist or an idealist; a Christian or a freethinker; I found that the more I learned and reflected, the less ready was the answer; until, at last, I came to the conclusion that I had neither art nor part with any of these denominations, except the last. The one thing in which most of these good people were agreed was the one thing in which I differed from them. They were quite sure they had attained a certain "gnosis," – had, more or less successfully, solved the problem of existence; while I was quite sure I had not, and had a pretty strong conviction that the problem was insoluble.[35]

Huxley then paid homage to the role which the Metaphysical Society had played in forcing him to come up with a term that described his own mindset:

> This was my situation when I had the good fortune to find a place among the members of that remarkable confraternity of antagonists, long since deceased, but of green and pious memory, the Metaphysical Society. Every variety of philosophical and theological opinion was represented there, and expressed itself with entire openness; most of my colleagues with *–ists* of one sort or another; and, however kind and friendly they might be, I, the man without a rag of a label to cover himself with, could not fail to have some of the uneasy feelings which must have beset the historical fox when, after leaving the trap in which his tail remained, he presented himself to his normally elongated companions. So I took thought, and invented what I conceived to be the appropriate title of "Agnostic." It came into my head as suggestively antithetic to the "Gnostic" of Church history, who professed to know so much about the very things of which I was ignorant; and I took the earliest opportunity of parading it at our Society, to show that I, too, had a tail, like the other foxes. To my great satisfaction, the term took, and when the *Spectator* had stood godfather to it, any suspicion in the minds of respectable people that a knowledge of its parentage might have awakened was, of course, completely lulled.[36]

Ironically, it was his fellow Metaphysical Society member Leslie Stephen who was to popularize the term – Huxley himself seldom used it.

---

35 Thomas Henry Huxley, *Agnosticism and Christianity and Other Essays* (Amherst, New York: Prometheus Books, 1992), 162.
36 Ibid., 163.

In one sense, "agnosticism" was a new expression of the age-old saying of Socrates that true wisdom consists in acknowledging one's own ignorance. Yet there is certainly much more to Huxley's coinage than a simple assertion of lack of knowledge. Some philosophers of the time, such as the aforementioned Herbert Spencer, went so far as to argue that in areas of metaphysics, *all* people should be agnostic, since the human mind can never have knowledge of the ultimate. "I don't know" shifts to "*We* don't know" and, even more, to "*No one* knows." Yet such an extreme view as the latter would seem to forestall any sort of evidentialism, since what would be the point of even looking for factual support to bolster a belief, if such support is by definition impossible to find?

Why did Huxley refrain from making a more positive argument, namely that belief in God's existence (*theism*) is not supported by evidence whereas lack of belief (*atheism*) in God's existence *is* consistent with our intellectual understanding? Huxley's avoidance of the term "atheism" was consistent perhaps with his desire to disassociate himself from all "isms", but there is another factor to consider – the ethical consequences of denial of God's existence. One constant concern expressed by members of the Metaphysical Society was a fear of atheism. As seen above, Huxley was eager to avoid making an explicit denial of God's existence. As Walter Houghton states:

> The decline of Christianity and the prospect of atheism had social implications which now seem curious . . . . It was then assumed, in spite of rationalist denials, that any collapse of faith would destroy the sanctions of morality; and morality gone, society would disintegrate. Mill described the age as one in which the opinion that religious belief was necessary for moral and social purposes was universal, and yet real belief was feeble and precarious –a situation well calculated to arouse anxiety.[37]

Most of the members of the Metaphysical Society, whatever their personal metaphysical views, shared a concern about the growing sense of religious disbelief, and the discussions tended to address the main challenges to traditional beliefs found in biology, mathematics, logic, and physics. A good number of the essays presented by the members dealt with the origins of morality and how to inculcate virtues among the public. Indeed, some of the agnostic members were willing to defend religious institutions for their ability to perform this service, even if they

---

37 Houghton, 58-59.

disagreed with the institutions' ultimate foundations in theology. James Livingston writes:

> There was a surprisingly widespread belief among Victorian intellectuals, including freethinkers, that with the demise of Christian doctrine there would be a serious crisis and decline in public morals. In a symposium in the first issue of *The Nineteenth Century* the question of "The Influence Upon Morality of a Decline in Religious Belief" was debated by a dozen eminent writers, including Fitzjames Stephen, Huxley, Clifford, Frederic Harrison, Dean Church, R. H. Hutton, and W. G. Ward. Clifford was the only contributor who did not predict moral decline.[38]

What perturbed many of the members of the Metaphysical Society was the fear that a general spread of disbelief would cause the lower strata of society to cease to be law-abiding citizens. In Houghton's words:

> What gave edge to these general speculations on the causal relationship of disbelief and disorder was their particular application to the lower classes. For "everyone" agreed that any discarding of the Christian sanctions of duty, obedience, patience under suffering, and brotherly love was obviously "fraught with grievous danger to property and the State." Nothing could illustrate that assumption more tellingly than the reviews of *The Descent of Man* (1871) in the most important newspapers, where Darwin was severely censured for "revealing his zoological [anti-Christian] conclusions to the general public at a moment when the sky of Paris was red with the incendiary flames of the Commune."[39]

One can see here echoes of the earlier views of Hume, who felt that the masses were incapable of evaluating evidence in a critical manner. Huxley (who acknowledged his own debt to his predecessor in his 1897 book *Hume*) was a political conservative who took pains to distance himself from the more radical exponents of the scientific revolution. Yet there were a good number of individuals – Clifford being one of them – who saw the decline in religious belief to be a great opportunity *for* moral development. Quoting again from Houghton:

> The disintegration of Christian theology and even religious belief which was so often agonizing was also an enormous relief. The new vision of a "scientific" universe was a nightmare – and it was a glorious dream, as men discovered that much or all of dogmatic Christianity was sheer superstition, thank God, and looked forward, with joyful anticipation in

---

38 Ibid., 36.
39 Ibid., 59.

some cases, to a new revelation of man's destiny. To put the situation another way, if modernism for most Victorians threatened to destroy the comforts of belief, for a substantial minority it promised to end the *dis*comforts of belief.[40]

Taking their cue from Mill's lead, the agnostics turned the tables on religionists. If religious beliefs were no longer to be taken as literally true, what force did they have as moral teachings? And, as Clifford was to write in his 1877 essay "The Ethics of Religion", what is the real moral meaning of "original sin"? "If God holds all mankind guilty for the sin of Adam", Clifford asserted, "if he has visited upon the innocent the punishment of the guilty, if he is to torture any single soul for ever, then it is wrong to worship him."[41]

Andrew Pyle, in his introduction to *Agnosticism: Contemporary Responses to Spencer and Huxley,* writes:

> In many respects, this seizing of the moral high ground by the anti-clerical party represents the heart of the debate over agnosticism. From the beginning, the agnostics appeal explicitly to such moral values as personal integrity, unselfishness, honesty, frankness, humility, and tolerance. The agnostics seek to portray themselves as intellectually honest in following the arguments wherever they may lead, as humble in frankly admitting their limitations, and as tolerant of the weaknesses of their fellow men. The defenders of the established Churches are represented, in sharp contrast, as standing for little more than pride and prejudice.[42]

It was in this intellectual setting that W. K. Clifford was to give his famous talk "The Ethics of Belief".[43]

---

40 Ibid., 48.
41 W. K. Clifford, "The Ethics of Religion" in *Lectures and Essays, Vol. II* (London: Macmillan and Co., 1879), 224.
42 Andrew Pyle, introduction, *Agnosticism: Contemporary Responses to Spencer and Huxley* (Bristol, England; Thoemmes Press, 1995), *xviii.*
43 For further information, see Timothy J. Madigan, introduction, *The Ethics of Belief and Other Essays* by W. K. Clifford (Amherst, New York, 1999), *ix-xxi.*

CHAPTER TWO

W. K. CLIFFORD: LIFE AND PHILOSOPHY

I. Biography

In 1946, the mathematician James R. Newman was asked to write an introduction to a reprint of W. K. Clifford's classic work (published posthumously), *The Common Sense of the Exact Sciences* (1885). Reminiscing about this in an article which appeared in the February 1953 issue of *Scientific American,* he noted his surprise at how few materials were available about this figure - a handful of scattered articles and obituaries, an entry in *The Dictionary of National Biography* written by Clifford's friend Leslie Stephen and a brief biographical preface to his collected works, written by his friend Sir Frederick Pollock. "This neglect of Clifford," Newman wrote, "is difficult to explain. He was not only one of the great mathematicians of his century but an original philosopher and a leader of British intellectual life in the Victorian age. Much of Clifford's thinking was ahead of his time. His mathematical work was prophetic, and its merit is still untouched . . . his philosophical ideas were rational and humane . . . An inspiring faith in the power of reason, and in human progress, guided Clifford's remarkably productive but tragically short life . . ."[1]

While his 1876 essay "The Ethics of Belief" continues to be often anthologized, there is still little discussion of the life and significance of this figure. Yet Clifford, although living only to the age of 33, made important contributions to the fields of mathematics, philosophy, and psychology. He was a rare combination of scientist and poet. In the words of William James: ". . . Clifford's mental personality belonged to the

---

1 James R. Newman, "William Kingdon Clifford", in *Scientific American,* February 1953, No. 188, 78.

highest possible *type* . . . The union of the mathematician with the poet, fervor with measure, passion with correctness, this surely is the ideal."[2]

1. Early Years

William Kingdon Clifford was born in Exeter, England on May 4, 1845. There is not much known about his early years, for as his friend Frederick Pollock wrote: "A soul eager for new mastery and ever looking forward cares little to dwell upon the past; and Clifford was not much apt to speak of his own earlier life, or indeed of his life at all."[3]

Clifford's father, also named William, was a bookseller, dealing largely in devotional material, and he raised his son to be a god-fearing Anglican. A man of some importance in the town, he also served as justice of the peace there. Clifford's mother, whose maiden name was Kingdon, died in September of 1854, when he was only nine. He inherited from her a constitutional weakness which perhaps led to his own early death from tuberculosis.

A precocious child, Clifford was educated at a small private school in Exeter until 1860, when at the age of 15 he was sent to King's College, London. Here Clifford revealed abilities not only in what would be his chosen profession, mathematics, but also in the fields of literature and classics – skills which he would continue to demonstrate for the rest of his life. His talents in the field of mathematics were evident at an early age, as can be seen in the following charming anecdote:

> The Reverend Percival Frost (author of the classic *Curve Tracing*) once boasted to his brother A. H. Frost (who had done missionary work in India) of the remarkable space perception possessed by the young William Kingdon Clifford. Now the brother had brought back with him from India a complicated three-dimensional puzzle in the form of a sphere composed of a number of cleverly interlocked pieces, and the challenge of the puzzle was to take it apart. A. H. could scarcely believe the incredible things Percival had said about the boy Clifford, and so he asked Percival to invite the youngster to tea and to see if he could unlock the three-dimensional puzzle. Forthwith the boy was invited and shown the puzzle. Without touching the puzzle, Clifford carefully looked it over for a few minutes,

---

2 William James, review of W. K. Clifford's *Lectures and Essays* and *Seeing and Thinking* in *Essays, Comments and Reviews* (Cambridge, Massachusetts: Harvard University Press, 1987), 356.
3 Frederick Pollock, "Biographical Introduction" to W. K. Clifford's *Lectures and Essays* (London: Macmillan and Co., 1886), 2.

and then sat with his head in his hands for a few more minutes. He then picked up the puzzle and, to A. H.'s astonishment, immediately took it apart.[4]

Having won a minor scholarship, in October of 1863 Clifford went to Trinity College, Cambridge, where he read mathematics. At the age of 18 he wrote two original papers in geometry which led his tutor, Percival Frost, to prophecy that he would gain a place among the leaders of science. But Clifford refused to limit his studies, and received honorable mention in classics, modern history and English literature. "The pursuit of knowledge for its own sake," Pollock writes, "and without even such regard to collateral interests as most people would think a matter of common prudence, was the leading character of Clifford's work throughout his life. The discovery of truth was for him an end in itself, and the proclamation of it, or of whatever seemed to lead to it, a duty of primary and paramount obligation."[5] This attitude would mark his most famous essay, "The Ethics of Belief."

Whatever tasks Clifford set himself to, he persevered until he had mastered them. He learned French, German and Spanish because he thought these important to his work in mathematics (and his knowledge of German would come to good use later as he helped to introduce and modify Kant's ideas to the English-speaking world); he also learned Arabic, Greek and Sanskrit because they were a challenge, and hieroglyphics because it was a riddle, and even Morse code and shorthand because he claimed to be interested in all methods of conveying thought.

Clifford's enthusiasm for learning occurred fortuitously. The latter half of the nineteenth century was a time of tremendous innovations in such fields as astronomy, biology, chemistry, mathematics, philosophy, and psychology - all areas in which he would both write and lecture about. But his discursiveness did have an impact on his achievements at Cambridge. To quote again from Newman:

> The catholicity of Clifford's interests and his independence of mind guided his reading even in mathematics. He would not permit himself to be strait-jacketed into the training routine for the competitive examinations known as the tripos. In England more than elsewhere the honours a student wins, or fails to win, at the university tag him for the rest of his life, especially if he follows an academic career. The unfortunate competitive aspect of the

---

4 H. Eves, *Mathematical Circles Squared* (London: Prindle, Weber and Schmidt, 1972), 81.
5 Ibid., 5.

tripos has long since been abandoned, but in Clifford's day to finish on top, to be "first wrangler", was coin for the future. To prepare for the competition one placed oneself in the hands of a special coach for a long and unbelievably arduous grind. Months of practice in intricate manipulations were intended to increase the rate at which one could solve, and more especially write out, the solutions to the problems. Tutors and students alike knew that Clifford could be first wrangler if he trained for this intellectual gymnastic. Clifford, too modest to know and caring less, with almost no preparation finished second wrangler.[6]

Still, Clifford was in good company. Other second wranglers included such noted mathematicians as Whewell, Sylvester, Kelvin and Clerk Maxwell. Clifford himself was most proud not of his intellectual gymnastics but rather his physical feats. Although slight in build, he had great strength, and was able to pull himself up on the bar with one hand. His class yearbook gave him the accolade as "one of the most daring athletes of the University", and his most accomplished feat, taken on a dare, was to hang by his toes from the cross bars of a church tower's weathercock, "a feat," writes John D. North is his entry on Clifford in the *Dictionary of Scientific Biography,* "befitting a High Churchman, as he then was."[7]

Clifford was indeed an ardent Christian in his early years, and underwent an experience several other devout men and women grappled with in the so-called "Victorian Crisis of Faith" - a loss of religious belief. For Clifford, though, unlike many others, this was a positive experience, and one that would become central to his concept of "the ethics of belief."

At Cambridge, Clifford was asked to join the Apostles, a secretive club of the 12 most outstanding students. Deep in the study of Aquinas at the time, he reveled in supporting Catholic doctrines by reference to scientific analogies. But the impact of evolutionary theory, which had been hotly debated since the publication of *On the Origin of Species* in 1859, altered his views. He no longer felt it necessary to explain scientific discoveries through the prism of existing religious tenets, and in fact came to see religious institutions as the chief obstacles to scientific advancement. At a time when those who would hold fellowships or teaching positions in the colleges in Oxford or Cambridge were expected to profess allegiance to

---

6 James R. Newman, introduction to W. K. Clifford, *The Common Sense of the Exact Sciences* (New York: Alfred A. Knopf, 1946), xxi.
7 John D. North, entry on "William Kingdon Clifford" in the *Dictionary of Scientific Biography* (New York: Charles Scribner's Sons, 1971), 322.

the Thirty-Nine Articles of Religion, this could be a career-destroying belief.

2. Academic Career

In 1865, the British Parliament declared that assent to the Thirty-Nine Articles was general rather than particular, which was perhaps of some benefit to Clifford, since it was just three years later, in 1868, that he was elected to a fellowship at Trinity, where he would reside until 1871. In the meantime, he had demonstrated his oratorical skills by winning the college declamation prize in 1866, with a discourse on Sir Walter Raleigh, in consequence of which he was appointed to deliver the annual oration at the college commemoration. He spoke in honor of Dr. Whewell, the late master of Trinity College, whom he praised for using his intellectual gifts to better the world. This was for Clifford a duty, which he would do his best to exemplify for the remainder of his own days. One of his first public lectures was given in March of 1868, to the Royal Institution, and was entitled "On Some of the Conditions of Mental Development". In it, he declaimed again upon the importance of a critical intelligence, and the upward development of the human mind. The lecture demonstrated the rhetorical abilities that would stand him in good stead for his entire career as a public speaker:

> What, in fact, are the conditions which must be satisfied by a mind in process of upward development . . .? They are two; one positive, one negative. The positive condition is that the mind should act rather than assimilate, that its attitude should be one of creation rather than acquisition . . . If the mind is artistic, it must not sit down in hopeless awe before the monuments of the great masters as if heights so lofty could have no heaven beyond them . . . The negative condition is plasticity: the avoidance of all crystallisation as is immediately suggested by the environment. A mind that would grow must let no ideas become permanent except such as lead to action. Towards all others it must maintain an attitude of absolute receptivity; admitting all, being modified by all, but permanently biased by none. To become crystallised, fixed in opinion and mode of thought, is to lose the great characteristic of life, by which it is distinguished from inanimate nature: the power of adapting itself to circumstances.[8]

---

8 W. K. Clifford, "On Some of the Conditions of Mental Development" in *Lectures and Essays,* p 70-71.

Clifford is here applying the theory of Darwinian organic evolution to human cultural development, well before most scientists - including Darwin himself - would have been comfortable in doing so. By the time he delivered this lecture, Clifford had come to the conclusion that the Christian religion, be it High or Low church, was an impediment to human intellectual growth. He saw quite clearly that the chief opposition to Darwin was coming from the pulpits, and he allied himself with T. H. Huxley, the biologist popularly known throughout England as "Darwin's Bulldog."

During his time at Cambridge, Clifford continued to couple his academic pursuits with membership in debating societies that sharpened his wits. He was a member of the Grote Club, which included other members who would make their mark on English society, including the economist Alfred Marshall, the philosopher Henry Sidgwick, and the logician John Venn. Marshall became a great friend of Clifford's, although he felt that Clifford "was too fond of astonishing people." In a memoir he wrote late in his life, Marshall described a typical meeting of the Club:

> For a year or two (1869) Sidgwick, Mosley, Clifford, Moulton and myself were the active members; and we all attended regularly. Clifford and Moulton had at that time read but little philosophy; so they kept quiet for the first half hour of the discussion, and listened eagerly to what others, and especially Sidgwick, said. Then they let their tongues loose, and the pace was tremendous.[9]

While at Cambridge, Clifford continued to write important mathematical papers, at the rate of three or four a year, with such titles as "On Syzygetic Relations among the Powers of Linear Quantics" and "On the Umbilici of Anallagmatic Surfaces", while keeping up with his membership in various social and fraternal organizations, as well as continuing his public lectures. Such lectures were by no means atypical of the times. Newman points out that "Great importance attached to popular or semi-popular lectures in the nineteenth century; every scientist, philosopher, and man of letters took to the lecture platform - Huxley, Kelvin, Mach, Helmholtz, Maxwell, Faraday, Davy, to mention at random a few of the scientists - to popularize learning and, often, to impart the first notice of new ideas and discoveries."[10] But Clifford, with his unique combination of scientific understanding and rhetorical persuasive skills, was considered a master.

---

9 Reported by Newman in *The Common Sense of the Exact Sciences*.
10 Ibid., xxii.

He gave most of his public lectures with only a few short notes as reference, revising them afterwards for publication. His obvious enthusiasm, and his desire to enlighten, as well as his great clarity, won over his audiences, even when his lectures dealt with the most abstruse topics in mathematics.

In 1870, Clifford demonstrated his more empirical interest in science by joining an eclipse expedition, which sailed to the Mediterranean. Clifford fell in love with the area, which he would visit again, in a fruitless effort at the end of his life in hopes of recovering his strength. The ship he was on, the *Psyche,* hit a rock near Catania, and was sunk, although all hands on board and the instruments were saved. In a letter written to Frederick Pollock's wife from Florence a few days after the wreck, Clifford wrote: ". . . I am so angry at the idiots who failed to save the dear ship - alas! My heart's in the waters close by Polyphemus's eye, which we put out."[11] It is interesting to note that a ship disaster was used as an illustrative point to begin his most famous essay, "The Ethics of Belief", written 6 years later.

In 1871 a chair in applied mathematics became available at University College, London. Clifford was recommended for the post by, among others, the eminent mathematician James Clerk Maxwell, who summarized the young man's abilities thusly:

> The peculiarity of Mr. Clifford's researches, which in my opinion points him out as the right man for a chair of mathematical science, is that they tend not to the elaboration of abstruse theorems by ingenious calculations, but to the elucidation of scientific ideas by the concentration upon them of clear and steady thought. The pupils of such a teacher not only obtain clearer views of the subjects taught, but are encouraged to cultivate in themselves that power of thought which is so liable to be neglected amidst the appliances of education.[12]

Clerk Maxwell had come to value Clifford's talents after coming in contact with him at the small, informal meetings of the London Mathematical Society, where - in the company of men whose abilities he greatly respected – Clifford rather uncharacteristically tended to remain silent. But when Clifford did speak, the cogency of his remarks were duly noted.

---

11 W. K. Clifford, "Selections from Letters, etc." in *Lectures and Essays,*   37.
12 Quoted by Pollock in the "Biographical Introduction" to *Lectures and Essays,* 10.

3. Non-Academic Activities

Clifford was appointed to the Professorship in Applied Mathematics at University College, London and would spend the remainder of his short career there. It was a congenial place for a freethinker like himself, since it was founded, in 1827, to be a secular institution, where professors would be free from swearing to any religious test. One of its founders was the famous Utilitarian philosopher Jeremy Bentham (1748-1832), whose educational influence was still in evidence there, as was his physical presence, since he had bequeathed his corpse to the college, where it resided at public meetings. The freethinker Moncure D. Conway noted in his autobiography that Clifford's "coming to London was a great event. At twenty-seven he was regarded by the leading scientific men as their peer, and he had gone through all the phases of religious faith into well-informed freedom. He had a winning personality, irresistible indeed, and in public speaking could charm alike the Royal Society or a popular audience. Our acquaintance made at Cambridge became friendship in London, and my wife and I used to attend the weekly evenings in his rooms when his friends - among them always Lady Pollock and her sons - gathered around him."[13]

Conway relates an amusing anecdote, which shows that Clifford was not taken in by the interest shown at this time by many of his fellow professors - including such members of the prestigious Metaphysical Society as Henry Sidgwick and A. J. Balfour - in so-called spirit mediums, who supposedly were able to commune with the dead. By this time, Clifford had become a fierce advocate of the view that there was no such thing as disembodied consciousness, and he delighted in debunking paranormal claims. On one occasion, he and Conway decided to test the psychic abilities of "the famous Williams", who was supposedly able to communicate with the dead and cause them to appear to the living:

> The *séance* was in my house. The method of Williams was that we should surround the table, finger hooked in finger; then in the dark he would make some excuse for changing the finger, and contrive to get those on each side of him to hook the forefinger and little finger of the same hand, leaving one of his hands free to do the tricks. Clifford had heard of that device, and warned me. When we had been seated for some time Williams said his finger held by Clifford was weary, and proposed to change it, but Clifford in a low voice declined on his side, as I did on mine. Whereupon Williams

---

13 Moncure D. Conway, *Autobiography : Memories and Experiences of Moncure Daniel Conway* (Boston and New York: Houghton Mifflin., 1904), 351.

raised the light and rushed out of the house, leaving his accordion and banjo, which I sent him next day. Several credulous ladies who had been victimised by Williams were present, and had the detection explained to them. Williams was broken up in London by this exposure, and the last I heard of him was at Rotterdam, where the Customs officers seized his paraphernalia of wigs, masks, rag hands, and phosphorus.[14]

While humorous, this story also is a good example of Clifford's almost evangelical desire to combat credulity and charlatanism, and his wish to, in Conway's words, "liberate the people of all classes from degrading dogmas." In this, he fought a battle in his time against colleagues who felt that psychic research was a legitimate area for scientists to explore. The field of psychology was just being formed at the time, and it was still unclear what the limits of its particular area of study would be. William James, for example (who would later be one of Clifford's strongest, if sympathetic, critics) not only wrote one of the earliest textbooks on psychology, but also devoted a good deal of his time and energy to the Society for Psychical Research, where he explored such purported phenomena as automatic writing, trance announcements and communications with the dead. Clifford would have none of this, and made it a special point to show how supposed psychics were guilty of using trickery of the basest sort to fool not only credulous believers but learned professors as well.

In addition, Clifford sought to limit the area of psychology's study to the brain and how it worked, rather than to explorations of disembodied consciousness. In his lecture entitled "Body and Mind", given in 1874, Clifford laid out his position regarding the brain's relationship to consciousness in his typically blunt way: ". . . we should have the highest assurance that Science can give, a practical certainty on which we are bound to act, that there is no mind without a brain . . . It is made of atoms and ether, and there is no room in it for ghosts."[15] As Janet Oppenheim writes in her study of the period, *The Other World: Spiritualism and Psychical Research in England, 1850-1914*: "Clifford's determination to keep psychology within the confines of scientific naturalism won wide endorsement."[16]

---

14 Ibid.
15 "W. K. Clifford, "Body and Mind" in *Lectures and Essays,* p 269-270.
16 Janet Oppenheim, *The Other World: Spiritualism and Psychical Research in England, 1850-1914* (Cambridge, England: Cambridge University Press, 1985), 240.

While his extracurricular affairs kept him busy, Clifford did not shirk his professional duties. He was punctilious about meeting all his academic obligations, but on one occasion he did take a voluntary leave of absence from his scheduled lecture, informing his class that he would be absent on important business which would probably not occur again. The occasion was his marriage, on April 7, 1875, to Lucy Lane. They were to have two daughters together, and it was by all accounts a happy marriage for both. Lucy was to outlive him by half a century, and became in her own right well known as a novelist and dramatist.[17] In addition, she was to become a close confidant of Henry James, brother of her husband's friendly nemesis William. She shared many of her husband's interests, and their home became a popular meeting place, not only for learned friends but also for the friends' children as well, for Clifford had a great fondness for the young. He devised a plan for the education of children, and it is a sad fact that he did not live long enough to educate his own two daughters. He also wrote fairy tales and nonsense verse, and delighted in putting on children's parties, where his laughter was as little constrained as that of the young ones he was entertaining.

A few months previous to his marriage, in June of 1874, Clifford was elected a Fellow of the Royal Society. He had previously turned down the offer, with the remark that he did not want to be respectable yet. Pollock writes that ". . . such was the absence in him of anything like vanity or self-assertion, that when his scruples were overcome, and his election took place, he was the last person from whom his friend heard of it. I did not know it myself till several months later."[18]

In the same year, Clifford was also elected to another exclusive organization, the Metaphysical Society. At 29, he was the youngest member ever inducted into the Society, the most famous of all Victorian discussion clubs, counting among its members such acclaimed individuals as William Gladstone, Alfred Lord Tennyson, T. H. Huxley, Archbishop (later Cardinal) Manning, and John Ruskin. Meetings were held nine times a year, usually at a hotel, where after dinner a paper would be given by one of the members with discussion - often heated - following. Chiefly concerned with the arguments for or against religious belief, the Society's discussions were of the highest caliber, and Clifford was flattered to be able to offer three papers before the Society, all of which were later

---

17 See Monte Chisholm's charming *Such Silver Currents: The Story of William and Lucy Clifford 1845-1929* for further information on Lucy's own rich and fascinating life after William's death.

18 Frederick Pollock, "Biographical Introduction" in *Lectures and Essays,* 12.

published and helped to make him a famous figure in his day. For Clifford, the exercising of intellectual abilities in the company of fellow critical thinkers (whether they shared his conclusions or not) was an opportunity not to be missed, and Pollock records that "When he came home from the meetings of the Metaphysical Society (attending which was one of his greatest pleasures, and most reluctantly given up when going abroad after sunset was forbidden him), he would repeat the discussion almost at length, giving not only the matter but the manner of what had been said by every speaker, and now and then making his report extremely comic by a touch of plausible fiction."[19] Even here, his natural exuberance could not be contained.

In the spring of 1876, the symptoms of lung disease began to manifest themselves. At first, Clifford attempted to ignore these signs, and continued on his breakneck schedule of teaching classes, writing scholarly papers on mathematics and popular essays on public issues, delivering lectures, and attending society meetings, as well as raising his family. He thought that he could train his body to endure such hardships, and was known to sit up all night, writing papers in a single sitting. In Pollock's poignant words, Clifford "fancied himself to be making investments when he was in fact living on his capital."[20] If he had been asked, as a naturalist and rationalist, it if was wrong to neglect the conditions of one's own health, then Clifford would have surely answered in the affirmative, but - like such other fellow freethinkers Thomas Huxley and Leslie Stephen - he constantly put his own well-being into jeopardy through his strenuous lifestyle and almost Herculean efforts.

It was only with great reluctance that Clifford finally faced up to the fact of his illness, and agreed to take six months' leave of absence. He and his wife spent the summer of 1876 in Algiers and the south of Spain, leaving their infant daughter in the care of family at home. Clifford enjoyed himself immensely in the former locale, practicing his Arabic and partaking of the custom of smoking a pipeful of *kif* in the marketplace (it brought tears to his eyes). He also attended a lecture on the Koran and Government, and was intrigued to hear the lecturer's claim that absolutism in government was a Turkish, not an Arabic, institution. This appealed to his republican sentiments, although he was skeptical about the claim's legitimacy.

Clifford had a less enjoyable time in Spain, where he felt he was constantly being cheated by the natives, and where he had to be on guard

---

19 Ibid., 14.
20 Ibid., 15.

against falsehoods. He wrote Pollock: "I think it possible that one Spaniard may have told me the truth: he had lost so many teeth that he left out all his consonants, and I could not understand a word he said."[21] As usual with Clifford, he could not resist blaming this sorry state of affairs on the pernicious influence of the ecclesiastic system which was so powerful in the Southern European countries. "I suppose it frightens people to be told that historical Christianity as a social system invariably makes men wicked when it has full swing. Then I think the sooner they are well frightened the better."[22] This was basically the sentiment Clifford had expressed to the Metaphysical Society three months earlier, in his April 11, 1876 address "The Ethics of Belief." He was to soften his views about the Spaniards later in his trip, taking an anthropological interest in the vendettas and sense of outraged personal dignity he witnessed, and noting that he only had stones thrown at him once, and they did not hit him.

4. The New Republic

In June of 1876, while Clifford and his wife were out of the country, *Belgravia: An Illustrated London Magazine* began serialization of a satiric work called *The New Republic,* a witty *roman a clef* poking fun at some of England's leading intellectuals, including Matthew Arnold, Benjamin Jowett, T. H. Huxley, Walter Pater, and John Ruskin. Originally published anonymously, it soon became known that the author was W. H. Mallock, a 26-year old member of the landed gentry, and an ultra-High Anglican, who was disturbed by the growing disbelief toward Christian doctrines being promulgated by religious liberals and agnostics. In 1877, *The New Republic* was issued as a two volume book, although no author's name was placed on it until the fourth edition, issued as one volume, appeared in 1878. Subtitled *Culture, Faith and Philosophy in an English Country House,* the book describes a weekend party in a country home, where leading representatives of science, religion and letters squabble among themselves over the meaning of life, and try to devise their own modern version of Plato's *Republic* (this was a particular dig at Jowett, the Master of Mallock's *alma mater* Balliol College, who had just recently published his own translation of the *Republic,* with a long introduction comparing Plato's Greece with nineteenth-century England, and bemoaning the prevalence of time-serving public officials, long-winded

---

21 W. K. Clifford, "Selections from Letters, etc." in *Lectures and Essays,* 41.
22 Ibid.

preachers and frivolous men of letters in both societies - Jowett, whom Mallock detested, is made to look particularly ridiculous in the novel).

W. K. Clifford appears in the novel, in the guise of Mr. Saunders, a ferocious advocate of scientific triumphalism and anti-religious manifestoes. While most of the characters are comic creations, Saunders is particularly outrageous, making inappropriate comments and drawing disapproving stares every time he opens his mouth. Clifford must have been well-known at the time, since Mallock fully expected his reading audience to grasp the specific personages he was skewering. Mallock wished to bring together champions of various positions he considered to be mutually wanting, and let them expose each others' inadequacies through their debates. He very skillfully used more or less the actual words of those he pilloried. As John Lucas points out in his introduction to the work: " . . . it is important to make the identifications correctly otherwise we shall not understand the point of Mallock's work, which is directed at specific issues, ideas, dogmas, creeds, and at the people who hold them. And very often, Mallock does not so much parody the originals as set their own words in carefully chosen and betraying contexts so that they condemn themselves."[23] This is especially true of Mr. Saunders' diatribes. Mallock must have been an avid reader of Clifford's popular essays, for Lucas adds that ". . . Saunders' almost hysterical hatred of orthodox religion accurately enough reflects the tone of much of Clifford's writing."[24] What particularly disturbed Mallock was the blithe way in which both Clifford and Huxley (who appears as Mr. Storks in the novel) seem indifferent to the suffering that would occur should Christian beliefs be swept away, and the shock that this would cause to morality. In reality, the two men were very concerned about this issue, although their conclusions about the death of Christianity tended to be differently stressed. In the novel, Saunders and Storks come across as perfect foils, the former constantly blurting out blunt pronouncements which the latter would prefer to state with more finesse.

At his first appearance in the novel, the character Saunders is represented as coming from Oxford. After a defense of progress as the most important goal of life, he is asked what enjoyment there might be if humans should eradicate all the evils of existence:

---

23 John Lucas, introduction to W. H. Mallock, *The New Republic: Culture, Faith and Philosophy in an English Country House* (Leister, England: Leister University Press, 1975), p 16-17.
24 Ibid., 24.

"I . . . believe," Mr. Saunders went on, "that as long as the human race lasts, it will still have some belief in God left in it, and that the eradication of this will afford an unending employment to all enlightened minds."[25]

To this, one of the female characters gasps that if such irreligious views are to be picked up at Oxford, *she* will see to it that her little boy will go to Cambridge when he grows up - a rather ironic comment, given that the model for Mr. Saunders was himself a product of a thorough Cambridge education. Saunders barrels on in his defense of progress, oblivious to the consternation he has caused at the dinner table, boldly asserting that "All our doubts on this matter . . . are simply due to that dense pestiferous fog of crazed sentiment that still hides our view, but which the present generation has sternly set its face to dispel and conquer. Science will drain the marshy grounds of the human mind, so that the deadly malaria of Christianity, which has already destroyed two civilisations, shall never be fatal to a third."[26] While extreme, this is almost an exact quote from Clifford's essay "The Unseen Universe", which appeared in the June 1875 issue of the *Fortnightly Review,* and which ended with a strong warning not to allow religious superstition to once again take hold in society: "That which you keep in your hearts, my brothers, is the slender remnant of a system which has made its red mark on history, and still lives to threaten mankind . . . Take heed lest you have given soil and shelter to the seed of that awful plague which has destroyed two civilisations, and but barely failed to slay such promise of good as is now struggling to live among men."[27] It is hard to fault Mallock for being uncharitable in his representation, since the real words of Clifford are even more ferocious than those of his fictional counterpart.

The comic highlight of the novel occurs later, after the ladies have left and the men have settled down for wine and cigars, when a discussion on sin occurs:

"Sin . . .", said Mr. Storks, "is a word that has helped to retard moral and social progress more than anything. Nothing is good or bad, but thinking makes it so; and the superstitious and morbid way in which a number of entirely innocent things have been banned as sin, has caused more than half the tragedies of the world. Science will establish an entirely new basis of morality and the sunlight of rational approbation will shine on many a thing, hitherto overshadowed by the curse of a hypothetical God."

---

25 Ibid.,   25.
26 Ibid.,   30.
27 W. K. Clifford, "The Unseen Universe" in *Lectures and Essays.*

"Exactly so," exclaimed Mr. Saunders eagerly. "Now, I'm not at all that sort of man myself", he went on, "so don't think it because I say this."

Everyone stared at Mr. Saunders in wonder as to what he could mean.

"'We think it, for instance," he said, "a very sad thing when a girl is as we call it ruined. But it is we really that make all the sadness. She is ruined only because we think she is so. And I have little doubt that that higher philosophy of the future that Mr. Storks speaks of will go far, some day, towards solving the great question of women's sphere of action, by its recognition of prostitution as an honourable and beneficent profession."

"Sir!" exclaimed Mr. Storks, striking the table, and glaring with indignation at Mr. Saunders, "I could hardly have believed that such misplaced flippancy –"

"'Flippancy! it is reasoned truth," shrieked Mr. Saunders, upsetting his wine-glass.[28]

While the real Clifford did not apparently address himself to the topic of the ethics of prostitution, certainly Huxley was often taken aback by the forthright approach with which his younger friend and colleague at the Metaphysical Society often expressed himself. Another person who would later express annoyance at Clifford's views regarding religion was Matthew Arnold, but in *The New Republic*, he comes across - if such a thing is possible - as even more buffoonish than Clifford. His character, Mr. Luke, is constantly sighing and shaking his head over the sad state of present affairs. John Lukas, in his introduction to the novel, states that ". . . Mallock's success here is very remarkable. It is not simply that he reproduces the cadences of Arnold's prose but that he devastatingly catches the pose of bitter-sweet weariness and fastidious rejection which characterizes much of Arnold's writing. And though it may at first glance seem odd that Mallock should so dislike Arnold's notion of the elite, and his desire to save religion as a force for good, a second look makes it clear that Mallock inevitably rejects both Arnold's assumption of the elite's classlessness and his insistence on reading the Bible as literature."[29] Clifford shared this disdain toward world-weariness and reverence toward the Bible as a moral repository, albeit for quite different reasons than Mallock. The words of Saunders in the novel, regarding the need to eradicate false doctrines and unsupported claims, are very much those of Clifford as well: "Let us get rid of what is evil before we introduce what is good. I should begin by getting rid of every belief that is not based upon

---

28 *The New Republic*, p 64-65.
29 John Lucas, introduction to *The New Republic*, p 20-21.

reason, and every sentiment whose existence cannot be accounted for."[30] No wonder Arnold was apt to shake his head in exasperation at Clifford's pronouncements. This is nicely captured in *The New Republic,* in a scene where Mr. Luke is trying to respond to the assertion of Mr. Stockton (based on the physicist and geologist John Tyndall, a popular lecturer of the day and a good friend of Huxley's, whose views regarding science he generally shared) that science would enrich religious sentiment by purifying it of its lesser qualities. "Mr. Luke was going to have answered; but worse even than Mr. Stockton's, Mr. Saunders hated accents now got the start of him."[31]

Mr. Saunders makes his last appearance in the novel when, after nervously discovering that he has misplaced his written disproof of God's existence, he rushes back to the assembled guests to announce in a disappointed voice that the housemaid had thrown it away, adding: "I am pleased to discover, however, that she previously read through a part; so it has not perished, I trust, without emancipating one spirit."[32] This distresses the other assembled guests, most of whom are freethinkers of various sorts, but who remain in agreement that the lower classes should not be made aware of such views. As Mr. Storks had stated during Saunders' absence: "Now, those are the sort of young fellows . . . that really do a good deal to bring all solid knowledge into contempt in the minds of the half-educated. There's a certain hall in London, not far from the top of Regent Street, where I'm told he gives Sunday lectures."[33]

5. Clifford as Freethought Activist

Clifford did indeed give several addresses to the Sunday Lecture Society, from 1872-75, and took a deep interest in its aims to popularize scientific findings and try to increase scientific literacy, as well as criticize religious dogmas and sacerdotal superstitions - all of which were of a piece to him. Meetings were held at St. George's Hall, Langham Place at 4:00 PM every Sunday from November to May, and Clifford was one of the more frequent lecturers. He gave talks on such topics as "Atoms", "The First and Last Catastrophe: A Criticism of Some Recent Speculations About the Duration of the Universe", "Body and Mind" and "Right and Wrong: The Scientific Ground of Their Distinction" to the Society. Upon

---

30 *The New Republic,* p 153-154.
31 Ibid., 226.
32 Ibid., 338.
33 Ibid., 290.

his return to England, he continued to address the Society. For instance, on March 4, 1877, he spoke on "The Bearing of Morals on Religion".

Clifford also remained a steady attendee of the Metaphysical Society's meetings, although he would not deliver another paper to it after the April 11, 1876 meeting, where he read "The Ethics of Belief." Due to the state of his health, he began to confine his extracurricular activities to writing reviews not previously delivered as lectures. He continued to tax his system, though, often writing late into the night, completing a long review entitled "Virchow on the Teaching of Science" (which appeared in the April 1878 issue of *Nineteenth Century*) in one night's sitting. His friend Leslie Stephen was to write of Clifford: "The disproportion between his great nervous energy and his constitutional weakness tempted him to dangerous efforts, both physical and intellectual. It was difficult to persuade him to adopt prudential measures, and he persevered even in his gymnastic exercises till after serious warnings."[34]

For all his ill health, Clifford's *joie de vie* could not be contained. He made it a point to edit all his own manuscripts, and was meticulous regarding punctuation. He also dabbled in mechanical inventions, going so far as to begin experiments on the construction of a flying machine. This led to an interest in kites, which caused some consternation when, during the Long Vacation of 1877, Clifford and his wife visited friends in Wales. After spending the whole morning laying out a great length of string in order to launch a kite of unusual dimensions, he was nonplused when, during a luncheon break, word came to him that a flock of sheep had become hopelessly entangled in his handiwork. Another engineering feat for which he was proud was designing a duck-pond near his home for a family of ducklings that had been frequenting a narrow ditch by the roadside. An over-officious government minister, claiming that the pond was an encroachment on the highway, filled it. Pollock: "Clifford regretted the duck-pond even more than the kite."[35]

One of the last projects Clifford worked on was especially near and dear to his heart. After discussions with Thomas Huxley and Moncure Conway, he came to the conclusion that a gathering of freethinkers from across the world should be held, the aim of which would be to liberate the peoples of all classes from degrading dogmas. Combining his republican sentiments with his scientific advocacy, Clifford was the driving force

---

[34] Leslie Stephen, entry on "William Kingdon Clifford" in *The Dictionary of National Biography,* Vol. IV, "Chamber-Craigie" (London: Oxford University Press, 1968), 539.
[35] Pollock, introduction to *Essays and Lectures,* p 31-32.

behind the Congress of Liberal Thinkers, which was held on June 13-14, 1878 at the South Place chapel in England, a few days after the commemoration of the centenary of Voltaire's death, for which a great festival was held in Paris on May 30th. According to Conway:

> Our congress brought together leading men from all parts of the United Kingdom, and some from other European countries, from India, and from America. Nearly all of these 400 congressmen (including several congresswomen) represented some congregation or society. We had Broad Churchmen, Unitarians, Secularists, Theists; and we had a tower of strength in my American friend, Wentworth Higgins. At the end of two days' discussion an association was formed, its aim being defined as:
>
> 1. The scientific study of religious phenomena. 2. The collection and diffusion of information concerning religious movements throughout the world. 3. The emancipation of mankind from the spirit of superstition. 4. Fellowship among liberal thinkers of all races. 5. The promotion of the culture, progress, and moral welfare of mankind, and of whatever in any form of religion may tend towards that end. 6. Membership in this Association shall leave each individual responsible for his own opinion alone, and in no degree affect his relations with other associations.
>
> The presidency of the association was conferred on Professor Huxley, and by him accepted. I remember well the satisfaction with which, referring to the eminent names in the membership, Huxley said: "Freethinkers are no longer to be simply bullied."[36]

Not everyone shared in the enthusiasm for this gathering of radical thinkers. In a manner rather typical of him, Matthew Arnold was quoted as saying: "I am strongly of the opinion that the errors of popular religion in this country are to be dispersed by the spread of a better and wider culture, far more than by direct antagonism and religious counter-movements."[37]

The leading figure, and the person who had done more than anyone else to organize such a gathering of iconoclasts, was not present. Sadly, 1878 was a hard year for Clifford. His father died in February, and that, coupled with the strain of his incredible schedule, brought about another collapse in April. He and Lucy once again set sail for the Mediterranean, with stays in Malta, Gibraltar, Venice and Monte Generoso, where some improvement finally set in by August, at which point he returned. The voyage necessitated his missing the Congress of Liberal Thinkers, where

---

36 Conway, p 352-353.
37 Ibid.

he was to have been the featured speaker. He had tried to prepare a talk to be read in his absence, but even this proved to be too much of a strain. On May 23 he sent a letter to Conway, which arrived while the Congress was in session, consisting of the following notes which he *would* have delivered if he had been able to address the Congress in person:

> Catholics are fond of saying that an age of atheism is approaching, in which we shall throw over all moral obligations, and society will go to ruin. Then we shall see what is the true effect of all our liberal and scientific teaching. As a matter of fact, however, even themselves admit that the public conscience is growing in strength and straightness, while the Catholic dogmas and organism are more and more repudiated. We may see reason to believe that the former of those facts is the cause of the latter. Part of modern unbelief is no doubt due to the wider knowledge of criticism of the so-called "evidence of Christianity," but in all ages sensible men have seen through that flimsy structure. Intellectual scepticism is not really more rife than it has been in many past periods. The main ground of hope for the masses is the moral basis of scepticism - 1, its revolt against mythology; 2, its revolt against the priestly organisation of the churches.
>
> As to the mythology, the dogma of eternal damnation is being quietly dropped, as not in the Jewish part of the New Testament; but it has been practically taught by the Christian organisation for sixteen centuries. Therefore the Christian organisation ought to be thrown away with it, for it is not "an opinion like another," but a wicked thing to believe.
>
> As to the priestly organisation, the practical effect of the Christian organisation, "the Church," has always been adverse to morality, and is now. The clergy is everywhere making more pronounced its revolt from the great principles which underlie the modern social structure. There is a strong antagonism between the Christian organisation and the Jewish ethical literature, which our moral sense approves. And I believe that, so far as the Christian organisation is concerned, the time has come for heeding again the ancient warning: "Come out of her, my people, that ye be not partaker of her sins, and that ye receive not her plagues."[38]

Vintage Clifford. There is no doubt that such a talk would have been well received by the assembled freethinkers. The association had several meetings at Huxley's home following the Congress, but without Clifford's guiding hand and boundless enthusiasm it could not continue, and it ceased to exist shortly after Clifford's death.

---

38 Ibid., 354.

6. Final Illness and Death

Clifford returned to England in August of 1878, looking haggard and still enfeebled by the tuberculosis that was killing him. Friends noted that his good spirits had not left him, but he was no longer capable of his usual exertions. He kept his wits about him, and did not recant from his previously-held views. When made aware of a newspaper report which claimed that he was converting back to Christianity in his final days, Clifford fired back a retort that, while his doctor had certified that he was ill, "twas not mental derangement."[39]

In his autobiography, Moncure Conway writes:

> Professor Clifford's ailment was consumption; during its rapid progress we were all under illusive hopes excited by his inexhaustible spirits. In September, 1878, it became certain that he would not recover. One day when my wife and I were on our way to visit the Cliffords, we met Huxley just from the house. His face was clouded with despair, and he exclaimed, "The finest scientific mind in England for fifty years is dying in that house." On entering we found Clifford in his armchair, serene and full of his habitual humour, his wife trying to smile. He had just been writing and showing her a skit after the style of Lucian which he repeated to us. It represented Christ and his disciples strolling through Hyde Park and subjected to questions by suspicious policemen. The talk between St. Peter and a policeman was exquisitely comical. Clifford spoke of St. George Mivart's claiming the favour of scientific men for his Catholic Church on the ground of its evolution from the moral and spiritual forces of the whole world; and also something he had read concerning the superiority of that church in bringing the humble people in contact with pictures and images. "This," he said, "is all ingenious and plausible - families all want some church or other to go to on Sundays; but the man is in doubt between competing sects: the Catholic Church steps forwards and says, 'I'm a pretty woman - choose me!'"[40]

While travel was dangerous, it became evident as the winter weather ensued that Clifford's only hope for survival was to leave England and once again venture to a warmer clime. He and his wife set sail for Madeira, Portugal in February of 1879. To its credit, the Senate of University College recommended that he keep his chair in Mathematics,

---

[39] Quoted in Bernard Lightman, *The Origins of Agnosticism: Victorian Unbelief and the Limits of Knowledge* (Baltimore: Johns Hopkins University Press, 1987), 122.
[40] Conway, 361.

and, provided that his health should improve, he be invited to lecture on special subjects not involving any strain to his system. The February 13, 1879 issue of *Nature* reported on a testimonial meeting held by a number of his friends, as a demonstration of their affection and admiration: "The friends of Professor Clifford, who has been compelled by ill health to relinquish active work and reside in Madeira, are anxious to present him with a substantial testimonial in public recognition of his great scientific and literary attainments. At a meeting held at the Royal Institution . . . it was resolved that a fund should be raised for the above-mentioned purpose, and that the sums received should be placed in the hands of trustees for the benefit of Professor Clifford and his family."[41] Among the signatories were T. H. Huxley, John Tyndall, Dr. William Spottiswood, president of the Royal Society, the mathematician H. J. S. Smith (who would edit the posthumous collection of Clifford's mathematical papers) and Sir Frederick Pollock (who, with Leslie Stephen, would co-edit the posthumous collection of Clifford's popular lectures and essays). According to Noel Annan, it was Stephen (who had been elected to the Metaphysical Society in 1877), in mourning from the recent death of his wife, who was instrumental in these efforts. "It was characteristic of Stephen," Annan writes, "that, when he was broken by Minny's death and spent his days in solitude, he roused himself to make one new friend who needed friendship and was enduring a harder fate than himself, the brilliant mathematician, William Kingdon Clifford, at that date almost at his last gasp from consumption. It was Stephen who got up a subscription to send him to Madeira in the vain hope that he might recover."[42] In a letter to Oliver Wendell Holmes, Jr., dated January 4, 1879, Stephen expressed his strong feelings for his young friend:

> Poor young Clifford, the eminent atheist & mathematician has about finished his career at the age of 32 or thereabouts. He has been breaking bloodvessels & going down the usual descent & at last his doctors have said he cannot live for more than 2 or 3 weeks if he stays here & as a last desperate chance, his poor wife is taking him out to Madeira. He will probably never get there, though he starts on Tuesday. I have been sitting with him a good deal in some poor little lodgings where they have been for the last three months & seen him visibly failing. He has been admirably brave & cheerful, though poor fellow, he will leave a wife & 2 little babies

---

41 Quoted by James R. Newman in his introduction to *The Common Sense of the Exact Sciences,* lvii.
42 Noel Annan, *Leslie Stephen: The Godless Victorian* (New York: Random House, 1984), 100.

with next to nothing, I fear. I could write a deathbed scene of an atheist who would scandalize the pious; for whenever the poor lad (he is really a boy in everything but ability) could talk, he enjoyed nothing so much as talk of a kind not calculated to edify believers. I believe, though I have to take it on faith, that he is really something astonishing as a mathematician; but he was delicate & utterly careless & has finally thrown his life away. I have grown very fond of him lately, for he is a good kindhearted simple creature & delighted in talking infidelity much as a schoolboy would enjoy breaking painted windows.[43]

Stephen continued to look after Clifford's family after his death, and befriended Lucy, who often stayed at his house in Cornwall. Annan's biography of Stephen is illustrated by charming cartoons which Stephen drew to entertain Clifford's young daughters, including one of a tired bear reading from *The Dictionary of National Biography* (of which Stephen was the general editor). One can imagine that the bear is reading Stephen's own entry on Clifford, which he was to write not long after Clifford's death.

Although he did have a few days of rest in the sun, Clifford sensed that his life was coming to an end. He knew a week before that his death could come at any time, yet, in Pollock's words: ". . . his interest in the outer world, his affection for his friends and his pleasure in their pleasures, did not desert him to the very last. He still followed the course of events, and asked for public news on the morning of his death, so strongly did he hold fast his part in the common weal and in active social life."[44] He gave careful directions for the disposal of his papers. He had a long-standing interest in the life and work of Spinoza (in 1877 he had been planning to lecture on this topic at the London Institution, but his health had not allowed it), so it is not surprising that Spinoza's great saying was often on his lips: "*Homo liber de nulla re minus quam de morte cogitate*"; "There is nothing over which a free man ponders less than death" (*Ethics,* P. IV, Prop. 67).

W. K. Clifford died on March 3, 1879, at the age of 33. His body was brought back from Madeira and buried in Highgate Cemetery, with an epitaph he had chosen from Epictetus: "I was not, and was conceived: I loved, and did a little work: I am not, and grieve not." Conway remarks: "There was some excitement about the admission into Highgate Cemetery

---

43 Leslie Stephen, *Selected Letters of Leslie Stephen,* Volume 1, edited by John W. Bicknell (Columbus: Ohio State University Press, 1996), 236.
44 Pollock, introduction to *Lectures and Essays,* p 19-20.

of this epitaph, but such was the love for Clifford that the objectors could not venture to encounter it."[45]

Perhaps the most fitting written memorial for Clifford could be found in a letter he wrote to Lucy, during their courtship, in 1874. It expresses quite nicely the type of person Clifford admired, and wished to emulate, and symbolically represents his oft-stated goal of helping humanity to advance from the worship of Christ to the appreciation of the possibilities inherent in the human species itself:

> ... the people in the middle ages had a closer connection between theory and practice; a fellow would get a practical idea into his head, be cock-sure it was right, and then get up and snort and just have it carried through. Nowadays we don't have prophets with the same fire and fervour and insight. To which it may be said that our problems are infinitely more complex, and that we can't be so cock-sure of the right thing to do . . . Still there is room for some earnest person to go and preach around in a simple way the main straightforward rules that society has unconsciously worked out and that are floating in the air; to do as well as possible what one can do best; to work for the improvement of the social organisation; to seek earnestly after truth and only to accept provisionally opinions one has not inquired into; to regard men as comrades in work and their freedom as a sacred thing; in fact, to recognise the enormous and fearful difference between truth and falsehood, right and wrong, and how truth and right are to be got at by free inquiry and the love of our comrades for their own sakes and nobody else's.[46]

This was an agenda that Clifford attempted to fulfill. If he held human beings up to high standards, then they were standards he himself never shirked from striving toward. It would be hard to find an example of a more earnest person, and it is not inappropriate to consider him to have been a preacher, albeit an unorthodox one to be sure. No Kantian ever extolled more highly the virtue of duty, nor more fervently advocated truth for truth's sake, and no Utilitarian showed greater concern for the well-being - both physical and mental - of the human species as a whole. As Pollock summarized his friend in the moving introduction to Clifford's *Lectures and Essays:* "If there was anything for which he had no toleration, and with which he would enter into no compromise, it was insincerity in thought, word, or deed. He expressed his own opinions plainly and strongly because he held it the duty of every man so to do; he

---

45 Conway, 361.
46 W. K. Clifford, *Lectures and Essays,* 22.

could not discuss great subjects in a half-hearted fashion under a system of mutual conventions . . . Being always frank, he was at times indiscreet; but consummate discretion has never yet been recognised as a necessary or even a very appropriate element of moral heroism. This must be borne in mind in estimating such passages of his writings as, judged by the ordinary rules of literary etiquette, may seem harsh or violent."[47] This is especially true in analyzing Clifford's most famous, and pugnacious essay, "The Ethics of Belief," which will be done in the next chapter. First though, it is important to look at Clifford's intellectual significance, and the contributions he made to the fields of mathematics, psychology and social sciences in general, as well as to philosophy.

7. Clifford's Contributions

1. Mathematics

The field in which Clifford truly excelled, and in which he made his signal contributions, was mathematics. He developed the theory of biquaterions, and linked them with more general associative algebras. His work showing how certain three parallels define a ruled second-order surface was honored by being labeled a "Clifford's surface". Two lines of the same type on the Clifford surface are equidistant from each other throughout their length and have infinitely many common perpendiculars of the other type. The parallel lines in elliptic space are called "Clifford parallels". His major contributions were in the area of geometry, where he was to write many highly technical papers. In his entry on Clifford in the *Dictionary of Scientific Biography,* John D. North writes:

> In mathematics, Clifford was first and foremost a geometer . . . Clifford left memorable results, as in his investigations of the geometrical consequences of extending a method of Cayley's for forming a product of determinants, in his research into quaternion representations of the most general rigid motion in space, and in his application of the techniques of higher-dimension geometry to a problem in probability. Simultaneously with Max Noether he proved (1870) that a Cremona transformation may be regarded as a compound of quadratic transformations, and toward the end of his life (1877) he established some important topological equivalences for Riemann surfaces. In all this, Clifford justifies the commonly

---

47 Pollock, introduction to *Lectures and Essays,* 14.

expressed belief of contemporaries that his early death deprived the world of one of the best mathematicians of his generation.[48]

Demonstrating a proficiency in his chosen profession which early marked him out for top honors, he never allowed his extracurricular activities to interfere with his pursuit of knowledge for its own sake. A practical man himself, in one of his earliest public addresses, the 1868 lecture "On Some of the Conditions of Mental Development", Clifford felt the need to defend abstruse mathematical researches which seemed to have no usefulness in-and-of-themselves. "The fact is," he asserted, "that the most useful parts of science have been investigated for the sake of truth, and not for their usefulness. A new branch of mathematics, which has sprung up in the last twenty years, was denounced by the Astronomer-Royal before the University of Cambridge as doomed to be forgotten, on account of its usefulness. Now it turns out that the reason why we cannot go further in our investigations of molecular action is that we do not know enough of this branch of mathematics."[49] One can see his wariness of Utilitarianism, although his argument is actually a defense of the possible long-term utility of research with no obvious physical application at the time.

Clifford's friend H. J. Stephen Smith, a noted geometer who held the Savilian chair at Oxford and who would help to edit his posthumous papers on mathematics, pointed out the clever way in which Clifford extended his love for geometry into the world as a whole:

> . . . to this his favourite science he attributed the widest imaginable scope, and at times regarded it as co-extensive with the whole domain of nature. He was a metaphysician (though he would only have accepted the name subject to an interpretation) as well as a mathematician; and geometry was to him an important factor in the problem of "solving the universe." Thus he was a geometer of a type peculiarly his own; and his dealings with the science were characterized by an amount of scepticism and an amount of faith which one would hardly expect to find combined in a mathematician.[50]

---

48 John D. North, entry on "W. K. Clifford" in *Dictionary of Scientific Biography* (New York: Charles Scribner's Sons, 1971), p 322-323.
49 W. K. Clifford, "On Some of the Conditions of Mental Development" in *Lectures and Essays,* p 70-71.
50 H. J. Stephen Smith, introduction to W. K. Clifford, *Mathematical Papers,* edited by Robert Tucker (London: Macmillan, 1882), xii.

While able to interact familiarly with learned mathematicians operating on the highest of levels, Clifford also wished to share his enthusiasm for the topic with a wider group, and felt a moral obligation to educate the general public. His natural gift for clarity of expression aided him in this endeavor. Leslie Stephen summarized his career in the following words:

> As a mathematical writer Clifford was marked by a keen power of imagination, rich in its suggestions of new lines of thought and discovery; he was a standing example of the fact that the true man of science, especially the mathematician, is the man of speculation, of tested theory, of keen, albeit disciplined imagination. His "Canonical Dissection of a Riemann's Surface," his theory of "Biquaternions," and his unfinished memoir "On the Classification of Loci," belong to the classics of mathematical literature. As a mathematical teacher Clifford did much (and his influence is still working) to revolutionise the teaching of elementary mathematics; he introduced into England the graphical and geometrical methods of Mobius, Culmann, and other Germans. His uncompleted textbook on "Dynamics," his fragmentary "Common Sense of the Exact Sciences," and the "Lectures on Geometry" represent especially the direction and novelty of his elementary teaching; its fundamental aim was not to teach a student the analytical solution of a problem, but to force him to think for himself.[51]

Ironically enough, Clifford's influence in promoting mathematical awareness would occur some six years after his death. In 1886, his friend and student Karl Pearson (1857-1936), himself a distinguished mathematician, completed Clifford's *The Common Sense of the Exact Sciences,* the aim of which was to explain modern scientific and mathematical thought to the uninitiated. Clifford's original plan was to produce a book called *The First Principles of the Mathematical Sciences Explained to the Non-Mathematical,* containing six chapters on *Number, Space, Quantity, Position, Motion,* and *Mass.* He completed the first two chapters, and saw them in proof, as well as the first portion of the chapter on Quantity, and nearly the entire chapter on Motion. Shortly before his death, he expressed the wish that the title should be changed to *The Common Sense of the Exact Sciences.* The job of revising and completing the work was at first to be done by Clifford's colleague at University College, London, R. C. Rowe, the Professor of Pure Mathematics, but he

---

[51] Leslie Stephen, entry on "W. K. Clifford" in *Dictionary of National Biography,* 540-541.

himself died in October of 1884, and the task was then given to Pearson, who consulted with Mrs. W. K. Clifford in order to complete the work in a way as true to Clifford's intentions as possible.

Pearson was to hold the same position as his mentor, being appointed Chair of Applied Mathematics and Mechanics at University College, London in 1884. Also like Clifford, he combined his mathematical acumen with a great interest in politics and social issues, giving public lectures and advocating for university reform. Becoming one of the leading experts on statistics, Pearson was to spend much of his later career as an advocate of the controversial science of human genetics. In her history of English social science from 1870-1914, Reba N. Soffer discusses Pearson's changing position regarding the best way to bring about a good society:

> Progressive reformers were entirely in sympathy with Pearson's dictum in 1885 that since social stability depended upon individual morality and that in turn depended upon education, it was a "'primary function of society to educate its members." But his post-Boer War rejection of nurture for a theory of determinism of nature directly contradicted everything that reformers believed. In part, Pearson's zealotry for eugenics as an escape from biological necessity came from an essentially religious feeling, made even stronger by his agnostic break with the Church of England, that wherever error existed it must be corrected.[52]

One can see how Pearson carried on not only Clifford's mathematical work, but also his campaign to reform society, albeit with methods Clifford might not have approved of. For all his eccentricities, Pearson was himself a first-rate mathematician. In a rather offbeat encomium to both Clifford and Pearson, E. T. Bell, in his book *The Development of Mathematics* (1945), writes: "Pearson's enthusiasm for W. K. Clifford's intuitive dynamics and physics, also for Clifford's violent hostility to traditional beliefs, influenced at least his earlier thinking. Both Clifford and Pearson were creative mathematicians; neither fitted the milk-and-water, namby-pamby 'great man' ideal of the 'great mathematician' which seems to be the accepted norm in historical accounts of mathematicians; and at least one of them would have hooted at the idea that he was, or was to become, an object of reverence to generations of students."[53]

---

52 Reba N. Soffer, *Ethics and Society in England: The Revolution in the Social Sciences 1870-1914* (Berkeley: University of California Press, 1978), 197.
53 E. T. Bell, *The Development of Mathematics* (New York: McGraw-Hill Book Company, Inc., 1945), 610.

The Common Sense of the Exact Sciences was much in line with Clifford's lifelong intention to make mathematics as assessible as possible to the general public. It became a bestseller for its original publisher, Kegan Paul, Trench, & Co., and in a reprinted edition published by Alfred A. Knopf in 1946, no less a personage than Bertrand Russell, in his preface, was to remark on the influence Clifford's writings had on him, and also on their continuing relevance to the spreading of mathematical knowledge:

> The copy of this book which I still possess was given to me by my tutor when I was fifteen years of age. I read it at once, with passionate interest and with an intoxicating delight in intellectual clarification . . . Now, having re-read it after fifty-seven years, many of them devoted to the subjects of which it treats, I find that it deserved all the adolescent enthusiasm that I bestowed upon it when I first read it . . .The subject of which this book treats - the basis of pure mathematics in logic and of applied mathematics in observation - is one in which immense progress has been made since the time when Clifford wrote, but knowledge of subsequent work only increases the reader's admiration for his prophetic insight. All that is said on the relation of geometry to physics is entirely in harmony with Einstein's theory of gravitation, which was published thirty-six years after Clifford's death . . . Clifford's book may not only still be read with great profit by young people interested in mathematics, but should also be studied with diligent admiration by all who are engaged in trying to make difficult ideas intelligible.[54]

High praise indeed, from another first-rate mathematician who shared Clifford's gift of clarity as well as his almost-evangelical desire to improve the lot of humanity.

Karl Pearson early on pointed out one of Clifford's most significant contributions to the field of mathematics. Clifford, he said, "may be regarded as marking an epoch in the history of this science in England. He was among the first by his writings to raise a protest against the analytical bias of the Cambridge school."[55] As an undergraduate at Cambridge, Clifford had become interested in the work on non-Euclidean geometry that had been done by Riemann and Lobachevski. His knowledge of languages, especially German, gave him a facility to understand these

---

[54] Bertrand Russell, preface to W. K. Clifford's *The Common Sense of the Exact Sciences,* p v-vi, viii.
[55] Leslie Stephen, entry on "W. K. Clifford" in the *Dictionary of National Biography,* 540.

foreign articles which many of his fellow English geometers lacked, and his natural curiosity and willingness to follow arguments to their logical conclusions even when such conclusions were not what he was initially prepared to accept made him receptive to the shocking implications of these works.

In a charming book called *For My Grandson: Remembrances of An Ancient Victorian,* Frederick Pollock discussed the climate at Cambridge when he and Clifford were students there: "We were too cocksure about lots of things. Many pages were written by great logicians wondering how we knew that Euclid's axioms were absolutely true. Some great mathematicians, my dear friend Clifford among them, had the courage to say we knew no such thing, and now we know they are not true for the space we live in, though near enough for common terrestrial purposes."[56]

This was an exiting time to be a student of mathematics, for fundamental changes were occurring in the field. First of all, there was a change in attitude regarding received wisdom. For more than 2,000 years, Euclid's geometry had been considered as an unquestioned certain body of knowledge. Up until the middle of the nineteenth century, geometry and arithmetic (both areas in which Clifford excelled) were considered to be the two main parts of mathematics, but algebra and analysis had since become established areas in their own right.

Another change was the way in which mathematical knowledge was imparted. Even in Clifford's day there was still a general attitude that one accepted a set of axioms without question, much as religious believers accepted the revealed truth of sacred scripture, but this no longer seemed an acceptable approach, given the innovations in the field. In the words of E. T. Bell: "We seem to have come a long way since 1873, when that erudite English historian of mathematics and indefatigable manufacturer of drier-than-dust college textbooks, Isaac Todhunter (1820-1884) counseled a meek docility, sustained by an avid credulity, as the path of intellectual rectitude: 'If he [a student of mathematics] does not believe the statements of his tutor, probably [in Todhunter's day at Cambridge] a clergyman of mature knowledge, recognized ability and blameless character - his suspicion is irrational, and manifests a want of the power of appreciating evidence, a want fatal to his success in that branch of science which he is supposed to be cultivating.'"[57] No man ever showed greater respect for adhering to evidence than W. K. Clifford, but such a

---

56 Sir Frederick Pollock, *For My Grandson: Remembrances of an Ancient Victorian* (London: John Murray, 1933), vii.
57 Bell, vi.

reverential attitude toward a purveyor of the truth rather than toward the truth itself went against everything he stood for, especially at a time when the long-accepted "truths" of his own area of expertise, geometry, were being questioned as never before. As Bell adds: "Each of five men - Lobachewsky, Bolyai, Plucker, Riemann, Lie - invented as part of his lifework as much (or more) new geometry as was created by all the Greek mathematicians in the two or three centuries of their greatest activity. There are good grounds for the frequent assertion that the nineteenth century alone contributed about five times to mathematics as had all preceding history."[58]

Clifford made his own significant contribution by becoming one of the leading exponents of the new non-Euclidean geometry. In 1873, for instance, he translated Riemann's "Habilitationsvortrag" into English and had it published in *Nature,* a mere six years after its original appearance. In his lecture delivered that same year, "The Philosophy of the Pure Sciences," Clifford asserted: "It was Riemann . . . who first accomplished the task of analysing all the assumptions of geometry, and showing which of them were independent. This very disentangling and separation of them is sufficient to deprive them for the geometer of their exactness and necessity; for the process by which it is effected consists in showing the possibility of conceiving these suppositions one by one to be untrue; whereby it is clearly made out how much is supposed."[59]

Clifford was well aware that he was living in an exciting time, and made the bold claim that "What Vesalius was to Galen, what Copernicus was to Ptolemy, that was Lobatchewsky to Euclid . . ."[60] He reveled in the possibilities of these new approaches. In Pollock's words: "He took much pleasure in the speculative constructions of imaginary or non-Euclidean systems of space-relations which have been achieved by Continental geometers, partly because they afforded a congenial field for the combined exercise of scientific intuition and unbridled fancy. He liked talking about imaginary geometry, as a matter of pure amusement, to any one interested in it. But at the same time he attached a serious import to it."[61]

---

58 *Ibid.,* p 15-16.
59 W. K. Clifford, "The Philosophy of the Pure Sciences" in *Lectures and Essays,* 228.
60 Ibid., 212.
61 Pollock, introduction to *Lectures and Essays,* p 10-11.

Geometry held a role in philosophy which was important enough that changes in the interpretation of geometrical knowledge could have strong ramifications. Philosophy of science was seen as closely tied up with the metaphysics of many other areas, so a change in the status of geometry could have a very far-reaching effect.[62]

Thus, the introduction of non-Euclidean geometry was not only a challenge to mathematicians - it also was a blow to those philosophers and theologians who held to the existence of necessary and universal truths in general. If even Euclid's geometry could be assailed, after thousands of years of being unquestioned, then what *else* might prove assailable? In particular, Kant's contention that space could be proved using the eternal truth of Euclidean geometry existing outside of our experience was no longer tenable, as Clifford was quick to point out.

Clifford, being in the forefront of this new approach to geometry, was also one of the first to announce the radical implications it had for philosophy, just as he was one of the first to announce the radical implications that Darwin's theory of evolution would have beyond the field of biology. Indeed, he made an explicit connection between non-Euclidean geometry and evolution in his epistemological speculations. Clifford can be considered a pioneer in the field of psychology, which was just emerging at that time as a field of study separate from philosophy.

2. Psychology

By following the lead of Riemann and Lobachevski, Clifford was atypical for his time in arguing that geometrical truth is a production of experience, for he saw that, in Howard E. Smokler's words, "through a change in the basic assumptions of microgeometry (geometry of the infinitesimally small) he could work out a system of geometry and physics which would clear up the anomalies in physical theory that existed in his day. He saw that a reformulation of microgeometry in non-Euclidean terms could achieve this result, and in this respect he anticipated, at least in part, Einstein's program."[63] He is given credit for anticipating Einstein's theory of gravitation, in his chapter "On the Bending of Space" in *The*

---

62 J. L. Richards, "The Reception of a Mathematical Theory: Non-Euclidean Geometry in England, 1868-1883" in *Natural Order: Historical Studies of Scientific Culture,* edited by Barry Barnes and Steven Shapin (London: Sage Publications, 1979),   146.
63 Howard E. Smokler, entry on "William Kingdon Clifford" in *The Encyclopedia of Philosophy*   (New York: Macmillan Press, 1966),   125.

Common Sense of the Exact Sciences and in remarks he made in a paper entitled "On the Space-Theory of Matter", in which he suggested that:

> (1) small portions of space *are* in fact of a nature analogous to little hills on a surface which is on the average flat; namely, that the ordinary laws of geometry are not valid in them. (2) That this property of being curved or distorted is continually being passed on from one portion of space to another after the matter of a wave. (3) That this variation of the curvature of space is what really happens in that phenomena which we call the *motion of matter*, whether ponderable or ethereal. (4) That in the physical world nothing else takes place but this variation, subject (possibly) to the law of continuity.[64]

Not all historians of science are willing to accord Clifford such high praise, however. E. T. Bell, for all his admiration of Clifford, writes: "This embryonic divination has been acclaimed as an anticipation of Einstein's (1915-1916) relativistic theory of the gravitational field. The actual theory, however, bears but slight resemblance to Clifford's rather detailed creed. As a rule, those mathematical prophets who never descend to particulars make the top scores. Almost anyone can hit the side of a barn at forty yards with a charge of buckshot."[65] While Clifford, of all people, would have agreed that the belief he would have beaten Einstein to the punch lacks sufficient evidence to be held as true, it is clear that had he lived he would have almost assuredly "descended into particulars" regarding an area that was still in his own estimation speculative.

Whatever the credit due him, Clifford's concern with the composition of matter related to the influence which Spinoza continued to have on him. And this was to lead to his own concern - one shared by his fellow freethinker T. H. Huxley - about the problem of consciousness. While the freethinkers were constantly being referred to as "materialists", both Clifford and Huxley took pains to avoid being thus labeled. Here is how Clifford himself saw the term as it applied to consciousness:

> Many eminent men have been so much impressed with the exact correspondence between what goes on in our minds and what goes on in our brains, that they have mixed up the two things; and they have used expressions, such as to say that thought is a secretion, as if it were a really mechanical thing which was produced by the brain, or even a mechanical

---

64 W. K. Clifford, "On the Space-Theory of Matter" in *Mathematical Papers*, 21-22.
65 Bell, 360.

state of motion produced by the motion of the brain in the same way as other machines produce states of motion in other things. Or they have said that the mental force is correlated with the natural forces, meaning that it can be produced out of natural forces. These expressions belong to the view that mental facts, states of consciousness, that the whole subject of the mind of man is a subject dealing with a material thing like his body. The view which regards mental facts as just a part of a train of material facts is commonly called materialism.[66]

While recognizing that the word "materialist" had been a term of opprobrium, this was not his reason for distancing himself from it. Rather, he found the hypothesis that mental facts and material facts are one and the same to be untenable. And yet, not wanting to be counted as a dualist, Clifford needed some way to subsume the two under one category. He came up with a rather tortured theory of "mind-stuff" - an infelicitous term and one rather ill-defined. He wrote about this in his essay "On the Nature of Things-in-Themselves", which was originally delivered as his first lecture to the Metaphysical Society, on June 9, 1874, and was later published in the influential journal *Mind,* in the January 1878 issue.

Like those other mathematician/philosophers Rene Descartes and Bertrand Russell, Clifford sought to analyze subjects by breaking them down into their simplest components, and he saw no reason why the universe itself could not be so analyzed. The basis unit of the universe, he argued, is something he called "mind-stuff." Feelings arise from a certain conjunction of such units, and the greater the complexity of the organism, the greater the amount of feeling. At a certain point in the continuum, consciousness arises, although it is difficult to ascertain where exactly the line can be drawn. Humans are unique in that they are aware of consciousness in other members of their same species. This is not an *object,* using Clifford's terminology, which would be a phenomenon presented to one's consciousness, but rather an *eject,* an inferred existence which is "thrown out" of one's own consciousness. Arising from such awarenesses of objects and ejects are *beliefs,* which concern the future sequence of feelings about these entities. "The existence of this table," he states, "as an object in my consciousness carries with it the belief that if I climb up on it I shall be able to walk about it as if it were the ground. But the existence of my conception of you in my consciousness carries with it

---

66 W. K. Clifford, *Seeing and Thinking* (London: Macmillan, 1890), 88.

the belief in the existence of you outside my consciousness, a belief which can never be expressed in terms of the future sequence of my feelings."[67]

Like Descartes, Clifford is veering dangerously close to solipsism here, which he recognizes, since he adds: "It may very well be that I myself as the only existence, but it is simply ridiculous to suppose that anybody else is. The position of absolute idealism may, therefore, be left out of count, although each individual may be unable to justify his dissent from it."[68] Still, the belief in the existence of other people's consciousness remains a constant, and is a guide to action. In addition, one also infers the existence of similar objects in other people's minds, so that the chair I see before me is an object, while the same chair is inferred by me to exist in the minds of those around me. It, too, is an eject. Clifford uses the term "social object" to refer to the complex symbolization of an infinite number of ejects related to the objects they resemble. He goes further, by questioning the existence of individual objects unconnected to ejects:

> Now, it is probable that the individual object, as such, never exists in the mind of man. For there is every reason to believe that we were gregarious animals before we became men properly so called. And a belief in the eject - some sort of recognition of a kindred consciousness in one's fellow-beings - is clearly a condition of gregarious action among animals so highly developed as to be called conscious at all.[69]

Consciousness, then, arises from feelings, which in turn arise from a combination of "mind-stuff". Although not all things possess mind or consciousness, they all do possess some small piece of mind-stuff, and when the elements of this come together in a large enough unit, there is the beginning of sentience: "As we go back along the line, the complexity of the organism and of its nerve-action insensibly diminishes . . . All this imagined line of organisms is a series of objects in my consciousness; they form an insensible gradation, and yet there is a certain unknown point at which I am at liberty to infer facts *out* of my consciousness corresponding to them. There is only one way out of the difficulty, and to that we are driven. Consciousness is a complex of ejective facts."[70]

Consciousness, Clifford further argued (using language similar to that which William James would employ in his *Psychology*), consists of a

---

67 W. K. Clifford, "On the Nature of Things-in-Themselves" in *Lectures and Essays,* p 275-276.
68 Ibid.
69 Ibid., 277.
70 Ibid., 284.

stream of feelings, including a feeling of personality. Showing his debt to Hume, he writes: "It seems to me that I find nothing in myself which is not accounted for when I describe myself as a stream of feelings such that each of them is capable of a faint repetition . . . It seems to me that this is a complete account of all the kinds of facts which I can find in myself . . . and if anybody finds any other kinds of facts in himself, it is an exceedingly important thing that he should describe them as clearly as he possibly can."[71]

Clifford's presentation of "ejects" and "mind-stuff" did not prove to be persuasive, nor did it have much effect on the contemporary discussions of consciousness in the pages of *Mind*. Still, there are definite similarities here with James' influential "stream of consciousness" approach, which would appear elsewhere a few years after Clifford's death. James was an avid reader of as well as a contributor to *Mind*.

One can also see in Clifford's discussion of "objects" and "ejects" a theory about the intellectual development of the human species, a concern first expressed in his 1868 lecture "On Some of the Conditions of Mental Development." In his 1874 essay "Body and Mind", he adds: "I have absolutely no means of perceiving your mind. I judge by analogy that it exists, and the instinct which leads me to come to that conclusion is the social instinct, as it has been formed in me by generations during which men have lived together; and they could not have lived together unless they had gone upon that supposition."[72]

In his 1875 essay "On the Scientific Basis of Morality", Clifford coined the term "the tribal self" to explain how a conception of another's mind becomes the starting point for morality - a conception which other living things do not seem to have. "A cat," he writes, "likes your hand, and your lap, and the food you give her; but I do not think she has a conception of *you*." Puckishly, he can't resist adding in a footnote: "Present company always excepted - I fully believe in the personal and disinterested affection of *my* cat."[73] The idea of the social instinct was key to his ethical writings, and was at the heart of his famous assertion: "it is wrong always, everywhere, and for any one to believe anything upon insufficient evidence." The pursuit of knowledge was a social issue, and one in which all members of the human species participate.

---

[71] W. K. Clifford, "Body and Mind" in *Lectures and Essays,* 258.
[72] Ibid., , 262.
[73] W. K. Clifford, "On the Scientific Basis of Morality" in *Lectures and Essays,* 292.

Clifford saw knowledge from a biological perspective, as growing out of a response from an organism to adjust to the world. Thus, even the axioms of geometry, once taken to be eternal, were themselves forms of experience. Furthermore, this construction has become transformed into neural capacities. In the words of Howard E. Smokler: ". . . Clifford conceived of the form-content distinction of knowledge as one relative to the biological development of the race. What is at one time the content of experience is later, through a biological process, transformed into a form of experience."[74] The principles of geometry and arithmetic, then, along with other laws, serve as ways of structuring human experience.

Mind was an ideal journal for the publication of Clifford's speculations regarding consciousness. It was founded in 1876 and financially supported by the psychologist James Bain. Previous to this, the only other outlet in Britain for discussions of consciousness was the *Fortnightly Review*, another frequent publisher of Clifford's essays, and one which was sympathetic to Clifford's agnostic position. *Mind,* the first journal to devote itself entirely to the newly-forming field of psychology, was more ecumenical in its approach. As Reba N. Soffer writes:

> *Mind* . . . was intended to provide publicity for the widest possible range of psychological and philosophical thought and practice. Even more, the new quarterly set out to stimulate public acceptance of psychology as a "scientific" subject. It was no coincidence that *Mind* was begun after the Royal Commission of Scientific Instruction in 1876 deliberately omitted from their survey the "Mental and Moral Sciences" on the grounds that they were not of sufficiently scientific interest.[75]

The editor of *Mind* was G. Croom Robertson, a colleague of Clifford's at University College, London, where he was Grote Professor of Mind and Logic, and also a fellow member of the Metaphysical Society. He had been elected to his position at University College in 1866, at the age of 24, in lieu of James Martineau, "whom George Grote had opposed on the ground that the position was incompatible with any clerical profession."[76] Grote was a good friend of Bain's, and it is likely that the latter suggested Robertson, his student and collaborator, for the position. It was also Bain who insisted, on condition of his becoming the financial backer of the project, that Robertson be named sole editor of *Mind.* Robertson shared

---

74 Howard E. Smokler, 124.
75 Soffer, 130.
76 Alan Willard Brown, *The Metaphysical Society: Victorian Minds in Crisis, 1869-1880* (New York: Octagon Books, 1973), 197.

not only academic interests with Clifford, but character traits as well, and a similar constitution and personal history. Alan Brown describes how his editing of the journal was combined with "heavy teaching obligations in University College and elsewhere. But his youthful precocity had left him fragile and sickly, and in consequence he never dared to overtax his strength. His health finally broke down almost completely; and he was tended like a brother in his last illness by his devoted friend Leslie Stephen. As with W. K. Clifford, his friends and admirers, who were many, were sure that if his health had been better he would have done great things . . . And perhaps *Mind,* which is still published and enjoys the highest prestige among philosophers, is a sufficient monument to Robertson's gifts."[77]

Robertson was careful not to let his own materialistic perspective dominate the journal. He treated psychology as a common ground for different philosophical schools to interact. "Rejecting uniformity or agreement," Soffer writes, "*Mind* provided an outlet for such developing and diverse concerns as human and animal neurology, language, pathological behavior, anthropology, animal psychology, and the relation between psychology, biology, and the physical sciences. *Mind's* great influence came from its freedom from both old traditions and new dogmas."[78] It was a perfect forum for Clifford to express his own systematic speculations regarding the origins and development of human consciousness. Beginning in 1879, the year of Clifford's death, one of its more frequent contributors was William James, later to become Clifford's most famed critic.

"On the Nature of Things-in-Themselves" is an article filled with undigested ideas, in which Clifford, influenced still by Spinoza, but also trying to adhere to the latest findings in evolutionary thought, gave his own theory of the basic composition of the universe. One wonders how the members of the Metaphysical Society must have reacted to the initial presentation of his paper, for his almost Berkeleyan idealistic argument that mind was the ultimate reality could not have been pleasing to either the traditional theists or the more-materialistically oriented agnostics and positivists present.

In Soffer's view, Clifford was an important, albeit transitional figure, in the development of psychology as an independent academic field. Comparing him to William James, who is often credited with being the most influential figure in this early stage of the discipline's development,

---

77 Ibid., p 202-203.
78 Soffer, 131.

she argues that Clifford was unable to break away fully from the older tradition of seeing mind as a passive, non-emotional entity, although he was certainly one of the first to apply Darwinian evolutionary principles to an understanding of how consciousness might have occurred in the first place. Although influenced by Herbert Spencer's view that the mind differentiates itself and becomes more integrated in its relation to other minds (Clifford's "ejects") as well as external things, he differed from Spencer in regarding the mind as creative rather than merely reactive. Soffer writes:

> Clifford came very close to the new psychology [promoted by James] in his understanding of mind as constantly inventive within a world known only through probable laws. But he remained a transitional figure because he believed absolutely in the existence of value-free truth.[79]

Clifford held that the scientific approach was the best way to reach knowledge which was objective. For him, consciousness is dependent upon a material basis, the brain, and - as was seen earlier in the story given by Moncure Conway - he had absolutely no sympathy with the sort of scientific investigation of psychics being done by James. In his attitude toward scientific advancement, he shared many similarities with Charles S. Peirce, the brilliant American philosopher and mathematician who was a friend to both Clifford and James, and who likewise chided the latter for his near-obsession with psychical research.

Clifford saw Darwin's writings as a scientific explanation for the continuing advancement of consciousness. His was a curious combination of Spinoza's monism, Kant's epistemology and Darwin's evolutionary theory. The philosopher of biology Michael Ruse has gone so far as to call Clifford "one of the first 'evolutionary epistemologists'", for he provided a way of understanding Kant's question "Given our *a priori* knowledge of certain mathematical principles, how is this possible?" by examining the possible origins of such knowledge. "Our ancestors," Ruse writes, trying to summarize Clifford's position, "may have had to work through various geometries by trial and error, whereas we can now know them instinctively," adding: "Emboldened by this sensible epistemological conclusion, Clifford then gave full rein to his metaphysical imagination."[80]

---

79 Ibid.
80 Michael Ruse, entry on "William Kingdon Clifford" in *The Oxford Companion to Philosophy* (Oxford: Oxford University Press, 1995), edited by Ted Honderich, 137.

Thus, it is appropriate to move from an examination of Clifford's significance in psychology to a look at his significance in philosophy, especially metaphysics, an area in which - unlike many of his agnostic colleagues - he was not afraid to tread.

3. Philosophy

Clifford's notion of "mind-stuff" and his bold speculations regarding the basic composition of the universe shows that, unlike most of the English philosophers of his time (or indeed even now), he was not adverse to metaphysics; perhaps his knowledge of German and his ability to read the works of German philosophers had inspired him. To be sure, he was no admirer of idle speculation or unscientific assertions. He once remarked of an acquaintance: "He is writing a book on metaphysics, and is really cut out for it; the clearness with which he thinks he understands things and his total inability to express what little he knows will make his fortune as a philosopher."[81] But Pollock, in his introduction to Clifford's *Lectures and Essays,* makes it clear that this remark did not express Clifford's total rejection of metaphysics as a vital area of exploration:

> He held that metaphysical and theological problems ought to be discussed with exactly the same freedom from preconceived conclusions and fearlessness of consequences as any other problems. And he further held that, as the frank application of the right method of search to the physical sciences has put them on a footing of steady progress, though they differ in the amount and certainty of the knowledge already won in their respective fields . . . But he never accepted, and I do not think he was ever tempted to accept, the doctrine that all metaphysical inquiries ought to be put aside as unprofitable. Indeed he went beyond most English psychologists, though in a general way he must be classed with the English school, in his estimation of the possibility of constructing a definite metaphysical system of scientific principles.[82]

No wonder he felt so at home in a debating group called The Metaphysical Society. Unlike his friends Huxley and Stephen, Clifford would not have found the group's name to be ironic.

In his extended critique of the leading Victorian agnostics, *The Origins of Agnosticism: Victorian Unbelief and the Limits of Knowledge,* Bernard Lightman repeatedly points out how defenders of the natural sciences

---

81 Pollock, introduction to *Lectures and Essays,* 21.
82 Ibid.

were themselves vulnerable to the weapon they wielded against organized religion: the limit of human knowledge. For how could they defend science without admitting that science was unable to provide a grounding for its own basic assumptions? He writes:

> Agnosticism was originally conceived of by Huxley as a powerful weapon to be used by science against the false pretensions of orthodox theology. Ironically, the marriage between agnosticism and scientific naturalism did not work out. As formulated by Huxley, Tyndall, Clifford, Stephen and Spencer, the agnostic position was peculiarly vulnerable in areas that could only embarrass such staunch defenders of the value of natural science . . . The sceptical element of the Victorian agnostics' thought made it difficult for them to demonstrate the reality and validity of the crucial scientific principles of the universality of the law of causation, the uniformity of nature, and the existence of an objective, external, natural world. In a sense, these three scientific axioms became articles of faith, for the agnostics could no more justify certainty in their existence than orthodox Christians could scientifically prove the actuality of the Son, the Father, and the Holy Ghost.[83]

Such an accusation would only be fair if, in fact, any of the agnostics claimed the *certainty* of the existence of such a "holy trinity." But this is not the case. All of them, for instance, were aware of Hume's telling critique of the notion of certainty, and none could provide any better argument than that of Kant - we are conditioned to accept it, although we cannot prove it. Still, Lightman is on the right track when he asserts that most of the agnostics, in their rallying cry for science, evaded any discussion of how to justify causation, the uniformity of nature and the existence of an objective world, either because they had no good arguments themselves, or because they wished to avoid all metaphysical speculation as unfruitful.

Yet Lightman himself shows that one agnostic - W. K. Clifford - not only *did* attempt to provide arguments for such metaphysical constructs, but positively relished the chance to cross swords with theologians on their own turf, and attempt to shift the field of play from their hands into that of the scientists. "Of all the agnostics," Lightman writes, "Clifford was the most aware of the epistemological difficulties generated by his agnosticism. He recognized that from his position the first principles of science could only be contingent, and therefore subject to revision."[84]

---

83 Lightman, 146.
84 Ibid., 161.

Quite rightly, Lightman adds: "Because he was the youngest of the agnostics, he had grown up under the influence of Darwin's views and was able to work out a truly evolutionary worldview . . . Clifford's refusal to base his notion of science on a Newtonian determinism is closely related to his adherence to probabilistic methods. The rise of statistical reasoning, even prior to quantum physics, was one of the factors leading to the decline and fall of causality in scientific explanation. The result for Clifford is a radical uncertainty in science which he cheerfully accepts."[85] As will be explored in the final chapter, Clifford was perfectly willing to use an "as if" approach to the reality of causation, the uniformity of nature and the existence of the external world.

One can see the systematic attitude which Clifford brought to his discussions of ethics, epistemology, and metaphysics. Even his notion of "ejects" and its role in consciousness was connected to his ethical concerns. In "On the Nature of Things-in-Themselves", he drew an explicit connection between ejects and the development of a concept of self in relationship to other selves: "I do not pause to show how belief in the Eject underlies the whole of natural ethic, whose first great commandment, evolved in the light of day by healthy processes wherever men have lived together, is 'Put yourself in his place.'"[86] He would explore this notion in detail (although omitting explicit references to "ejects") in his essays "On the Scientific Basis of Morals", "Right and Wrong: The Scientific Ground of Their Distinction", "The Ethics of Religion" and "The Ethics of Belief."

Clifford's concern with ethics, then, as best expressed in these above-mentioned essays, is of a piece with his logical, epistemological and metaphysical concerns. He was far more of a systematic thinker than he is usually given credit for. It was his own hope that, before his death, he would be able to publish an extended book, in which he would express a synthetic approach to philosophy, entitled *The Creed of Science.* He had been impressed early on by Herbert Spencer's work, but found it too speculative, and not grounded sufficiently in the scientific findings of the day. Above all, Clifford wished to provide a scientific understanding of human morality, one not beholden to previously-existing religious arguments, which he felt had tended to impede the understanding by crystallizing it in dogmas and outmoded explanations.

If Michael Ruse is correct that Clifford was one of the earliest exponents of "evolutionary epistemology" it is surely the case that he was

---

85 Ibid., 171.
86 Ibid., "On the Nature of Things-in Themselves" in *Lectures and Essays,* 278.

equally one the earliest exponents of "evolutionary ethics." In his book *The Temptations of Evolutionary Ethics,* Paul Lawrence Farber writes: "One of the first to discuss the ethical implications of Darwin's work was William Kingdon Clifford"[87], this at a time when Darwin himself (and even "Darwin's bulldog," T. H. Huxley) preferred to avoid such speculations for fear they would further retard the acceptance of the scientific evidence for the theory itself. Clifford's ethical views, especially as these relate to his previously-discussed work in mathematics, epistemology and metaphysics, will be explored in detail in the next chapter. But one further quote from Farber is important in grasping the project which Clifford was expressing in "The Ethics of Belief" and other of his popular lectures and essays. "Clifford's interest in a new foundation for ethics," Farber holds, "and a new philosophical perspective from which to view society reflected more than his own personal tastes. The 1870s were a period during which intellectuals reexamined their cultural assumptions . . . Even for the supporters of such monumental change as Clifford, there was considerable ambiguity. For many of those who were willing to eradicate Christianity as a force in the modern world, the loss of Christian morality was perceived to be an intolerable impoverishment of humanity. Much of the creative thought of the late nineteenth century was directed in one form or another at attempting to resolve this dilemma."[88] Reba Soffer states that Clifford "strenuously promoted the nineteenth-century conviction that science . . . was benevolent . . . Ethical views are not determined by, nor do they depend upon, the vagaries of individual choice. Clifford advised moralists to study the source and substance of ethics scientifically, through an analysis of institutions and the way they perpetuate certain values while rejecting others."[89] To conclude this chapter on Clifford's significance, I would like to look at the role he played in furthering the acceptance of the institutionalization of science in Victorian England.

8. Clifford as an Apologist for Science

In his essay "Scientific Discourse as an Alternative to Faith," George Levine points to one central, and often overlooked, practical reason why the Victorian agnostics were so warlike in their approach to theology. The

---

[87] Paul Lawrence Farber, *The Temptations of Evolutionary Ethics* (Berkeley: University of California Press, 1994), 22.
[88] Ibid., 25.
[89] Soffer, 134.

very role of education was being reconsidered. He writes: "The naturalists' pugnacity was not unreasonable in a society that was only slowly and reluctantly allowing them serious professional status . . ."[90] Clifford and his associates were self-conscious propagandists struggling on behalf of a profession which still had to find a place for itself in the culture, and which needed to make a definite break from ecclesiastical control. "At stake was the possibility of science in a culture that preferred *a priori* authority, and took the idea of the unity of nature as unproblematic . . . Science, that is to say, threw everything in doubt, at the same time as it was arguing strenuously that at last a positive method had been found to clear things up."[91] The older model of education, which had lasted since the 17th Century, still connected an unchanging body of scientific knowledge with a dogmatic religious structure. Professors at Oxford and Cambridge were expected to be clergymen, and they were required to uphold time-honored traditions. Clifford, with his inherent rebelliousness, was far more at home in the explicitedly secular University College. His love of education for its own sake was evident in the public lectures he gave so frequently, and in his scheme "to issue a series of little school manuals whose lessons would be designed to help 'kids find out things for themselves.'"[92]

Even during his student days at Cambridge, as he shared his enthusiasm for non-Euclidean geometry with those around him, Clifford was concerned more about imparting a method of learning rather than revealing pre–conceived answers, and felt that there are compensating intellectual pleasures which help individuals to deal with parting from old beliefs. In a notebook he kept at the time, Clifford expressed himself in the same sort of religiously-tinged language that would dominate his later essay "The Ethics of Belief": "Whoever has learnt either a language or the bicycle can testify to the wonderful sudden step from troublesome acquirement to the mastery of new powers, whose mere exercise is delightful . . . This I say, is especially and exceptionally true of the pleasures of perception. Every time that analysis strips from nature the gilding that we prized, she is forging thereout a new picture more glorious than before, to be suddenly revealed by the advent of a new sense whereby we see it – a new creation, at sight of which the sons of

---

90 George Levine, "Scientific Discourse as an Alternative to Faith" in *Victorian Faith in Crisis* (Stanford, California: Stanford University Press, 1990), edited by Richard J. Helmstadter and Bernard Lightman, 231.
91 *Ibid.,* 252.
92 James R. Newman, "William Kingdon Clifford" in *Scientific American,* 81.

God shall have cause to shout for joy . . . Doubtless there shall by and by be laws as far transcending those we know as they do the simplest observation. The new incarnation may need a second passion; but evermore it is the Easter glory."[93]

There was thus more to Clifford's defense of science than a purely professional interest. A concern for the betterment of the human condition was ever-most in his mind. Like many of his contemporaries, both religious or naturalistic, he was troubled by the societal problems which the Industrial Revolution had helped to bring about. As Reba Soffer describes the period in England following 1870, almost every intellectual was motivated by a passionate search for some new basis for ethical and social obligation "among the ruins of older faiths", and were guided by:

> . . . a commonly declared need for some compelling ethic of personal social obligation that had developed from the late 1860s within a small, closely knit, homogenous community of energetic, thinking people centered mostly in the universities. This community came of age convinced that it bore the responsibility for discovering and carrying out a program of individual and social reform. Although the development of a reformist social science necessarily required the availability of epistemological and scientific models to support reformist aspirations, the sufficient condition for such a development lay in the intense sense of duty that the emerging reformers shared.[94]

No one expressed a sense of duty more than W. K. Clifford did. For him, the duty to tell the truth, and correlate beliefs to evidence, was an obligation that all must adhere to, and the method which best enabled humans to achieve this was the scientific one. He coupled this with his republican political views, and truly did hold that the liberation and advancement of the human species was dependent upon its breaking away from ecclesiastic control through assimilating the scientific method as much as possible. Science would be the means through which human progress would be best accomplished. There was no greater apologist, or lyricist, for science than W. K. Clifford. Consider the story with which he ends his essay "Body and Mind":

> What is the domain of Science? It is all possible human knowledge which can rightly be used to guide human conduct. In many parts of Europe it is

---

93 Quoted in Frederick Pollock, "Biographical Introduction" in *Lectures and Essays,* p 27-28.
94 Soffer, 6.

customary to leave a part of the field untilled for the Brownie to live in, because he cannot live in cultivated ground. And if you grant him this grace, he will do a great deal of your household work for you in the night while you sleep. In Scotland the piece of ground which is left wild for him to live in is called "the good man's croft." Now there are people who indulge a hope that the ploughshare of Science will leave a sort of good man's croft around the field of reasoned truth; and they promise that in that case a good deal of our civilising work shall be done for us in the dark, by means we know not of. I do not share this hope; and I feel very sure that it will not be realised: I think that we should do our work with our own hands in a healthy, straightforward way. It is idle to set bounds to the purifying and organising work of Science. Without mercy and without resentment she ploughs up weed and briar; from her footsteps behind her grow up corn and healing flowers; and no corner is far enough to escape her furrow. Provided only that we take as our motto and our rule of action, Man speed the plough.[95]

There is no better expression of *Clifford's* hope for humankind than his essay "The Ethics of Belief", which will be examined in detail in the following chapter. For himself, surely the personal ideal he sought to exemplify is expressed in his 1875 essay "The Unseen Universe", where, after disparaging the desire for some future immortal life where intelligence would be released from its bodily imprisonment, he extolled the virtues of those who worked to better human life here on earth: "But for you noble and great ones, who have loved and laboured not for yourselves but for the universal folk, in your time not for your time only but for the coming generations, for you there shall be life as broad and far-reaching as your love, for you life-giving action to the utmost reach of the great wave whose crest you sometimes were."[96]

These were the sentiments behind his essay "The Ethics of Belief".

---

95 W. K. Clifford, "Body and Mind" in *Lectures and Essays,* p 272-273.
96 W. K. Clifford, "The Unseen Universe" in *Lectures and Essays,* p 164-165.

CHAPTER THREE

AN ANALYSIS OF "THE ETHICS OF BELIEF"

"The Ethics of Belief" was delivered as an address to the Metaphysical Society on April 11, 1876. Although it stands on its own, it was partly an extension of the debate which had occurred during the previous five meetings of the Society. On November 9, 1875, the jurist J. Fitzjames Stephen had given a talk entitled "Remarks on the Proof of Miracles". The scientist W. B. Carpenter, on December 14, 1875, next gave an address entitled "On the Fallacies of Testimony in Relation to the Supernatural". Thomas Huxley continued the debate on January 11, 1876 with his talk "The Evidence of the Miracle of the Resurrection", for which the discussion continued at the next meeting on February 15, 1876 (the only paper read before the Society which was felt to warrant two meetings). And on March 14, 1876, the philosopher Shadworth Hodgson spoke on "The Pre-Suppositions of Miracles". Clifford was in attendance and was a full participant in the discussions at all of these meetings, and he wrote his essay so that it would further the rationalistic criticism of miracles and supernatural evidence which the previous papers had developed.

Like most of the talks given to the Society, "The Ethics of Belief" was shortly thereafter published. Clifford took advantage of the opportunity to expand upon his oral presentation, and to address some of the criticisms that were brought out in the Society's discussions. "The Ethics of Belief" was printed in the January 1877 issue of *Contemporary Review, XXXIX*. It was later reprinted in his posthumously published *Lectures and Essays* (1879).

1. The Ethics of Belief

Clifford begins his essay with a description of a ship owner who allows a vessel badly in need of repairs to nonetheless go out to sea. The owner dismisses from his mind any doubts as to its seaworthiness. The ship, laden with passengers, goes down in mid-ocean, killing all aboard. Clifford holds that the owner is morally culpable for their deaths, because he had no right to believe on such evidence as was before him that the ship could make the journey. This alone might be an uncontroversial assertion. But Clifford goes further. He adds that even if the ship *had* made it safely to shore, the owner would still have committed an immoral action.

This might lead one to assume that Clifford's argument for evidentialism is essentially deontological—one has a duty to apportion one's beliefs to the evidence, regardless of the consequences. Perhaps he is claiming that consequences should not be considered when evaluating the morality of one's actions. However, later in the essay, Clifford pursues a more teleological line of argument, declaring that belief is not a private matter. There are serious detrimental effects when one makes decisions for which the evidence is not persuasive. The repercussions relate to both the person involved and the society to which that person belongs. Believing for unworthy reasons not only weakens a person's powers of self-control, but also adversely affects one's community of fellow-believers. They, too, are likely to fall into the habit of believing merely because it makes them feel better, rather than seriously pursuing the best evidence available. The example set by those who refrain from serious inquiry into beliefs will have a snowball effect. Were this to continue, Clifford asserts in rather alarming tones, humankind itself would soon sink back into savagery.

"The Ethics of Belief" is divided into three sections: 1. "The Duty of Inquiry"; 2. "The Weight of Authority"; and 3. "The Limits of Inference".

2. The Duty to Inquire

In this first section, one can see the Kantian influence on Clifford. Clifford had read Kant, and was in agreement with at least some of the latter's ethical views. Clifford's familiarity with German gave him an advantage over many of his fellow Englishmen who were attempting to grapple with Kant's Critical Philosophy. As Andrew Pyle points out:

> The history of the reception of Kant's thought in England would make a fascinating story. The barriers to overcome were formidable: few Englishmen read German; Kant's prose proved hard to read and almost impossible to translate; his reputation for impenetrable obscurity went ahead of him and ensured that few even bothered to try. (Herbert Spencer, for example, read no German and had to absorb Kant at second hand).[1]

---

[1] Andrew Pyle, introduction to *Agnosticism: Contemporary Responses to Spencer and Huxley* (London: Thoemmes Press, 1995), xi-xii.

It is in the section on "The Duty to Inquire" that Clifford introduces his ship owner example. "What shall we say of him?" Clifford asks. "Surely this, that he was verily guilty of the death of those men."[2] Yet what is the basis of this guilt? The ship owner is sincere in his belief that the ship is sound—"but the sincerity of his conviction can in no wise help him, *because he had no right to believe on such evidence as was before him.*"[3]

This is the crux of the matter. Clifford is addressing here the manner in which individuals acquire their beliefs. But he then deviates from a purely deontological approach, by focusing upon the effect which ill-conceived and badly-formulated beliefs have upon the community.

One notes here for the first time a central aspect of the essay overall—the frequent use of religious language. Consider the following, which occurs early on in the first section: "He who truly believes that which prompts him to an action has looked upon the action to lust after it, he has committed it already in his heart."[4] This is a veiled reference, if not a parody, of Jesus' famous words, that to lust after a woman in one's heart was to actually commit adultery. Furthermore, Clifford states that the social bonds that keep humans together are a "sacred trust", and that beliefs are a "sacred faculty" which prompt the decisions of the will.[5] This bond is "desecrated" when given to unproved and unquestioned statements. It is "sinful" to hold a belief not supported by evidence, because such a belief has been stolen in defiance of our duty to humankind.[6] It will lead to the destruction of society, which is "wicked". Those who hold beliefs without question have committed "one long sin against mankind."[7] And finally:

> If this judgment seems harsh when applied to those simple souls who have never known better, who have been brought up from the cradle with a horror of doubt, and taught that their eternal welfare depends on *what* they believe, then it leads to the very serious question, *Who hath made Israel to sin?*[8]

Why does Clifford use such religious rhetoric? One reason perhaps is to be ironic, in that he is actually arguing against the holding of religious

---

[2] W. K. Clifford, "The Ethics of Belief" in *Lectures and Essays* (London: Macmillan and Co., 1886), 339.
[3] Ibid. 339-340.
[4] Ibid., 342.
[5] Ibid., 342-343.
[6] Ibid., 344.
[7] Ibid., 346.
[8] Ibid.

beliefs in general. Another reason would be to outrage devout religious believers, who would be offended by such profane use of sacred terms. But there is also a rhetoric strategy at play here. Clifford recognized that such language would resonate with his readers, almost all of whom would have been raised in traditional Christian households. Bernard Lightman, in his book *The Origins of Agnosticism: Victorian Unbelief and the Limits of Knowledge* (1987), points out that this style was utilized by many anti-religious essayists, whose "use of biblical language and ideas can be interpreted as a purely polemical strategy since prose shaped by biblical style and rich with allusions drawn from Holy Scripture had a powerful effect on the Victorian public."[9]

But there is more to it than this. By using such words as "sin" and "sacrilege", Clifford turns the tide on religious moralizers. He demands hard work, demonstrates a concern for others, and castigates those who do not encourage people to act their best. His strategy is in line with the claim made by David Berman (see chapter one) that John Stuart Mill had inaugurated the "ethics of belief" debate by claiming that it was nonbelievers who most closely lived up to the ideals of hard work, honesty, and intellectual integrity which religious believers claimed to espouse. In a sense, Clifford is giving new meaning to the phrase "holier than thou."

As will be seen in the next chapter, the usage of theological terms was a strategy also followed by Clifford's contemporary, Friedrich Nietzsche, in such polemic works as *The Anti-Christ, Thus Spake Zarathustra,* and *Ecce Homo.* Like Nietzsche, Clifford at times could be said to have philosophized "with a hammer."

Clifford ends "The Duty to Inquire" with a nice prelude to the following section, which discusses the significance one may place upon authority. He quotes two prominent English poets in support of his own rather harsh emphasis on duty. First of all, John Milton (1608-1674): "A man may be a heretic in youth; and if he believe things only because his pastor says so, or the assembly so determine, without knowing other reason, though his belief be true, yet the very truth he holds becomes his heresy." And next, Samuel Taylor Coleridge (1772-1834): "He who begins by loving Christianity better than Truth, will proceed by loving his own sect or Church better than Christianity, and end in loving himself better than all." It is clever of him to use two Christian authors to support his own views. And one can see here a perhaps ironic usage of the argument from authority which Clifford is to criticize in the next section.

---

[9] Bernard Lightman, *The Origins of Agnosticism: Victorian Unbelief and the Limits of Knowledge* (Baltimore: Johns Hopkins University Press, 1987), 120.

3. The Weight of Evidence

One charge against Clifford which was levied by such later critics as William James was that his evidentialism leads ultimately to complete inaction. Waiting for compelling evidence might in fact lead one to do nothing at all. Yet Clifford himself recognized the danger of becoming a universal skeptic, "doubting everything, afraid always to put one foot before the other until we have personally tested the firmness of the road."[10] It would be foolhardy to deprive ourselves of the vast body of knowledge that has been accumulated over the centuries and time-tested for its accuracy. Indeed, the basic thrust of "The Ethics of Belief" as a whole is to *protect* this body of knowledge from corruption, and not to ignore it or take it for granted. Yet clearly, given its scope, it would be impossible for one person to test even one hundredth part of it through experimentation or observation. Therefore, the problem of relying upon authority needs to be addressed. What kind of evidence does authority provide, and does this satisfy Clifford's own dictate that beliefs improperly grounded should be judged as immoral?

According to Clifford, the search for truth has been the best approach to gather information, especially concerning beliefs related to proper conduct: "Those men who have nearly done their duty in this respect have found that certain great principles, and these most fitted for the guidance of life, have stood out more and more clearly in proportion to the care and honesty with which they were tested, and have acquired in this way a practical certainty."[11] This does not mean that the beliefs are necessarily true, but rather that they have passed the test of time. No bad consequences will follow from self-control in belief-formation. In fact, beliefs about good and bad actions in dealing with other people, as well as how to deal with other animals and the natural world, are constantly being tested and verified. For instance, the beliefs about which berries are poisonous versus which are healthy can be found in books written by naturalists. If the information in several such books tallies, then it is acceptable to believe the information.

What Clifford is most concerned about in this essay, though, are beliefs based upon authority in which independent verification is discouraged. In the above example, one is perfectly capable of testing the information found within the books, even though it would be perilous to do so. But some beliefs are treated in a different manner. He lists three approaches which discourage verification: 1. Acts of faith; 2. The

---

[10] Ibid., 347.
[11] Ibid.

unanimity of paid advocates; 3. The suppression of contrary evidence. These are all suspect, because they shield propositions from being examined. All engage in an improper usage of authority.

But Clifford does not claim that no actions can be based upon beliefs for which one lacks certainty. He writes: "There are many cases in which it is our duty to act upon probabilities, although the evidence is not such as to justify present belief; because it is precisely by such action, and by observation of its fruits, that evidence is got which may justify future belief."[12] This is in direct conflict with the criticism William James will later make, that Clifford's evidentialism leads to a paralysis of action. In fact, for Clifford, the habit of conscientious inquiry is the very basis for proper action.

Clifford states that one has a duty to act upon probabilities. He delineates when it is proper to: 1. Believe something on the testimony of others; and 2. Believe something which goes beyond all human experience.

To understand the first point, he asks: When can one dismiss the testimony of another as being unworthy? Individuals who make improper claims do so either because they are misinformed, or because they are lying. Therefore, it is proper to evaluate the *character* of an individual. Three points need to be considered: the person's *veracity,* the person's *judgment,* and the person's *knowledge.* One can see here similarities with the views expressed in David Hume's controversial essay "On Miracles", of which Clifford was well acquainted. In this 1776 essay, published *after* Hume's death to spare him from the consequences of questioning such a fundamental aspect of religious faith as belief in miracles, the following famous words appear:

> We frequently hesitate concerning the reports of others. We balance the opposite circumstances which cause any doubt or uncertainty; and when we discover a superiority on any side, we incline to it, but still with a diminution of assurance, in proportion to the force of its antagonist. This contrariety of evidence, in the present case, may be derived from several difference causes; from the opposition of contrary testimony; from the character or number of the witnesses; from the manner of their delivering their testimony; or from the union of these circumstances. We entertain a suspicion concerning any matter of fact when the witnesses contradict each other; when they are but few or of a doubtful character; when they have an interest in what they affirm; when they deliver their testimony with hesitation, or, on the contrary, with too violent asseverations. There are

---

[12] Ibid.

many other particulars of the same kind, which may diminish or destroy the force of any argument derived from human testimony.[13]

Two main questions, in Clifford's view, need to be asked regarding any human testimony: "Is the person honest?" and "Might the person be mistaken?" Answering "Yes" to the former does not give any strength to the latter. An excellent moral character is not sufficient evidence for accepting a person's statement as true, especially when it is about matters which that person cannot possibly have known. To illustrate this, Clifford very cleverly uses a religious example—not from Christianity, but rather from Islam. "A Mohammedan, for example, will tell us that the character of his Prophet was so noble and majestic that it commands the reverence even of those who do not believe in his mission."[14] Even if one grants the Mohammedan the benefit of the doubt and agrees to the Prophet's exemplar moral character, there are other explanations for his visions. It could be a matter of hallucination, or a dream. Put yourself in the Prophet's place—how might *you* interpret such visions? Clifford writes: "It is known to medical observers that solitude and want of food are powerful means of producing delusion and of fostering a tendency to mental illness."[15]

The use of the Prophet Mohammed was an ingenious one. The members of the Metaphysical Society, and the readers of the *Contemporary Review*, would be unsympathetic to Islamic prophecies, and therefore willing to dismiss them. But the strategy Clifford is using is similar to that which Voltaire had used in his 1728 play *Mahomet the Prophet, or Fanaticism*. Robert L. Myers, in his discussion of Voltaire's veiled message, explains:

> As early as 1718 . . . Voltaire expressed the conviction that the power of the Church rests primarily upon the credulous attitude of the unenlightened people. Throughout his career, therefore, he strove with unfailing energy to put an end to ignorance, bigotry, and prejudice, to enlighten his fellow countrymen in every area of thought. . . . Ostensibly drawing a portrait of the historical Mahomet (he even dared to dedicate the play to Pope Benedict XIV, who accepted the honor), Voltaire's satire is not limited to the Moslem religion bur reaches out to touch Christianity itself.[16]

---

[13] David Hume, "On Miracles", in *Hume on Miracles,* edited by Stanley Tweyman (London: Thoemmes Press, 1996), 3-4.
[14] Ibid. 348.
[15] Ibid., 350.
[16] Robert L. Myers, introduction to Voltaire's *Mahomet the Prophet or Fanaticism,* translated by Robert L. Myers (New York: Frederick Ungar, 1964), v-vii.

One imagines that, even if not personally acquainted with that particular work of Voltaire's, Clifford was well aware of the usefulness of critiquing non-Christian beliefs as a way of getting Christians to begin to examine their own beliefs.

Sounding somewhat like a pragmatist, Clifford goes on to write: "Belief belongs to man, and to the guidance of human affairs: no belief is real unless it guide our actions, and those very actions supply a test of its truth."[17] But does this mean that the acceptance of Islam as a system of belief would thereby justify its claims? Certainly Islam has succeeded in convincing millions of adherents of its truth:

> The fact that believers have found joy and peace in believing gives us the right to say that the doctrine is a comfortable doctrine, and pleasant to the soul; but it does not give us the right to say that it is true. And the question which our conscience is always asking about that which we are tempted to believe is not, "Is it comfortable and pleasant?" but, "Is it true?" That the Prophet preached certain doctrines, and predicted that spiritual comfort would be found in them, proves only his sympathy with human nature and his knowledge of it; but it does not prove his superhuman knowledge of theology.[18]

Clifford is much closer to Bertrand Russell here—the comfort of beliefs is no justification of their truthfulness or falseness. One major problem with theological claims is that there are so many of them, and they do not agree. There has been more than one Prophet extolling claims about the nature of God, the afterlife and how to live a good existence. How does one determine which, if any, of these Prophets to follow? And secondly, how might one separate what is true from what is false when examining a specific Prophet's teachings? If no human is infallible, then it is up to a community of believers to help appraise each other's claims:

> It is hardly in human nature that a man should quite accurately gauge the limits of his own insight; but it is the duty of those who profit by his work to consider carefully where he may have been carried beyond it. If we must needs embalm his possible errors along with his solid achievements, and use his authority as an excuse for believing what he cannot have known, we make of his goodness an occasion to sin.[19]

---

[17] Ibid.
[18] Ibid., 351.
[19] Ibid., 352.

"Sin"—Clifford here returns to his usage of religious language, so prominent in the previous section. Continuing in this vein, he points out that followers of the Buddha have an even greater right to appeal to their founder's good moral character, and to the positive effects of adhering to his teachings—not the least of which is a disinclination to persecute others who do not accept the Buddha's teachings. Again, while never explicitly mentioning the ways in which Christians have often attempted to force their beliefs upon others through strength of arms (he is still here referring to *Islam*), it is hard to miss the oblique argument.

Clifford then switches to a different point—the need to at least theoretically be able to independently verify the claims of an authority. There is no ground for accepting on authority a statement which no human can be expected to verify. A chemist, who is trained in the field of chemistry, may claim that a certain substance is comprised of various other substances in a certain proportion. If I do not know anything that would lead me to question his moral character (such as his tendency to poison his patients), and if I am myself unlearned in the field of chemistry, and *if I can be made to understand the process by which he came to know this,* then and only then: "I may never actually verify it, or even see any experiment which goes towards justifying it; but still I have quite reason enough to justify me in believing that the verification is within the reach of human appliances and powers, and in particular that it has been actually performed by my informant."[20]

The beliefs thus formed are a common property to all human beings. They are valid for all, and can be tested by anyone who so chooses. The results will always be the same. The chemist's authority is only valid because his claims can and are put to the test with great frequency. This time-honored body of beliefs has been formed through intellectual struggle. We have a solemn duty to use it properly.

There is a need to differentiate traditions which welcome inquiry from those which shirk from it. If the only reason to believe a claim is that everyone has believed it for a long time, then that is not sufficient. Indeed, the person who raises questions about the belief is a greater benefactor to that society than those who continue to accept it unthinkingly (although Socrates was unable to convince his Athenian jury as to the self-evident nature of this claim). Clifford, again relying on a religious example, talks of a medicine man who orders his tribe to kill their cattle so that the sacred medicine will work. If there is no way to test the medicine, then the one who questions this may even have the duty to go into the holy tent and break the medicine.

---

[20] Ibid., 353.

"The rule which should guide us in such cases is simple and obvious enough: that the aggregate testimony of our neighbours is subject to the same conditions as the testimony of any one of them."[21] Ten million Frenchmen *can* be wrong! In fact, while one person making a claim most likely has the means to know whether it is true, the same cannot be said for masses of people.

Traditions build up the common experience of human beings. They act as guides for proper behavior, and as frameworks for our thoughts. In the moral world, for example, it gives us the conceptions of right in general, of justice, of truth, of beneficence, and the like. "These are given as conceptions", Clifford adds, "not as statements or propositions; they answer to certain definite instincts which are certainly within us, however they came there."[22]

Rules arise from this moral sense, but they still require further inquiry, since what establishes these rules is often the word of an authority figure. Here Clifford gives an example which might have come to him from his reading of Herbert Spencer (1820-1903):

> Until recently, the moral tradition of our own country – and indeed of all Europe – taught that it was beneficent to give money indiscriminately to beggars. But the questioning of this rule, and investigation into it, led men to see that true beneficence is that which helps a man to do the work which he is most fitted for, not that which keeps and encourages him in idleness; and that to neglect this distinction in the present is to prepare pauperism and misery for the future.[23]

Such questioning of practices actually helps to widen and strengthen the concept of benevolence. One makes a distinction between the instinct, and the intellectual conception of it. It is necessary to continually raise questions about the latter, for without doing so one would be left with codes of regulations which are not understood.

The method of investigation needs to clarified: "In regard, then, to the sacred tradition of humanity, we learn that it consists, not in propositions or statements which are to be accepted and believed on the authority of the tradition, but in questions rightly asked, in conceptions which enable us to ask further questions, and in methods of answering questions."[24]

There follows more use of religious language: "He who makes use of its results to stifle his own doubts, or to hamper the inquiry of others, is

---

[21] Ibid., 357.
[22] Ibid.
[23] Ibid.
[24] Ibid., 359.

guilty of a sacrilege, which centuries shall never be able to blot out."[25] The ending of this section sounds very much like a sermon. Indeed, one can even read the essay as a whole as a sort of secular sermon, written to exhort people to use their intellectual powers to the utmost, and refrain as much as possible from relying upon authority as the basis of their beliefs.

4. The Limits of Inference

In this final section of "The Ethics of Belief", Clifford touches upon a topic which was at the very heart of the debating Society to which he was speaking: metaphysical beliefs. In the area of metaphysics, one is dealing with claims that by their very nature are unverifiable. How can one test what is beyond not only one's own experience, but the experience of all human beings?

Clifford begins by making the point that every belief, to some extent, goes beyond our immediate experience. In order to have beliefs at all, one needs to make some metaphysical assumptions, such as the assumption that the future will be like the past. Another such assumption is the uniformity of nature. We do not experience this, yet without assuming it, we cannot hold any beliefs at all. One must also assume the reliability of memory, and one must assume that the future will be like the past:

> We find also that men do not, as a rule, forge books and histories without a special motive; we assume that in this respect men in the past were like men in the present; and we observe that in this case no special motive was present. That is, we add to our experience on the assumption of a uniformity in the characters of men. Because our knowledge of this uniformity is far less complete and exact than our knowledge of that which obtains in physics, inferences of the historical kind are more precarious and less exact than inferences in many other sciences.[26]

We must presume the uniformity of nature, but we have no right to believe it. It is a precondition of belief-formation, rather than properly a belief itself.

5. Criticisms of "The Ethics of Belief"

There are several criticisms one can make of "The Ethics of Belief". First, nowhere does Clifford define what he means by "belief". Second, at

---

[25] Ibid.
[26] Ibid., 362.

no point in the essay does he discuss the *adequacy* of evidence. What constitutes "sufficient" evidence to support a belief? Third, Clifford's bold assertion that it is not possible to sever beliefs from actions seems itself unsupported. Where is the evidence to bolster this claim? And finally, where is the evidence to support the claim that every belief we hold is significant? These two statements seem to be more blanket assertions than well-reasoned claims. Clifford could well be said to be going beyond the evidence himself here.

Nonetheless, "the Ethics of Belief" touched a nerve, and became the focal point of discussion not only of members of the Metaphysical Society, but also from other noted contemporaries. The next section will address how these individuals grappled with the various points made by this provocative essay.

CHAPTER FOUR

CLIFFORD'S CONTEMPORARY CRITICS

I. The Metaphysical Society

1. *The Nineteenth Century*

W. K. Clifford's "The Ethics of Belief" received an immediate response after its publication in 1877. Some of the leading intellectuals of the era, such as Matthew Arnold, were quick to revile him as a dangerous and facile unbeliever, while colleagues such as Thomas Huxley sprang to his defense. The controversy over what Clifford said in his essay did not abate even after his death in 1879, and was to receive its most famous response almost twenty years after its publication, in the famous essay by William James, entitled "The Will to Believe."

According to the Metaphysical Society's historian Alan Willard Brown, the publication of Clifford's "The Ethics of Belief" in the January 1877 issue of *The Contemporary Review* "created a storm of controversy among religion-minded men."[1] Alexander Strahan, its pious editorial director, resigned in protest because of it, feeling that Sir James Knowles, the Metaphysical Society's founder, "was guilty of allying both himself and the review with the forces of atheism and materialism."[2] Knowles reacted by founding his own journal, the *Nineteenth Century* that same year, inviting Clifford to become a regular contributor. Knowles issued an advertisement and prospectus about the new publication that boldly asserted its policy of maintaining an open forum for the expression of all responsible opinion; appended to it were the names of 104 distinguished men who had consented to be contributors, including all the then-members of the Metaphysical Society, as well as Matthew Arnold, G. H. Lewes, and John Henry Newman.

---

[1] Alan Willard Brown, *The Metaphysical Society* (New York: Columbia University Press, 1947), 180.
[2] Ibid., 181.

While partly responsible for the formation of one of the Victorian era's most distinguished journals, Clifford may also have been instrumental in the Metaphysical Society's demise. Brown writes that:

> We must observe, however, that from that time on some of the more conservative members of the Metaphysical Society began to attend less regularly and that the years of the Society's decline lie not far ahead. . . . the popular idea of the Society as a force undermining the faith and principles of old England became too widespread for social comfort.[3]

The Metaphysical Society did not long outlive Clifford, its final meeting being held on November 16, 1880. Huxley, with his usual turn of phrase, claimed that it died from too much love.

2. Metaphysical Society Responses

"The Ethics of Belief" managed to capture clearly and succinctly the main positions of those members of the Metaphysical Society who represented the empirical tradition. In addition, its appearance in 1877 was the culmination of a vigorous debate occurring within other learned societies and intellectual journals. As James Livingston writes in *The Ethics of Belief: An Essay on the Victorian Religious Conscience*:

> The debate over the ethics of belief in the 70's produced some of the most provocative and important modern writing on the subject of belief. In the 70's alone these writings included Newman's *Grammar of Assent* (1870), Henry Sidgwick's *The Ethics of Conformity and Subscription* (1870), Mill's essay on *Theism* (1874), John Morley's *On Compromise* (1874), James Fitzjames Stephen's *Liberty, Equality, Fraternity* (1874), Leslie Stephen's *Essays on Freethinking and Plainspeaking* (1873) and *An Agnostic's Apology* (these essays originally appeared in the *Fortnightly* during the 70's; the book was published in 1893), and the papers . . . read before the Metaphysical Society and reprinted in various periodicals during the decade.[4]

Clifford's essay was to become the most famous and oft-reprinted of all the Metaphysical Society papers. This was due partly to his own usage of what his friend Leslie Stephen called the "plainspeaking" style – even

---

[3] Ibid., 182.
[4] James C. Livingston, *The Ethics of Belief: An Essay on the Victorian Religious Conscience* (Talahassee, Florida: American Academy of Religion, 1974), 18.

those who were not aware of the ongoing debates within the Society could grasp his meaning and the intent of his arguments. Unlike some of the papers given to the Society earlier, Clifford made no attempt to seriously examine the claims of the "intuitionist" members, who argued that there are many truths which cannot be demonstrated but which everyone accepts unconditionally (this was the thrust of Cardinal Newman's influential book *The Grammar of Assent,* which claimed that, while in the exact sciences demonstrative proof was required, in issues of an ultimate or moral nature which demand immediate action, the convergence of probabilities could justify certitude). Perhaps, as a regular attendee of the Society, he felt that such a recapitulation of the intuitionists' arguments would be redundant, but the lack of such nuanced discussion perhaps helped to make his own essay seem more persuasive than it might otherwise have been. As Livingston points out:

> In the mid 1870's the intuitionists were called upon to answer a relentless series of attacks on the logic and morality of their theory of religious knowledge. The severest and most provocative statement of the new morality of belief was made by W. K. Clifford before the Metaphysical Society on 11 April 1876. He entitled the paper "The Ethics of Belief." While it lacked any consideration of the actual arguments of the intuitionists which marked the essays by Fitzjames and Leslie Stephen, it became, because of the simplicity of its rigorous principles, the classic statement of the new ethic of belief.[5]

Not surprisingly, the intuitionists were quick to respond. The most pointed counterargument came from the Catholic convert and defender of Newman, William George Ward, editor of *The Dublin Review.* According to Alan Willard Brown: "Ward was the most skillful logician of the English ultramontane Catholics and the most unrelenting antagonist of the empiricists and scientists in the Society."[6] Like Clifford a regular attendee at Society meetings, Ward had himself given a noted talk to the Society on December 15, 1869 (a few years before Clifford became a member), entitled "On Memory as an Intuitive Faculty". In that talk, Ward had struck at what he considered to be the empiricists' own Achilles heel – the assumption that memory was a reliable source for justified beliefs. Such justification, he argued, must itself be intuitive rather than proved.

Admitting that "The Ethics of Belief" had excited considerable attention, Ward wrote an article entitled "The Reasonable Basis of

---

[5] Ibid., 27.
[6] Ibid., 11.

Certitude", which appeared in the *Nineteenth Century* as a direct response to Clifford. He wrote: ". . . the thesis which I oppose is exhibited by different authors in different shapes: by none other certainly in so extreme a shape, as by Professor Clifford."[7] Using copious quotations from "The Ethics of Belief", Ward addressed what he took to be its central position, that no proposition can be morally justified it if is not supported by adequate evidence. To show the absurdity of this, he presents his own scenario:

> Let us apply this doctrine to a concrete case. Some agricultural labourer is sober, honest, chaste; and carefully educates his children in the same habits. (I need hardly say that if I were describing a virtuous man, there are other qualities on which I should lay even greater stress than on those mentioned in the text. I should represent him as living in the fear and love of God, and training his children in that fear and love. In argument, however, with Professor Clifford I cannot dwell on this, as he is not generally understood to hold Theistical doctrine.) But he is very fond of cricket; and is quite confident that the eleven of his own village are far superior to the eleven of another village whom they often encounter. This opinion is entirely unfounded; nor has it been engendered in his mind by any attempt at impartial inquiry, but exclusively by local prejudice and *esprit de corps*. According to Professor Clifford, this man is "desecrating belief, that sacred faculty;" he is "laying a stealthy train in his inmost thoughts which may some day leave its stamp on his character for ever;" he is making himself "father to the liar and the cheat." I am slow to credit a writer of undoubted ability with such a position as this; but for the life of me I cannot see what else he means.[8]

Ward was thus one of the first to point out that the hyperbolic aspects of "The Ethics of Belief" made it difficult to evaluate at face value. "Professor Clifford's article then – I must really think – is so manifestly exaggerated and unreasonable," he adds, "that I should be doing injustice to the general body of my opponents by taking him as in any sense their representative."[9] Still, Clifford's main points are in concordance with other empiricists like the Stephens and Huxley, in that it shares what Ward considers to be vast metaphysical assumptions – namely, the uniformity of nature and the reliability of memory. Returning to the arguments he had

---

[7] William George Ward, "The Reasonable Basis of Certitude" in *The Ethics of Belief Debate,* edited by Gerald D. McCarthy (Atlanta: Scholars Press, 1986), 172.
[8] Ibid.,172-173.
[9] Ibid., 174.

made in 1869, Ward proposed that the mind itself adds special powers to help supply the grounds of reasonable belief. James C. Livingston writes:

> Ward and several others regarded Clifford's rigorous ethic of belief to be not only founded on a vast metaphysical assumption but unreal and thus empty when considered in relation to common experience. . . . Ward pointed out that the philosophy of men like the Stephens, Huxley, and Clifford implies the theory "that the mind has only a power to criticize grounds of belief *independently* existing, and not itself to supply grounds of reasonable belief."[10]

Interestingly enough, Ward concludes his article with a brief discussion on whether it is advisable for religious believers to read the writings of such "infidels" as Clifford:

> And now in conclusion I would apply what has been said to a theological question of the most vital importance, which Professor Clifford also treats in his own characteristic way. Every Christian teacher, whether Catholic or Protestant, impresses a sacred duty on the mass of believers, that they shall not read infidel books or otherwise allow themselves to doubt the truth of Christianity. We Catholics in particular not only are forbidden by the Church to read anti-Catholic treatises – unless we are exceptionally fitted to do so without peril to our faith – but we account it a moral sin in any one who has really embraced the Faith to permit himself one deliberate doubt of its truth.[11]

This was indeed one of Clifford's strongest objections – that religious institutions deliberately prevent their members from investigating religious doctrines or reading the arguments of individuals who did not belong to the same congregation. Ward hastened to add that the Index of Forbidden Books and other means of censoring ideas were not opposed to the use of reason, but only to its misuse. To provoke doubt in matters of faith is to commit the grievous sin of rebellion against God's special gift. In this, Ward is using "sin" not in the ironic sense of Clifford, but in the literal sense of a deliberate act against God's wishes. While Ward no doubt felt he was one of the special few who was "exceptionally fitted" to both read and argue against anti-Catholic tracts, one can see here the sort of impasse which Richard Rorty would later call "an end to discussion." For Clifford, blocking the road to inquiry is the real cause of grievous harm; for Ward, provoking doubts that might imperil one's immortal soul

---

[10] Livingston, 29.
[11] Ward, "The Reasonable Basis of Certitude", 184.

is the ultimate sin to be prevented. This impasse would soon lead to the demise of the Metaphysical Society itself – rather than, as Huxley put it, "dying from too much love", it died when its most vocal members ceased to have a common language in which to discuss metaphysical issues at all.

Another theistic responder to Clifford's "The Ethics of Belief" was Richard H. Hutton. Alan Willard Brown describes Hutton in this way: "As one of the most active contributors to the Society's debates and one of those most constant in attendance, he bore more of the burden of defending the theistic postulate than many of the churchmen and did so with dialectical skill and ironic wit."[12] Hutton, co-editor of the influential weekly journal the *Spectator,* had in fact delivered the very first address to the Metaphysical Society, on June 2, 1869, a criticism of Herbert Spencer's theory of morality. Hutton's own theistic views were shaped by Unitarianism. Although he was sympathetic to the positions of Ward and Newman he never converted to Catholicism, nor in fact pledged himself to any specific faith. In his 1877 paper "Professor Clifford on the Sins of Credulity", Hutton, like Ward, took exception to Clifford's ethical attack on "credulity":

> Professor Clifford strikes at the very basis of his own ethics when he calls all belief which is either not founded on producible evidence at all, or when challenged, produces, as Columbus produced, evidence for itself which is not worth the paper on which it is written, - credulity, and brands it as both mischievous and dishonest. The simple fact is that the best and most binding faiths we have, faiths not only at the basis of popular religion, but also at the basis of domestic strength and peace, are founded on precisely such evidence as this at which Professor Clifford levels his most bitter shafts.[13]

For Hutton, "incredulity" could be as morally suspect as "credulity" – one needs to examine the motives involved rather than simply the act of believing. Regarding Clifford's example of the shipowner, Hutton points out that any moral evaluation must take into consideration the shipowner's self-interest. He allowed the ship to sail even though he had reason to believe it to be unseaworthy because of his financial interests. "It is the tainted motive", Hutton writes, "which makes the credulity and the incredulity alike evil."[14]

---

[12] Brown, 111.
[13] R. H. Hutton, "Professor Clifford on the Sins of Credulity" in *Aspects of Religious and Scientific Thought* (New York: MacMillan., 1899), 62.
[14] Ibid., 60.

While exciting strong criticisms among certain of the Society's members, Clifford also had his defenders. In addition to his good friend and supporter Thomas Huxley (the *bete noir* of Ward and Hutton), there were also the Stephen brothers, Fitzjames and Leslie. The former had been a member of the Metaphysical Society since 1873 and a frequent lecturer and participant thereafter. He was also one of the strongest critics of Newman's *Grammar of Assent*. Fitzjames Stephen was to deliver seven papers to the Society. His pugnacity ultimately made him a disruptive factor there. Like Clifford, with whom he shared common epistemological but not political views (Stephen was an arch-conservative jurist), he had a flair for phraseology which delighted his fellow freethinkers and infuriated his theistic opponents. To quote Livingston:

> Stephen was one of the most intrepid critics of the religious belief of his day and produced some of the sharpest and most telling arguments against the Newman-Ward ethic of belief. The inheritance of an evangelical conscience would not allow him to bide any compromise with an honest admission of agnosticism in religious belief. He abhorred any creed held on grounds of its truth. To propose beliefs on any other grounds than rational evidence, he said, "is like keeping a corpse above ground because it was dearest and most beloved of all objects when it was alive."[15]

No doubt Clifford would have appreciated that particular description of nonrational beliefs.

Leslie Stephen was elected to the Metaphysical Society in 1877, and, unlike his older brother Fitzjames, did not become a very active member. As a professional journalist, he did not have the time to devote to meetings, and he joined it at a time when it was already in decline. He did, however, give two addresses to the Society, each of which specifically addresses the challenges to the empirical position which Ward and Hutton had made against Clifford. Stephen had already arrived at a view very close to that of Clifford's "Ethics of Belief". In Livingston's words:

> In 1877 Stephen wrote three long papers on the logic and morality of belief, each pitting Locke's doctrine against that of Newman. Stephen's thesis is Locke's: belief must be proportioned to evidence which is open to or in the common possession of reasonable men.[16]

---

[15] Livingston, 22.
[16] Ibid, 24.

His first talk to the Society, on June 12, 1877, was entitled "Belief and Evidence". This was, as Alan Willard Brown points out, "a further contribution to the questions raised by Clifford on April 11, 1876, which, however, Leslie Stephen had not heard at the Society, for he was not then a member. But he had probably read it in its expanded form in *Contemporary Review,* January 1877; or he could have seen either the manuscript or the version printed for the Society."[17]

In this talk, Stephen reiterated the views earlier expressed by papers delivered by his brother Fitzjames, as well as Clifford's "The Ethics of Belief". Ward and Newman, he argued, deliberately confused certitude with probability. The former had given a brilliant analysis on how people are convinced by arguments, but had evaded discussion on what constitutes the laws of *right* belief. Granting that there are situations where absolute suspension of judgment might be impossible (an admission which Clifford also made in "The Ethics of Belief"), Stephen still held that one must differentiate between objective certainty and subjective conviction.

In this essay, as well as in the second address he gave to the Society on March 11, 1879, entitled "The Uniformity of Nature", Stephen also addressed the criticism of empiricists that they utilized intuitions and unprovable assertions in much the same way as did the intuitionists and religionists they so strongly criticized:

> How that proposition [the uniformity of nature] is to be logically established, or whether it can be logically established at all, is a question needless to be discussed. In any case, the belief is assumed in every step of every argument about matters of fact. To deny it is to fall into absolute scepticism, for it is to cut out the very nerve of proof in every proposition drawn from experience. . . . We cannot stir a step in any kind of reasoning about facts without implying the universal postulate. To reason in such matters is to assume the uniformity of Nature.[18]

Like Clifford, Stephen was willing to grant that empiricists utilized certain metaphysical assumptions, such as the uniformity of nature, but such assumptions must be utilized by *all* reasonable people, lest one become a universal sceptic. But the uniformity of nature cannot be equated with metaphysical beliefs that vary widely from religion to religion, and often from person to person, such as the goodness of God, the existence of the soul, and the nature of the afterlife.

---

[17] Brown, 333.
[18] Leslie Stephen, "Belief and Evidence" in *The Ethics of Belief Debate,* 105.

While sharing many of the same epistemological views, Stephen's motives were not identical to Clifford's. Like his brother Fitzjames, Leslie was a political conservative. Furthermore, as Alfred William Benn writes in his *History of English Rationalism in the Nineteenth Century*:

> ... Leslie Stephen's implacable hostility to the popular religion in all its forms seems to have arisen less from its untruth, which was the all-important motive with George Eliot and Clifford, than from its unreality. What provoked him was not that religion gave an answer to the problem of existence which experience showed to be illusory, but that the answer left every difficulty unsolved, and was felt to be illusory by the believers themselves. When agnostics are twitted with their confession of utter ignorance about what lies beyond experience, their best apology is that Christians, when pressed by philosophical enquiries, have to confess an equal ignorance, to fall back on an ultimate acknowledgement of the same impenetrable mystery, with the addition of encumbrances from which genuine agnosticism is free.[19]

Stephen also upheld a rather conservative personal ethics. In a letter he wrote to Julia Prinsep Stephen on January 20, 1887, he commented on the desire of a freethinker to publish one of Clifford's early works critical of marriage:

> Some of Lucy's freethinking friends, that Mathilde Blind for instance, want her to publish an early scrap of Clifford's containing speculations about marriage. I am glad to say that she objects & I have spoken as strongly as I can about it. It would be very unfair to him, as I tell her, and, as I do *not* tell her, it would be most unfair to her, as she would clearly be held responsible & nothing could be worse than to give any pretext for accusing her of supporting immoral opinions. I shall say some more about it but I think there is no danger.[20]

With the demise of the Metaphysical Society in 1880, the ethics of belief debate shifted to other domains. Clifford's article continued to be the focal point for this discussion. As Livingston writes:

> The debate of the 1870's continued into the next decade and beyond – but the zealous positivism of men like Clifford failed to enlist vigorous new

---

[19] Alfred William Benn, *The History of English Rationalism in the Nineteenth Century*, Volume II (New York: Russell & Russell, 1962), 385.
[20] Leslie Stephen, *Selected Letters of Leslie Stephen*, Volume 2, edited by John W. Bicknell (Columbus: Ohio State University Press, 1996), 344.

recruits. What Noel Annan has called "the curious strength of positivism" did not lose its hold on English thought, but it was challenged on many fronts. Influential men of letters and teachers like Matthew Arnold, T. H. Green and John and Edward Caird directed their considerable skills to opposing positivist empiricism and to establishing the warrants of religious belief on the solid ground of experience.[21]

Matthew Arnold (1822-1888), whose poem "Dover Beach" lamented the receding of "the sea of faith", was one of Clifford's most vocal critics. Religious beliefs, while literally untrue, Arnold felt, are nonetheless useful in that they keep the masses from becoming despondent. Clifford had vigorously opposed the view that intellectuals could successfully deal with the demythologizing of religious beliefs but the common people should continue to be taught that such myths are true. Such concepts as hell, original sin, and vicarious sacrifice were pernicious, Clifford held. Rather than giving real comfort from existential fears, they exacerbated such fears, by focusing constant attention on them. In "The Ethics of Religion", Clifford referred thusly to people like Arnold:

> But there is something to be said also to those who think that religious beliefs are not indeed true, but are useful for the masses; who deprecate any open and public argument against them, and think that all skeptical books should be published at a high price; who go to church, not because they approve of it themselves, but to set an example to the servants . . . . If we grant to you that it is good for poor people and children to believe some of these fictions, is it not better, at least, that they should believe those which are adapted to the promotion of virtue? Now the stories which you send your servants and children to hear are adapted to the promotion of vice.[22]

Like Clifford himself, Arnold is parodied in the book *The New Republic*, where his defense of a Christianity stripped of all myth is presented in the person of "Mr. Luke": "'It is true that culture sets aside the larger part of the New Testament as grotesque, barbarous, and immoral; but what remains, purged of its apparent meaning, it discerns to be a treasure beyond all price. And in Christianity - such Christianity, I mean, as true taste can accept - culture sees the guide to the real significance of life, and the explanation,' Mr. Luke added with a sigh, 'of that melancholy which in our day is attendant upon all clear sight.'"[23] This

---

[21] Ibid., 31.
[22] Clifford, 373.
[23] Mallock, *The New Republic,* 31.

is a spot-on reproduction of Arnold's fastidious advocacy of a Christianity without Christ.

In his 1883 book *God and the Bible,* Arnold, referring to Clifford's attacks on Christianity, wearily commented: "One reads it all, half sighing, half smiling, as the declamation of a clever and confident youth, with the hopeless inexperience, irredeemable by any cleverness, of his age. Only when one is young and headstrong can one thus prefer bravado to experience, can one stand by the Sea of Time, and instead of listening to the solemn and rhythmical beat of its waves, choose to fill the air with one's own whoopings to start the echo."[24]

This condescending attitude toward Clifford, based on his "inexperience" and "youth", is a two-edged sword. One could mention in response the following lines from Friedrich Nietzsche's *Thus Spake Zarathustra*: "Verily, that Hebrew died too young whom the preachers of slow death honor . . . . As yet he knew only tears and the melancholy of the Hebrew, and hatred of the good and the just - the Hebrew Jesus . . . . Believe me, my brothers! He died too early; he himself would have recanted his teaching, had he reached my age."[25] Tradition tells us that Jesus of Nazareth, like Clifford, met his end at the age of thirty-three.

Yet another critic of Clifford's was the physiologist George John Romanes, a good friend of Darwin's and Huxley's and the initiator in 1892 of a famous annual lecture at Oxford. An agnostic himself, Romanes sought to distance himself from Clifford's more assertive atheism. Frank Miller Turner writes:

> In 1885 Romanes delivered the Rede Lecture at Cambridge. In the course of this address, he defined the concept of pure agnosticism that he employed against both dogmatic religion and dogmatic naturalism. He told his audience, "If it be true that the voice of science must thus of necessity speak the language of agnosticism, at least let us see to it that the language is pure; let us not tolerate any barbarisms introduced from the side of aggressive dogma." The "aggressive dogma" to which Romanes referred was that of W. K. Clifford, one of the most articulate naturalistic writers. Clifford had suggested that the agnostic should simply disregard the question of the existence of God. Romanes argued that the pure agnostic

---

[24] Matthew Arnold, *God and the Bible,* edited by R. H. Super (Ann Arbor, Michigan: The University of Michigan Press, 1970), . 380-381.
[25] Nietzsche, *The Portable Nietzsche,* 185.

could not in good conscience ignore the question because the existence of God remained a rational though empirically unverifiable possibility.[26]

A similar attempt to mark a division between aggressive theism on one hand and aggressive atheism on the other would later be argued by the philosopher John Dewey, in his famous lecture *A Common Faith*, delivered at Yale in 1933. While not mentioning Clifford specifically (Dewey had in mind more contemporary freethinkers like Bertrand Russell), *A Common Faith* also tries to put theistic arguments in an area where they can be theoretically discussed while being empirically unverifiable.

As a final note on W. K. Clifford's influence on his own contemporaries, it is interesting to note that theologians of the time continued to read and reflect upon "The Ethics of Belief". James Livingston makes the following remarkable point:

> In 1911 J. M. Thompson, Dean of Divinity of Magdelen College, Oxford, published *The Miracles of the New Testament,* in which he frankly rejected the miracles of the Virgin Birth and the physical Resurrection. The book caused an outcry and Thompson's license to teach was removed by the Bishop of Winchester, and Gore, now Bishop of Oxford, refused him permission to officiate in his diocese. Thompson was deeply concerned over what he felt was a new and dangerous lack of respect for truth in the church. "We need to remind ourselves," he said, "very seriously of our responsibility for our beliefs," and concluded by commending to his readers the words of W. K. Clifford: "It is wrong in all cases to believe on insufficient evidence; and where it is a presumption to doubt and to investigate, there it is worse than presumption to believe."[27]

What Clifford would have thought about being championed by a Dean of Divinity and pilloried by a friend of Darwin's and Huxley's can only be surmised. It is a great tragedy that this premier polemicist, who loved nothing more than a good argument, did not live long enough to be able to engage personally with his critics. The most famous of these, William James, would help to continue discussion well into the next century of "The Ethics of Belief" by making it, and Clifford himself, a frequent target of his criticism.

---

[26] Frank Miller Turner, *Between Science and Religion* (New Haven: Yale University Press, 1974), 150.
[27] Brown, 47.

II. "The Will to Believe" and "The Fixation of Belief"

1. William James

The most interesting response to "The Ethics of Belief", and surely the most well-known, was a belated one. It came from the American philosopher and psychologist William James (1842-1910). His 1896 essay "The Will to Believe" is usually presented as the premier response to Clifford. In the words of John Passmore: "James's main thesis can be very simply stated: men cannot help going beyond the evidence . . . . In other words, down with Clifford!"[28]

Yet presenting the two essays as if they are diametrically opposed is misleading. For both Clifford and James *shared* many concerns, and the two essays, in their own ways, advocate a rigorous concept of intellectual honesty. Clifford and James agreed that dogmatic assertions and beliefs too-easily accepted needed to be vigorously opposed.

Although "The Will to Believe" is James' most well-known examination of Clifford, his interest in the latter's work precedes that essay by several years. In 1880, the year after Clifford's death, James reviewed his posthumously published works *Lectures and Essays* and *Seeing and Thinking*. The review begins:

> It is impossible to read these volumes without taking an even greater interest in the human character they reveal than in the matters of which they treat. The author was cut down last March at the age of thirty-three. Many who have read hastily and at long intervals the essays here gathered together may have caught the impressions of a genius too iconoclastic to be sympathetic, too fond of paradoxical statement to be wise, too eager for battle to be fair; but the massive effect of all the essays taken together and combined with the personal account of Clifford in the introduction strongly modifies this feeling.[29]

As is often the case when James at first heaps high praise on another writer, the review then shifts to a more critical tone, as he chastises Clifford for his pugnacious tone and his overemphasis on the "creed" of science. Such a creed, rather than being purely objective, is itself a case of "mere subjective capriciousness", and is not one which can inspire or

---

[28] John Passmore, *A Hundred Years of Philosophy* (Baltimore: Penguin Books, 1968), 101.
[29] William James, *Essays, Comments, and Reviews* (Cambridge, Massachusetts: Harvard University Press, 1987), 356.

motivate the general public, being at one and the same time too austere and too passionate. "What we complain of," James adds, "is that Clifford should have been willing . . . to use the conjuring spell of the name of Science, and to harp on Reverence for Truth as means whereby to force them on the minds of simple public listeners, and so still more bewilder what is already too perplexed. Splintered ends, broken threads, broken lights, and, at last, broken hearts and broken life! So ends this bright romance!"[30] All this from a man who pokes fun at *Clifford's* rambunctious style. James would continue to use such florid tones, while taking Clifford to task for using quite similar rhetorical flourishes, in his later essay "The Will to Believe".

"The Will to Believe" was originally delivered as an address to the Philosophical Clubs of Yale and Brown, and was published in *The New World* in June of 1896. A defense not so much of the *will* but rather *the right* to believe, James uses the long-dead Clifford as his primary foil throughout. Like Clifford's own "The Ethics of Belief", James' talk was delivered to a specific audience, whom he sought to influence. His fear, he told the assembled students, was that they were being affected by the "Harvard freethinking and indifference" of his own institution. He came prepared to give a "sermon" on the justification of faith. Like Clifford, James had a fondness for using religious language in a secular context.[31] James expressed the hope that the students' minds were more open than those of his own students at Harvard.

What James was fearful of was that the rising positivistic attitude of the sciences was having a deleterious impact on religious belief, by closing off proper understanding of the role which religion plays in the general society. As Ellen Kappy Suckiel puts it in her book *Heaven's Champion: William James's Philosophy of Religion,* James felt that:

> In light of their intellectual commitments, scientific rationalists find it easy to reject religious claims; but a deeper approach to the issues of religion will reveal that their perspective is unnecessarily exclusionary. Scientific rationalists exhibit a bias, or prejudice, in that they consider questions to be closed which legitimately may be regarded as open . . . James believes that scientific rationalists display both an overly narrow conception of

---

[30] Ibid., 360-361.
[31] In "Ethics and Evidentialism: W. K. Clifford and 'The Ethics of Belief'" (*The Journal for the Critical Study of Religion, Ethics, and Society*, Volume, 2, Number 1, 9-18), I argue that Clifford's essay can best be understood as a "secular sermon", and that his usage of religious language was a deliberate rhetorical strategy to get his readers to reexamine their set beliefs.

what may count as scientific evidence, as well as an overly broad conception of the legitimate domain of science. He thinks that they beg the question against religion, by disallowing, in advance, the possibility of the kinds of conclusions that richer conceptions of justification and evidence would permit. Although they view themselves as open-minded and rational, scientific rationalists often maintain their position with an unusual level of self-assurance and complacency, at times even arrogance, adopting a condescending stance toward religious believers. Typical of the scientific rationalists to whom James objects are W. K. Clifford and Thomas Huxley.[32]

It is precisely because James was himself committed to empiricism, and to a scientific outlook, that he so objected to the writings of men like Clifford. Yet the differences between them regarding the *ethics* of belief have been exaggerated. For they shared many similar views regarding the nature of belief and how best to cultivate justified beliefs. Both agreed that beliefs are voluntary, and within our control. Both talked about beliefs using moral terms. And, most significantly, both felt that the search for evidence is a necessary condition for defending beliefs. As Graham Bird, in his 1986 book *William James,* argues:

> James had no wish to dispute every aspect of Clifford's thesis. Though he rightly complains of Clifford's strident yet querulous tone, he nevertheless also referred to some aspects of his view as 'healthy' and would have echoed it for most cases of belief. James would not have wished to query the thesis that wherever possible we should proportion our beliefs to the available evidence. But he also thought that there were legitimate exceptions to Clifford's universal condemnation to be found among moral and religious belief. Even in that context James did not think that all beliefs of these kinds were legitimate exceptions. His concern was principally to identify as clearly as possible the conditions under which such exceptions could be validated. But he also thought that Clifford's view rested on a general misconception about the nature of belief.[33]

James, then, argued that Clifford's account of belief formation and preservation was inadequate, in that it did not take note of the role which the "passional" interests play in such a process. For James, Clifford epitomized the "intellectualist" or rationalist point-of-view. The strategy emphasized by Clifford was inadequate, for it failed to take into

---

[32] Ellen Kay Suckiel, *Heaven's Champion: William James's Philosophy of Religion* (Notre Dame, Indiana: University of Notre Dame Press, 1996), 9.
[33] Graham Bird, *William James* (New York: Routledge & Kegan Paul, 1986), 162.

consideration other aspects of human motivation. The actual psychology of human beings is influenced to a large extent by our "passional" and volitional nature. In order to understand the nature of belief, one must examine general assumptions, prejudices, and personal temperments, all of which are in turn affected by historical and societal contingencies. As James would put it, most of the beliefs we hold, be they moral, religious or factual, are held on trust as an unexamined credit balance. Indeed, even the high regard which some humans, such as Clifford, place on pursuing the truth as something highly desirable is itself influenced by our passional nature as much as by our intellectual nature. "Our belief in truth itself, for instance, that there is a truth, and that our minds and it are made for each other, - what is it but a passionate affirmation of desire, in which our social system backs us up?"[34]

In James' critique of Clifford's ethics of belief, he holds that the chief difference between them is marked by the advice each man offers regarding intellectual inquiry. For Clifford, the prime motivating force is to avoid error; for James, it is to discover truth. The first attitude is conservative, holding on to each precious belief which has been hard-won through proper examination. James compares Clifford to a general who marshals his forces and refuses to enter battle, thereby losing the war. The second attitude is adventurous, risky and fraught with peril - the kind of rugged individualism that James felt *he* exemplified. There are situations in which we are presented with a "genuine option", a choice between alternative beliefs, which cannot be decided by a preponderance of evidence one way or the other. In such cases, one has a right to decide to believe the option which most satisfies one's passional nature. James lays out three conditions for such exceptions to Clifford's "cautious" approach to belief-formation. The options must be:
1. Live rather than dead (each hypothesis is a real possibility to the subject).
2. Forced rather than avoidable (there is no possibility of *not* choosing).
3. Momentous rather than trivial (the decision will have a marked influence on one's life).

A "genuine" option, then, is one which is live, forced, and momentous. It is only in this admittedly limited category of beliefs that exceptions to Clifford's rule - apportion beliefs to the evidence - are allowable. In addition, such beliefs can be held without adequate evidence only where a decision *cannot* be made on intellectual grounds. This is to say that

---

[34] William James, "The Will to Believe" in *Essays on Faith and Morals* (New York: Longmans, Green and Co., 1947), 40.

intellectual inquiry must first take place, and must reach a genuine dilemma, where a preponderance of evidence cannot decide the issue. It is still illegitimate, in James' view, to believe on passional grounds *without* first engaging in intellectual inquiry, a key point which is often overlooked by commentators.

Is James' presentation of Clifford's argument a fair one? Was Clifford the sort of "scientific rationalist" who sought to prevent the acceptance of religious beliefs?

According to Graham Bird, James is unfair in his treatment of Clifford's agnosticism, the withholding of belief in God's existence until such time as evidence can decide the case:

> James ascribes to Clifford the motive of sheltering atheism under the guise of agnosticism, because he believes that to be an agnostic in such matters is to lose the potential benefits of the belief. But it is not easy to see why we may suspend judgment in science but cannot do so in religion without losing potential benefits.[35]

James is mistaken, for it is by no means clear that agnostics, in his words, "wilfully agree to keep their willing nature out of the game." Rather, they are careful to distinguish between what they desire to be true and what they can hold to be true due to proper evidence. Suckiel rejoins: "If the question of whether to believe in God were an exclusively intellectual one, James grants that it would be possible to withhold judgment. But he believes that agnosticism, while *theoretically* a distinct alternative, is, from a *pragmatic* perspective, in terms of the concrete role religious belief plays in the individual's life, no different from atheism."[36] This was apparently a belief of James' which met his own threefold criteria, but he himself admitted that for Clifford, such a choice might not be a live one. In fact, belief in God had indeed been a live option for Clifford, who broke from a sincere form of Christian fundamentalism before becoming a spokesperson for the agnostic position.

For all their differences over religion, James and Clifford are both concerned with belief-formation and the best strategies to follow in order to have beliefs that adhere to the truth. Perhaps the usual assumption that Clifford and James were diametrically opposed in their views regarding the ethics of belief is itself a belief that does not adhere to the evidence. A

---

[35] Bird, 167.
[36] Suckiel, 29.

careful reading of both essays, and an understanding of each man's underlying philosophical assumptions, is needed.

James C. S. Wernham, in his book *James's Will-to-Believe Doctrine: A Heretical View,* raises the pertinent question as to whether James' *Will to Believe* is in fact a response at all to Clifford's "The Ethics of Belief". Wernham writes:

> It is widely held that Clifford's "The Ethics of Belief" is the foil for James's will-to-believe doctrine, that his papers on that subject are best illumined when read against the background of Clifford's own essay. The claim is not more than a half-truth and perhaps less. The reason is this. Clifford's paper, unlike James's one, is admirably well named. It is about ethics, about duty. It is an ought-not-to-believe doctrine and the "ought" is unquestionably moral. Further, it is about belief and belief only, not about deciding to act, not about guessing or gambling, not about taking something as an hypothesis. Clifford's paper will illumine James's one, then, only if and in so far as it also is about ethics and about belief.[37]

Yet in seeking to criticize James, Wernham is himself unfair to Clifford. For Clifford too was interested in action. He felt that one cannot separate beliefs *from* actions. "The Ethics of Belief" is not only about the overlap between ethics and epistemology. Indeed, it strongly advocates the progress of human knowledge, and the hope for the betterment of human society.

Wernham argues that "The Will to Believe" presents a caricature of Clifford's theory of inquiry. James makes it seem as if Clifford's inquirer is a wholly passive individual, doing everything he/she can to eliminate personal feelings or desires.

> If the inquirer must be entirely passive, he must have no desires, must put no questions, must make no conjectures. Clearly, however, any inquirer must have some desire to find out, and he who puts no questions gets none answered; he who makes no conjectures gets none either confuted or confirmed. The wholly passive mind is not the ideal inquirer. Clifford knows it as well as James does. One of his subtitles is "The Duty to Inquire." The duty not to believe is not, for him, the duty to do nothing, to sit patiently waiting. It is the duty to go on inquiring, the duty, in other words, to make conjectures and to test hypotheses. James' portrayal of him is just a convenient whipping-boy, a figment of James' imagination . . .[38]

---

[37] James C. S. Wernham, *James's Will-to-Believe Doctrine: A Heretical View* (Montreal: McGill-Queen's University Press, 1987), 69.
[38] Ibid., 73.

Clifford never makes it a point that one should refrain from acting if one does not have complete or sufficient evidence. He makes a distinction between believing a proposition and acting upon it, which is consistent with his advocacy of our duty to inquire. It is often only *by* acting, by treating a proposition as if it were true, that one can come upon evidence to either support or refute it. But Clifford denies that one must truly believe such a proposition in order to act upon it. This would give a premature end to the process of inquiry:

> Why, then, does James read him as he does, read him so badly? The answer is that he reads into him his own view that no one acts on p who does not believe it. Give him that and it follows that the inquirer, the gambler, anyone who acts on p, also believes it. If the evidence does not favour p, he believes on insufficient evidence and what he does falls under Clifford's condemnation . . . By a nice irony, it is Clifford who gets the last laugh, however. Critics have read James's essay as a moral right-to-believe doctrine, as a reply to Clifford's moral duty-not-to-believe one. They have read it, in short, as a rival *ethics* of belief. It is that, in part, but in minor part. Taking Clifford as the foil distorts James's essay by highlighting the moral thesis and by putting the rest in shadow.[39]

Putting caricature aside, then, *are* Clifford and James offering rival ethics of belief theories? George Mavrodes, for one, denies that this is the case. Rather, he argues, James' approach is fully compatible with Clifford's:

> In making this claim . . . I do not intend to deny that James construed himself as disagreeing deeply with Clifford. Apparently he did think of things in that way. Nor do I deny that James and Clifford may have disagreed "in their hearts." I am claiming only that the positions which they actually put forth in these essays are consistent.[40]

The question which Clifford does not address is: How does one make a decision where there is an insufficiency of evidence? In cases where the evidence is not persuasive either way, Clifford's essay gives no real advice. This is where James "Will-to-Believe" argument offers complementary support:

---

[39] Ibid., 74.
[40] George I. Mavrodes, "Intellectual Morality in Clifford and James" in *The Ethics of Belief Debate,* edited by Gerald D. McCarthy (Atlanta: Scholars Press, 1986), 205.

> Our initial inclination, I suppose, is to think that Clifford tells him not to believe p. James himself certainly seems to think of Clifford in that way. And it seems likely that there is where Clifford's heart lay. His treatment of the examples in his paper has that tone about it. But his principle, as he actually states it, and the arguments which he gives for it, do not at all have that consequence. They do not tell our hypothetical inquirer not to believe p. They simply do not tell him what he should do at all, what would be within the bounds of intellectual morality . . .[41]

Clifford leads one to assume that there is a scale of evidence, and that at some point a threshold is reached whereby the evidence should lead any virtuous inquirer to believe a given proposition. But at no point does Clifford offer an argument for how to find such a threshold. According to Mavrodes, James' "Will-to-Believe" argument provides an answer for the threshold problem. It develops Clifford's principle by trying to delineate a strategy for belief-formation.

Mavrodes makes mention of Clifford's defense of a virtue theory approach to belief formation. "Clifford also suggests in some places," he writes, "that what is crucial to the morality of believing is not so much the truth of the belief, or the nature of its consequences, but the moral character to which it leads."[42] Surely one must differentiate between beliefs that are of the utmost importance and those that are of minor concern. An active pursuit of knowledge, in order to be *ethical,* has to make some distinctions:

> Once we recognize that not all truths are created equal, as it were, then it seems evident that we cannot express the goal of the cognitive life simply in terms of truth. The importance of what we believe must somehow be worked into it, and maybe some other (and even more obscure) elements as well. And the formulation of the goal must make room for the fact that a year of work for a tentative opinion about some things makes more sense than a minute spent for practical certainty about other things.[43]

All of this, Mavrodes holds, leads us back in James' direction. "Much more than with most epistemologists," he writes, "one has the feeling that James is sensitive to the complex reality of the human cognitive situation in the world, and to the profundity (and obscurity, too) of the human cognitive enterprise."[44] According to Mavrodes, Clifford gives a radical

---

[41] Ibid., 212.
[42] Ibid., 215.
[43] Ibid., 219.
[44] Ibid.

yet incomplete rule for leading a proper intellectual life; James provides a method for completing this rule.

But this still does not answer why James himself went out of his way to belittle Clifford's argument, nor why he himself held that the will to believe doctrine was a counter-example to, rather than a completion of, Clifford's ethics of belief. One reason, perhaps, has to do with the *intent* of James' lecture. He feared that members of his audience were being unduly swayed by the scientistic atmosphere of the times - an atmosphere which Clifford, in his own way, had done much to foster. He felt that the moral courage of his audience was being sapped. In Suckiel's words: "From the vantage point of his role as a philosopher who was able to influence public sentiment, James offered pragmatic alternatives as appropriate options to help combat the passivity and ennui of his generation . . . In order successfully to challenge prevailing orthodoxies and create philosophical movement in the minds and hearts of his audiences, James was diplomatic enough to tailor his remarks to their assumptions, interests and concerns."[45] Ironically enough, it was just such an urge to "challenge prevailing orthodoxies" that motivated Clifford to write "The Ethics of Belief" - the orthodoxies both men railed against were different, but the desire to promote freedom of thought and conscience was the same.

Like Wernham, David A. Hollinger has recently argued that a close reading of the two essays shows that James is markedly unfair in his presentation of Clifford's arguments. In Hollinger's words:

> . . . we seem unwilling to forgive the chief target of James's righteous wrath in "The Will to Believe," the English mathematician W. K. Clifford. James's dispatching of Clifford was so effective that commentators on "The Will to Believe" rarely even read the arguments of the thinker James was most concerned to answer. Clifford's historical significance is, thanks to James, akin to that of some of Socrates' more obliging stooges. He was foolish enough to voice opinions that a wiser intellect could refute with wholesome and lasting effects.[46]

Hollinger adds that James was able to present such a caricature primarily because his opponent had been eighteen years in the grave by the time James published "The Will to Believe". Clifford, perhaps more

---

[45] Suckiel, 91.
[46] David A. Hollinger, "James, Clifford, and the Scientific Conscience" in *The Cambridge Companion to William James,* edited by Ruth Anna Putnam (New York: Cambridge University Press, 1997), 70.

than James himself, relished a good fight, and was not the type to avoid responding to criticisms.

As seen earlier, Clifford never advocated the type of passivity James attributed to him. What he protested in "The Ethics of Belief" was the shielding of propositions from critical inquiry. Hollinger adds: "James thus dealt with Clifford through the classic device of appropriation and effacement: he appropriated for himself the more sensible qualifications that Clifford had built into his own argument to begin with, and then effaced these commonsense caveats from his summary of Clifford."[47]

Certainly the key difference between James and Clifford regarded a *special* type of belief - those relating to religion. Religious beliefs are particularly sensitive to examination, *because* they so often provide comfort and support. Hollinger asserts:

> Not every impression James left about Clifford was misleading. Clifford was truly less respectful than James of the religious beliefs of the masses of humankind, beyond as well as within the Christian tradition. James was correct to identify Clifford as the voice for a sensibility different from his own . . . Clifford was unattractively eager to carry the torch of the Enlightenment into the prayer room in the hopes of embarrassing some pious, if misguided soul.[48]

But what was Clifford's *intent* in being so provocative? Perhaps it was to break the logjam of conservative dogmas, which were no longer appropriate to the times.

James was concerned about protecting religious beliefs from the caustic process of inquiry so ruthlessly advocated by Clifford. Yet James, like Clifford himself, was a man of science. He wished to understand the varieties of religious experience. His own theistic beliefs were themselves quite unorthodox, and the God he avowed was by no means coextensive with the Christian deity believed in by most members of the society of his day. As Richard Gale points out, in his essay "Pragmatism Versus Mysticism: The Divided Self of William James", the type of moralistic religion James felt most comfortable with was that of "meliorism", "according to which it is a real possibility that if we collectively exert our best moral effort good will win out over evil in the long run . . . This religion of meliorism, which steers a course midway between optimism

---

[47] Ibid., 72.
[48] Ibid., 73.

and pessimism, is the one that James attempts to reconcile with science and tough-mindedness in general . . ."[49]

James' religious views were themselves unconventional - he certainly was not a believer in the Christian religion as it was understood by most members of his audience. Interestingly enough, Clifford, in "The Ethics of Belief", was careful *not* to directly attack Christianity. Hollinger writes:

> Clifford had not attacked theism directly, nor was he forthright in his approach to Christianity. "The Ethics of Belief" was a passionate vindication of critical inquiry, and a vociferous attack on the habit of accepting, unexamined, the truth-claims that come to us from political or religious authority, social custom, or undisciplined feeling. Clifford's essay bears more comparison than it has received to a great American apotheosis of scientific method that appeared in the same year, Charles Peirce's "The Fixation of Belief" (1877). Peirce brought science to bear on the entirety of belief, explicitly including religious belief, and he did so with a spirit of moral rectitude.[50]

Let us then turn to an examination of Peirce's notion of "inquiry", and its connections with Clifford's ethics of belief.

2. Charles Peirce

Charles Sanders Peirce (1839-1914) knew both James and Clifford. The former was his lifelong friend and supporter. The latter shared many of Peirce's interests, such as logic and mathematics. We know that Peirce read "The Ethics of Belief". Max H. Fisch examined Peirce's library and noted: "In Clifford's *Lectures and Essays* only 'The Ethics of Belief' is underlined . . ."[51] The two men met during Peirce's visit to England in 1875, where they engaged in lively discussion on Peirce's work on the logic of relations. Edward Livingstone Youmans, editor of *Popular Science Monthly,* was also in London at the time, and wrote home to his sister that "Charles Peirce isn't read much on this side. Clifford, however, says he is the greatest living logician, and the second man since Aristotle

---

[49] Richard M. Gale, "Pragmatism and Mysticism: The Divided Self of William James" in *Philosophical Perspectives 5, Philosophy of Religion, 1991*, 256.
[50] Ibid., 75.
[51] Max H. Fisch, *Peirce, Semeiotic, and Pragmatism* (Bloomington, Indiana: Indiana University Press, 1986), 53.

who has added to the subject something material, the other man being George Boole, author of the Laws of Thought."[52] High praise, indeed.

It was Youmans who published one of Peirce's most seminal papers, "The Fixation of Belief", in November of 1877. This was almost exactly the same time as Clifford's "The Ethics of Belief" appeared. Interestingly enough, like Clifford's paper, which had originally been delivered as an address to the Metaphysical Society, Peirce's essay had also begun as a paper, delivered in 1872 to the similarly-named Metaphysical Club. Peirce was concerned about the origin and defense of belief. To make this clear, his essay points out that:

> Belief does not make us act at once, but puts us into such a condition that we shall behave in some certain way, when the occasion arises. Doubt has not the least such active effect, but stimulates us to inquiry until it is destroyed . . .
>
> The irritation of doubt causes a struggle to attain a state of belief. I shall term this struggle *Inquiry,* though it must be admitted that this is sometimes not a very apt designation.
>
> The irritation of doubt is the only immediate motive for the struggle to attain belief . . . With the doubt, therefore, the struggle begins, and with the cessation of doubt it ends. Hence, the sole object of inquiry is the settlement of opinion.[53]

Peirce then goes on to give a careful explication of different strategies individuals use in order to allay doubts. Some rely on "the method of tenacity", doggedly refusing to pay attention to any evidence that might go against cherished beliefs. Others rely on "the method of authority", referring to reliable sources to overcome their doubts. Still others use "the *a priori* method", whereby they rely upon internal feelings to bring them back to a state of belief. And a small number of people use "the method of science", whereby they actively search for evidence, and treat all of their beliefs as potentially changeable. The fourth category is the only one wherein doubt is actually cultivated.

---

[52] Joseph Brent, *Charles Sanders Peirce: A Life* (Bloomington, Indiana: Indiana University Press, 1993), 119.

[53] Charles S. Peirce, "The Fixation of Belief" in *Philosophical Writings of Peirce,* selected and edited with an introduction by Justus Buchler (New York: Dover, 1955), 10.

Peirce even-handedly purports that all four strategies have their virtues. Yet, like Clifford, he cannot help but point out that the sort of shielding of beliefs - especially religious beliefs - one might accept in one's own case looks unacceptable when applied to people of other cultures:

> Let them ask themselves what they would say to a reformed Mussulman who should hesitate to give up his old notions in regard to the relations of the sexes; or to a reformed Catholic who should still shrink from reading the Bible. Would they not say that these persons ought to consider the matter fully, and clearly understand the new doctrine, and then ought to embrace it, in its entirety? But, above all, let it be considered that what is more wholesome than any particular belief is integrity of belief, and that to avoid looking into the support of any belief from a fear that it may turn out rotten is quite as immoral as it is disadvantageous.[54]

Such talk of immorality is resonant of Clifford's vigorous assertions in "The Ethics of Belief". And Peirce goes on to add that, while the other methods have their merits, the virtue of a clear logical consistency, while costly, is in many ways the highest virtue. In flowery language that again reminds one of Clifford's more purple passages, Peirce ends "The Fixation of Belief" thusly:

> The genius of a man's logical method should be loved and reverenced as his bride, whom he has chosen from all the world. He need not condemn the others; on the contrary, he may honour them deeply, and in doing so he only honours her the more. But she is the one that he has chosen, and he knows that he was right in making that choice. And having made it, he will work and fight for her, and will not complain that there are blows to take, hoping that there may be as many and as hard to give, and will strive to be the worthy knight and champion of her from the blaze of whose splendours he draws his inspiration and his courage.[55]

Such a knight in shining armor is very much in line with Clifford's virtuous inquirer, putting all beliefs to the test. But Peirce was careful to point out that this was not a model that *all* humans could aspire to, nor was it appropriate in all contexts. Unlike Clifford and his honest workman in the alehouse, Peirce felt that humans could be placed in different categories, corresponding to how they formed and defended their beliefs. In a later essay, "The Scientific Attitude and Fallibilism", he argued that

---

[54] Ibid., 21.
[55] Ibid.,. 21-22.

the community of inquirers consisted of different types. As was his usual practice, he held that there are *three* such universal classes of believers:

> If we endeavor to form our conceptions upon history and life, we remark three classes of men. The first consists of those for whom the chief thing is the qualities of feelings. These men create art. The second consists of the practical men, who carry on the business of the world. They respect nothing but power, and respect power only so far as it is exercised. The third class consists of men to whom nothing seems great but reason . . . For men of the first class nature is a picture; for men of the second class, it is an opportunity; for men of the third class, it is a cosmos, so admirable, that to penetrate to its ways seems to them the only thing that makes life worth living. These are the men whom we see possessed by a passion to learn.[56]

Contra Clifford, Peirce held that we *cannot* question all of our beliefs. Theoretical doubt does not bring about the type of inquiry that practical doubt causes - it does not irritate.

The aesthetically minded believer tends to rely on feelings, intuitions, and instincts, and generally holds on tenaciously to previously accepted postulates. This type of person is easily moved by poetry and rhetoric. The practical person focuses on concrete, short-term situations, and is only interested in examining fundamental principles if there is (in William James' famous term) some "cash value" to doing so. Such people seek order and opportunity, and often rely upon the method of authority to fix their beliefs. Unlike the third class of believers, the first two both fear and abhor chance and uncertainty. The aesthete and the businessperson distrust the thoroughgoing fallibilism of the scientific attitude, and are unlikely to be moved by appeals to reason.

For all his advocacy of a "community of inquirers", Peirce, at least at the time of writing "The Fixation of Belief," showed little sympathy for the vast body of individuals. The masses, he felt, could not be moved by the spirit of inquiry that motivated scientific thinkers. Thus, his "community of inquirers" applied primarily to scientific inquirers. He himself felt aloof from most members of society. In his biography of Peirce, Joseph Brent writes:

> Peirce, at this point of his philosophical development, saw no reason to import ethics into inquiry. Ethics was limited to implications drawn from

---

[56] Charles Peirce, "The Scientific Attitude and Fallibilism" in *Philosophical Writings of Peirce,* edited and with an introduction by Justus Buchler (New York: Dover Publications, Inc.), 42.

the ideal of truth as embodied in a community of inquirers, and the individual partook in knowledge only as a member of it. Outside the sacred circle, since worthless there, the individual was not bound by ethical considerations . . .This moral blindness cost Peirce dearly. It was twenty years before he proposed the doctrine that logic, and therefore pragmatism, depended on ethics in the larger sense.[57]

Still, no philosopher more boldly asserted the prime importance of inquiry to human society. In his stirring words, Peirce proclaimed: "Upon this first, and in one sense this sole, rule of reason, that in order to learn you must desire to learn, and in so desiring not be satisfied with what you already incline to think, there follows one corollary which itself deserves to be inscribed upon every wall of the city of philosophy: Do not block the way of inquiry."[58]

Did Peirce, in "The Fixation of Belief" and Clifford, in "The Ethics of Belief", therefore share a similar aim? Douglas Anderson, in his book *Strands of System: The Philosophy of Charles Peirce,* states:

> On the surface, it seems plausible to suppose that Peirce's project is akin to Clifford's. However, careful reading suggests a crucial difference. Peirce was interested not so much in "ethically" policing present beliefs as in identifying the method that could address the settlement of opinion in the long run.[59]

Anderson adds: "Foreshadowing his later thinking, Peirce seems to want to strike a middle ground between James' willing to believe and Clifford's stringent, scientistic "ethics of belief.""[60] Yet the strategies of these three thinkers are not so opposed as is usually presented. All of them offer a defense of inquiry.

Hollinger shows that James, under the influence of Peirce, *did* apply critical inquiry to religious beliefs in his later career, although remaining wary of Clifford's "robustious pathos" to the end.

> During the decade between "The Will to Believe" and *Pragmatism* James came to accept more fully an idea he had long suspected was true but had often resisted: that scientific discourse was the field on which the culture of the future would be determined. James had recognized from the start

---

[57] Brent,. 118-119.
[58] Peirce, "The Scientific Attitude and Fallibilism", 54.
[59] Douglas Anderson, *Strands of System: The Philosophy of Charles Peirce* (West Lafayette, Indiana: Purdue University Press, 1995), 83.
[60] Ibid.

that his dispute with Clifford had to do with what structure of plausibility would prevail in the world's most advanced societies. But until around the turn of the century James episodically indulged the hope - displayed the most openly in "The Will to Believe" - that a doctrine of separate spheres would preserve a place in which traditional religious emotions could continue to flourish unintimidated.[61]

The intent of all three men was to defend the *right* to inquire, and to oppose orthodox ways of thinking that impeded such progress. As Louis Pojman phrases it:

Perhaps it is misleading to call Clifford's theory an "ethics of belief", for he does not fault the belief but the *way* it was arrived at. What he is advocating is an *ethics of investigation* or of intellectual inquiry. There are certain rules in evidence gathering which have moral significance: e.g., being impartial, gathering a wide sample of evidence, being open to criticism, and checking one's results. If one adheres to these processes, the likelihood is that one will have an optimal set of beliefs. Even if it turns out that some of our beliefs are false, we still maintain the integrity of truth seekers, and our experience is that in the long run this is the best way to insure true beliefs.[62]

Such concern with the integrity of truth seeking is also, as we have seen, of great import to both James and Peirce, as well as to Clifford. All three men, each in his own way, offered strategies for keeping clear the way of inquiry.

III. Clifford's Later Contemporaries

1. Friedrich Nietzsche

On the subject of religion Clifford was something of a fanatic. Not only did he speak of the clergy as enemies of humanity, and of Christianity as a plague, but he also attacked all belief in God. He was thus more akin to some of the writers of the French Enlightenment than to the Nineteenth Century English agnostics, who were generally polite in what they said about religion and its official representatives. And he has been compared not inaptly with Nietzsche. (Frederick Copleston, S.J.)[63]

---

[61] Hollinger, 80.
[62] Louis Pojman, *Religious Belief and the Will* (New York: Routledge & Kegan Paul, 1986), 77.
[63] Frederick Copleston, S.J., *A History of Philosophy, Vol. VIII: Modern Philosophy* (New York: Image Books, 1994), 115.

Although contemporaries, William Kingdon Clifford (1845-1879) and Friedrich Nietzsche (1844-1900) were unaware of each other's work. Yet in many ways, they were soulmates in the battle to free the minds of human beings from outmoded superstitions, each of whom could rightly be said to have "philosophized with a hammer" in his quest to announce a Post-Christian ethics in Western civilization.

Clifford is today much less known than his German counterpart. Yet in their own time it was Nietzsche who was obscure - Clifford was something of a celebrity, as seen previously, even being parodied in the popular novel of the day, *The New Republic*.

One can note many similarities in the background of the two thinkers. They both were child prodigies, astounding those around them with their precocious knowledge. Also, both were deeply religious in their youth (Clifford was raised an Anglican, Nietzsche a Lutheran) and knew the Bible almost by heart at an early age - an attribute that would prove useful to them in their later anti-Christian polemical works. Although most remembered for their writings on ethics, epistemology and metaphysics, neither was by training or profession a philosopher. As mentioned earlier, Clifford was a mathematician, while Nietzsche was a Professor of Classical Philology at the University of Basel. Their professorial careers ended in the same year, 1879, with Nietzsche's resignation due to ill health and Clifford's untimely death.

Perhaps more to the point, Nietzsche's and Clifford's writing styles show remarkable similarities. They each utilized aphorisms and short, witty sentences to get their points across. They were blunt in their assertions, resorting frequently to symbolic phrases and exaggeration for effect. Consider these excerpts from Clifford's "The Ethics of Belief": "He who truly believes that which prompts him to an action has looked upon the action to lust after it, he has committed it already in his heart"[64]; "Whoso would deserve well of his fellows . . . will guard the purity of his belief with a very fanaticism of jealous care, lest at any time it should rest on an unworthy object, and catch a stain which can never be wiped away"[65]; and the following:

> If a man, holding a belief which he was taught in childhood or persuaded of afterwards, keeps down and pushes away any doubts which arise about it in his mind, purposely avoids the reading of books and the company of men that call in question or discuss it, and regards as impious those

---

[64]Ibid., 342.
[65]Ibid., 343.

questions which cannot easily be asked without disturbing it - the life of that man is one long sin against mankind.[66]

Note the use of such religious phrases as "lust . . . in his heart", "purity of belief", and "sin". Like Nietzsche, Clifford could not resist shocking his audience with sacrilegious or ironic usages of sacred words. Surely, the author of *The Anti-Christ* and *Ecce Homo* would have appreciated Clifford's approach.

Yet neither of them engaged in such rhetorical flourishes merely for shock effect. They each felt that the religion of Christianity, which had dominated the Western world for over 1,800 years, was played out, and was no longer appropriate to modern industrialized societies. Clifford would have heartily agreed with the proclamation of Nietzsche's madman in *The Gay Science*: "God is dead and we have killed him." And he would have further agreed that the real question was whether or not humans could prove to be *worthy* of so great a deed. Clifford saw the end of Christianity as a golden opportunity to promote the growth of human intelligence. In a later essay, "The Decline of Religious Belief", Clifford admitted that the loss of theistic belief could be painful. With a touch of elegance, he writes: "We have seen the spring sun shine out of an empty heaven, to light up a soulless earth; we have felt with utter loneliness that the Great Companion is dead. Our children, it may be hoped, will know that sorrow only by the reflex light of a wondering compassion. But to say that theistic belief is a comfort and a solace, and to say that it is the crown or coping of morality, these are different things."[67]

For Clifford, as for Nietzsche, the religious beliefs of human beings had once been reasonable hypotheses to explain the natural world and its wonders. But the rise of scientific investigation had shown that these answers, while often satisfying, were unsubstantiated or often plain wrong. If the facts no longer supported cherished beliefs, then for the good of human progress such beliefs had to be shed.

A characteristic which both men shared, perhaps due to their own initial attraction to the profession, was an abhorrence of clergy. Much like Nietzsche's remark that one should remember to wash one's hand after shaking that of a priest, Clifford was unqualified in his denunciation of clerics of all stripes. He felt that the priesthood was a means for a privileged few to gain power over the masses, through obfuscations and trickery. Priests, he stated, deliberately keep people in the dark, like the

---

[66]Ibid., 346.
[67]Ibid., 389.

rulers of Plato's cave, and prevent the free and open discussion of ideas that go against their set dogmas.

In his essay "The Ethics of Religion", Clifford sounds very Nietzschean indeed: "I can find no evidence that seriously militates against the rule that the priest is at all times and in all places the enemy of all men . . . . If there is one lesson which history forces upon us in every page, it is this: *Keep your children away from the priest, or he will make them the enemies of mankind.*"[68] No wonder Father Copleston, in the quote above, considered him something of a fanatic, as well as close to Nietzsche in spirit. "How gladly one would exchange the false claims of priests", Nietzsche writes in *Human, All Too Human,* "- that there is a God who demands the Good from us, who is guardian and witness of each act, each moment, each thought, who loves us and wants the best for us in every misfortune - how gladly one would exchange these claims for truths which would be just as salutary, calming, and soothing as those errors!" Yet he then adds a very UnCliffordian caveat:

> But there are no such truths; at the most, philosophy can oppose those errors with other metaphysical fictions (basically also untruths). But the tragic thing is that we can no longer *believe* those dogmas of religion and metaphysics, once we have the rigorous method of truth in our hearts and heads, and yet on the other hand, the development of mankind has made us so delicate, sensitive, and ailing that we need the most potent kind of cures and comforts - hence arises the danger that man might bleed to death from the truth he has recognized.[69]

Clifford would have had none of such despair. The masses had been hidden from the truth for too many centuries. The methods of science now made it possible for them to become educated, and to gain the knowledge which priests and rulers had kept from them. The truth could only strengthen society, by forging bonds based on justified beliefs. Like his friend Thomas Huxley, Clifford spent much of his free time giving public lectures to the working class, and writing textbooks to explain to them, in understandable language, the current findings in biology, geometry and physics. He would have been appalled by Nietzsche's offhanded comments about the inability of most humans to give up the dogmas of religion and theology.

---

[68] Ibid., 382.
[69] Friedrich Nietzsche, *Human, All Too Human: A Book for Free Spirits*, translated by Marion Faber, with Stephen Lehmann (Lincoln, Nebraska: University of Nebraska Press, 1996), . 77-78.

While denouncing the priestcraft in general, and Christianity in particular, both Clifford and Nietzsche expressed admiration for the life and teachings of Jesus of Nazareth ("Using the expression somewhat tolerantly, one could call Jesus a 'free spirit'", the latter wrote in *The Antichrist*). Yet, in Clifford's praise for Jesus, one can see the important *difference* between his ethics and Nietzsche's:

> The moral teaching of Christ, as partly preserved in the three first gospels, or - which is the same thing - the moral teaching of the great Rabbi Hillel . . . is the expression of the conscience of a people who had fought long and heroically for their national existence. In that terrible conflict they had learned the supreme and overwhelming importance of conduct, the necessity for those who would survive of fighting manfully for their lives and making a stand against the hostile powers around; the weakness and uselessness of solitary and selfish efforts, the necessity for a man who would be a man to lose his poor single personality in the being of a greater and nobler combatant - the nation.[70]

For Clifford, ethics was the study of the growing communal sense of human beings, uniting together to deal with the problems presented to them by the natural world. The nation was the repository for the accumulated wisdom of the tribe. Humans should strive together to increase this bank of wisdom, and fight against attempts to breach their solidarity. Here Clifford takes on an apocalyptic tone, stating: "It seems to me quite possible that the moral and intellectual culture of Europe, the light and the right, what makes life worth having and men worthy to have it, may be clean swept away by a revival of superstition."[71]

Nietzsche was far less sanguine in his estimation of the masses' ability to increase their storehouse of knowledge, or their willingness to give up the pleasures of superstitious belief. Far more than Clifford, he was a solitary being, living for long periods in ill-heated, rented rooms while toiling over books that were little read at the time. Clifford, on the other hand, delivered public addresses to large crowds, in addition to publishing articles in some of the most popular journals of his day. A family man, with a devoted wife and two daughters, as well as a general love for children (he even composed children's verses), Clifford would not have appreciated Nietzsche's scathing misanthropic pronouncements. Surrounded by many friends, several of whom did not share his own views, Clifford

---

[70]Clifford, 377.
[71]Ibid., 380.

naturally felt that team-spirit and mutual aid were the key supports to an ethics that encouraged all humans to excel.

Earlier than almost anyone else, Clifford saw the implications of Darwinian evolution to human ethics. Paul Lawrence Farber writes: "One of the first to discuss the ethical implications of Darwin's work was William Kingdon Clifford. . . . For Clifford, Darwin provided a revolutionary perspective, which, like the non-Euclidean geometry that shattered the belief in an eternal and fixed geometry, undermined traditional beliefs."[72] In addition, Clifford's ethics was strongly influenced by both the duty-based approach of Kant and the utilitarianism of Bentham and Mill. Humans, Clifford argued, had a moral obligation to apportion their beliefs to the evidence, and in doing so, they thereby increased the greater good of society. Nietzsche spurned both of these philosophies: each was, in his view, just an attempt to continue Christianity without Christ. His was closer to a virtue ethics approach, in line with the Aristotelian emphasis on character development. Also, unlike many neo-Darwinians, Nietzsche did not believe that evolution implied the inevitable progress of humankind. The stupidest and lowest men were more likely than not to propagate, and thereby marginalize the wise few. Yet Nietzsche did have a hope that these wise few *might* be able to lead the masses forward:

> The butterfly wants to break through his cocoon; he tears at it, he rends it: then he is blinded and confused by the unknown light, the realm of freedom. Men who are *capable* of that sorrow (how few they will be!) will make the first attempt to see if mankind *can transform itself* from a *moral* into a *wise* mankind. In those individuals, the sun of a new gospel is casting its first ray onto the highest mountaintop of the soul; the fog is condensing more thickly than ever, and the brightest light and cloudiest dusk lie next to each other. . . . Everything in the sphere of morality has evolved; changeable, fluctuating, everything is fluid, it is true: but *everything is also streaming onward* - to one goal. Even if the inherited habit of erroneous esteeming, loving, hating continues to govern us, it will grow weaker under the influence of growing knowledge: a new habit, that of understanding, non-loving, non-hating, surveying is gradually being implanted in us on the same ground, and in thousands of years will be powerful enough perhaps to give mankind the strength to produce wise, innocent (conscious of their innocence) men as regularly as it now produces unwise, unfair men, conscious of their guilt.[73]

---

[72] Paul Lawrence Farber, *The Temptations of Evolutionary Ethics* (Berkeley: University of California Press, 1994), 23.
[73] Ibid., .75-76.

Even though both men used Darwin as a starting point, Clifford was not willing to wait thousands of years. The time to change was *now,* and Darwin's startling theory was the means to do so. By accepting evolution, the human species could better understand and appreciate itself, as well as take an active role in shaping its own future development.

In many ways, Clifford exemplified what Nietzsche was to call, in his book *Human, All Too Human,* "a free spirit." Published in 1878, the year after Clifford's "The Ethics of Belief" saw print, *Human, All Too Human* marks Nietzsche's break from his romantic past, and defends the ideals of the Enlightenment:

> A man is called a free spirit if he thinks otherwise than would be expected, based on his origin, environment, class, and position, or based on prevailing contemporary views. He is the exception: bound spirits are the rule; the latter reproach him that his free principles have their origin either in a need to be noticed, or else may even lead one to suspect him of free actions, that is, actions that are irreconcilable with bound morality. . . . Incidentally, it is not part of the nature of the free spirit that his views are more correct, but rather that he has released himself from tradition, be it successfully or unsuccessfully. Usually, however, he has truth, or at least the spirit of the search for truth on his side: he demands reasons, while others demand faith.[74]

Nietzsche's free spirit is a lonely wanderer - a voice crying in the wilderness - a concept quite different from Clifford's public-minded challenger. The tragic irony is that, while desiring to aid his fellow human beings, "the bound spirits", he cannot help but alienate them. "Free spirits, pleading their cause before the tribunal of bound spirits", Nietzsche adds, "have to prove that there have always been free spirits and that freethinking therefore has permanence; then, that they do not want to be a burden; and finally, that on the whole they are beneficial to bound spirits. But because they cannot convince the bound spirits of this last point, it does not help them to have proved the first and second."[75]

The urge to convince *all* people to question their beliefs was key to Clifford's character. Much more than Nietzsche, he was socially-oriented. Believing on false assumptions, or out of a desire for comfort, was not only pernicious for individual development - it was also detrimental to society, since "no man's belief is in any case a private matter which concerns himself alone. Our lives are guided by that general conception of

---

[74] Nietzsche, *Human, All Too Human,* . 139-140.
[75] Ibid., 142.

the course of things which has been created by society for social purposes."[76] Credulity sapped the strength of this communal vitality:

> ... if I let myself believe anything on insufficient evidence, there may be no great harm done by the mere belief; it may be true after all, or I may never have occasion to exhibit it in outward acts. But I cannot help doing this great wrong towards Man, that I make myself credulous. The danger to society is not merely that it should believe wrong things, though that is great enough; but that it should become credulous, and lose the habit of testing things and inquiring into them; for then it must sink back into savagery.[77]

The possibility that Western society could easily collapse, and return to the barbarism of the Middle Ages, was ever on Clifford's mind. He blamed Christianity for this initial fiasco, and feared that a return to "sacerdotal Christianity", which many of his contemporaries such as Edward Manning and William Gladstone were advocating, would destroy the slow and steady progression of scientific knowledge that had only begun since the 1600s. Intellectual honesty would be overthrown, and the habit of truth-speaking would be weakened. "This system," he wrote, "if it should ever return to power, must be expected to produce worse evils than those which it has worked in the past. The house which it once made desolate has been partially swept and garnished by the free play gained for the natural goodness of men. It would come back accompanied by social diseases perhaps worse than itself, and the wreck of civilised Europe would be darker than the darkest of past ages."[78]

Clifford's friend and biographer Frederic Pollock felt that the former's enthusiasm for Darwin and natural selection, coupled with his public concern, had led him to develop a new system of ethics "combining the exactness of the utilitarian with the poetical ideals of the transcendentalist."[79] He was a collectivist in his thinking, as opposed to Nietzsche's individualistic ethics. Clifford urged all people to take an active role in making humankind fitter, and better able to survive in a changing environment:

> At one time Clifford held that it was worth our while to practise variation of set purpose; not only to avoid being the slaves of custom, but to eschew

---

[76] Clifford, 342.
[77] Ibid., 345.
[78] Ibid., 393.
[79] Pollock, introduction to Clifford's *Lectures and Essays*, 25.

fixed habits of every kind, and to try the greatest possible number of experiments in living to increase the chances of a really valuable one occurring and being selected for preservation.[80]

Although dubious that the vast majority of people could follow such a process, Nietzsche too espoused a kind of "experimentalism." As David Wisdo writes: "Nietzsche himself seems to think that the pursuit of intellectual honesty involves the cultivation of a kind of existential skepticism and that one should *always* be willing to call into question one's most cherished ideals and values."[81]

Both Clifford and Nietzsche had an ethics of belief, demanding that people treat each and every belief as capable of being changed or discarded in light of new evidence. Their opinions of the masses differed, but their own love for the truth made them epistemic comrades. While their influence has been disproportionate, Clifford's having significantly diminished and Nietzsche's having risen just as dramatically, they continue to demonstrate the virtues of a pursuit of truth. Each was a frustrated systematic philosopher, and they planned to put their various writings into a definite structure. Sadly, death in Clifford's case, and insanity in Nietzsche's, prevented them from doing so. To paraphraseZarathustra's comment on Christ: Verily, they died too young.

2. Karl Pearson

One person who did a great deal to keep alive Clifford's name and influence was Karl Pearson (1857-1936), his successor as chair of applied mathematics at University College, London. Pearson completed the work on Clifford's *The Common Sense of the Exact Sciences,* which was published in 1885, the year after his appointment. In addition to continuing Clifford's work in mathematics, Pearson was also a strong rationalist, authoring in 1888 *The Ethic of Freethought, a Selection of Essays and Lectures*. Like Clifford, he was a frequent public lecturer, and shared his predecessor's high hopes for the betterment of the human condition through scientific advancement.

Pearson had studied mathematics at King's College, Cambridge, Clifford's *alma mater*, where in 1879 (the year of Clifford's death) he became Third Wrangler in Mathematics. In 1880, Pearson became a

---

[80] Ibid.
[81] David Wisdo, *The Life of Irony and the Ethics of Belief* (Albany, New York: State University of New York Press, 1993), 67.

Fellow of the college. He studied law at Heidelberg and Berlin, and was called to the bar in 1881 (although he never practiced). In Germany, he became acquainted with Ernst Mach, who later dedicated his *Science of Mechanics* to him. Pearson's interest in the works of Lasalle and Marx convinced him of the rightness of socialism, and upon his return to England, he became involved in radical reform movements. His appointment to the chair of applied mathematics and mechanics at University College, London, occurred in 1884 and he held the post until 1911, when he was then appointed to the new chair of eugenics at the college; he retired in 1933.

One of Pearson's first projects was to complete the work on which Clifford had been laboring at the time of his death, which was to have been entitled *The First Principles of the Mathematical Sciences Explained to the Non-Mathematical.* Clifford's plan was to have six chapters: *Number, Space, Quantity, Position, Motion,* and *Mass.* He had finished the chapters on Number and Space, most of the chapter on Motion, and the first part of the chapter on Quantity. Shortly before his death, Clifford decided to shorten the title to *The Common Sense of the Exact Sciences.* R. C. Rowe, his colleague at University College, London, where he held the chair in pure mathematics, took on the task of revising and completing the manuscript, but his own death in 1884 once again stalled the project. The publishers, Kegan Paul, Trench & Co. then requested Pearson to finish the work. In his preface, he wrote: "It was with no light heart, but with a grave sense of responsibility that I undertook to see through the press the labour of two men for whom I held the highest scientific admiration and personal respect."[82]

Pearson wrote the chapter on "Position", and a good deal of "Quantity" and "Motion." He consulted with Clifford's widow to make sure that the arrangement of the chapters was according to her husband's plans, and checked all of the notes and slips of paper in Clifford's handwriting that pertained to the work in progress. Upon publication, the work was an immediate success and it remained in print for many years, giving Clifford a posthumous fame in his own field which he might otherwise have lacked. In the preface, Pearson wrote humbly of his own contributions to the book: " . . whatever there is in them of value I owe to Clifford; whatever is feeble or obscure is my own."[83] He added: "My sole desire has been to give to the public as soon as possible another work of one

---

[82] Karl Pearson, preface to *The Common Sense of the Exact Science* by William Kingdon Clifford (New York: Alfred A. Knopf, 1946), xiv.
[83] Ibid.

whose memory will be revered by all who have felt the invigorating influence of his thought. Had this work been published as a fragment, even as many of us wished, it would never have reached those for whom Clifford had intended it."[84]

In his introduction to the 1946 reprint of the book, the mathematician James R. Newman pointed out the influence which it had had over the years:

> To laud *The Common Sense of the Exact Sciences* would be superfluous. It is known to every student of the physical sciences; leading scientific works contain references and quotations; it is most often mentioned in writings on popular science and the philosophy of science. . . . Much of the book exhibits Clifford's (and Pearson's) extraordinary virtuosity in the art of making hard things seem easy. Throughout, one feels the impulsion, the intellectual range and vigour of Clifford's spirit.[85]

With the exception of Clifford's friends Leslie Stephen and Frederick Pollock, Pearson did more than anyone to make sure that Clifford would not be forgotten.

In his own famous work, *The Grammar of Science* (1892), Pearson continued to pay homage to his predecessor. As John Passmore puts it: "In those parts of *The Grammar of Science* which concern themselves with the concepts of mechanics Pearson is, as he says, developing the hints which Clifford had dropped; but Pearson, not Clifford, supplied the details."[86] Pearson quotes Clifford several times within the text. He mentions Clifford's notion of *mind-stuff* (albeit adding that it is not a concept he himself espouses), and devotes an entire section to Clifford's concept of *ejects*, writing:

> Clifford has given the name *eject* to existences which, like other-consciousness, are only inferred, and the name is a convenient one. At the same time it seems to me doubtful whether the distinction between *object* (what might possibly come to my consciousness as a direct sense-impression) and *eject* is so marked as he would have us believe.[87]

---

[84] Ibid., xvi.
[85] James R. Newman, introduction to *The Common Sense of the Exact Sciences*, .lix-lx.
[86] John Passmore, *A Hundred Years of Philosophy* (Baltimore, Maryland, 1966), 323.
[87] Karl Pearson, *The Grammar of Science* (London: J. M. Dent & Sons Ltd., 1951), 47.

Furthermore, in his discussion of "The Canons of Legitimate Inference", Pearson refers the reader who wishes to pursue the subject further to Clifford's essay "The Ethics of Belief." As his own writings clearly demonstrate, Pearson was sympathetic to much of what Clifford states in that famous work. He, too, felt that morality was progressing through natural selection, and those societies which stressed education and cooperation were most likely to overcome the debilitating influence of outmoded religious doctrines. He argued that as tribal-identification became feebler through human migrations, the social sympathies became extended to strangers, thus building stronger bonds. These instincts of fellow-feeling "guide us to those principles of conduct, duty to self, duty to society, and duty to humanity, which our forefathers were taught to think of as the outcome of supersensuous decrees or of divine dispensations, and which some even of their children still regard as due to mysterious tendencies to righteousness, or to some moral purpose in the universe at large."[88]

However, Pearson was less sympathetic to Clifford's dabbling in metaphysics, no matter how rationally-based. Pearson shared with Mach a dismissive attitude toward any speculation on ultimate reality, and he has been rightly called a precursor of the logical positivist movement.[89] Yet, he continued Clifford's exploration of the hypothesis of the uniformity of nature. Reba Soffer writes:

> Clifford's mathematical disciple Karl Pearson extended his mentor's use of probability by maintaining that the uniformities or "laws" we experience, the supposedly invariable sequences of natural phenomena, are only the sequence of our sensations. What we call "invariable" is nothing more than the result of our experience projected into a probable future. The so-called laws of nature are really laws of thought dependent upon the ordering powers of perception and not upon either sensations themselves or upon laws of matter. Every "natural law," then, is a description of the way in which our sensations occur; it is never their cause.[90]

---

[88] Ibid., 307.
[89] Passmore adds cheekily that A. J. Ayer's *"Language, Truth and Logic* contains little that is unfamiliar to readers of Continental positivism: but it created something of a sensation in England where such familiarity was by no means widespread, and even the positivism of Clifford and Pearson seems to have been forgotten. People heard with a sense of shock that metaphysical propositions are neither true nor false, but nonsense." Passmore, 582.
[90] Reba N. Soffer, *Ethics and Society in England: The Revolution of the Social Sciences 1870-1914* (Berkeley, California: University of California Press, 1978), 133.

Another concept which Pearson shared with Clifford was that of the herd instinct. In 1900, he wrote *National Life from the Standpoint of Science,* which attempted to prove that altruism was a natural product of this affectionate instinct, and served as the basis for ethics.

Although he had begun his career as an ardent socialist, who preached the doctrine of continuous progress, by the turn of the century Pearson had become far less optimistic. His public career shifted from mathematics to eugenics. In 1911, he became the successor to his friend Francis Galton as chair of eugenics at University College. According to Reba Soffer: "In part, Pearson's zealotry for eugenics as an escape from biological necessity came from an essentially religious feeling, made even stronger by his agnostic break with the Church of England, that wherever error existed it must be corrected."[91] Pearson no longer felt that education would be sufficient to bring about increased social stability and moral progress. Direct measures had to be taken to ensure that those less biologically fit did not continue to breed in disproportion to the more intelligent. He felt that civilization was best served by the advancement of the white race, and held that eugenic policies rather than renewed educational opportunities offered the most hope for the world. Although this marked a break from some of his earlier positions, Pearson had touched upon such views even in *The Grammar of Science,* where he wrote: "It is a false view of human solidarity, a weak humanitarianism, not a true humanism, which regrets that a capable and stalwart race of white men should replace a dark-skinned tribe which can neither utilize its land for the full benefit of mankind, nor contribute its quota to the common stock of human knowledge."[92] One sees here a disturbing side to Pearson's emphasis on increasing the "common stock of human knowledge." One can only speculate as to whether or not Clifford himself would have accepted his disciple's move toward social planning through eugenics.

3. Bertrand Russell

One of those who benefited greatly from Pearson's completion of *The Common Sense of the Exact Sciences* was Bertrand Russell (1872-1970). In his charming preface to the 1946 reprint, Russell paid homage to Clifford, his fellow mathematical pioneer:

---

[91] Soffer, 197.
[92] Pearson, *The Grammar of Science,* 310.

> The copy of this book which I still possess was given to me by my tutor when I was fifteen years of age. I read it at once, with passionate interest and with an intoxicating delight in intellectual clarification. From that day until I came to write this Preface, I had not looked at the book. Now, having re-read it after fifty-seven years, many of them devoted to the subjects of which it treats, I find that it deserved all the adolescent enthusiasm that I bestowed upon it when I first read it.[93]

High praise indeed from a man not noted for his charitable attitude toward those with whom he disagreed.

Clearly, Russell had an affinity for Clifford, especially his style of writing. "Clifford," he continued, "possessed an art of clarity such as belongs only to a very few great men - not the pseudo-clarity of the popularizer, which is achieved by ignoring or glozing over the difficult points, but the clarity that comes of profound and orderly understanding, by virtue of which principles become luminous and deductions look easy."[94]

This was an attribute which another great man - Russell himself - demonstrated throughout his long career. In fact, Nicholas Griffin, in his book *Russell's Idealist Apprenticeship,* speculates that "Clifford's skills as a popularizer, which Russell held in high esteem, may have served as a model in Russell's own popular writings."[95]

While it is perhaps not strictly correct to consider Russell a contemporary of Clifford's, one should note that, had he lived, Clifford would have only been 42 at the time Russell read his book in 1887. Russell often considered himself to be the last of the Victorians, and felt strangely out of place in the post-World War II era.

Russell was aware of the Metaphysical Society, as can be seen in the following amusing anecdote from his 1949 essay "The Victorian Age": "The Metaphysical Society, which consisted of a small collection of eminent men, debated in correct Parliamentary style the question of the existence of God. A member who had not been present enquired anxiously of one who had: Well, is there a God? To which the answer was: Yes, we had a very good majority."[96]

---

[93] Bertrand Russell, preface to *The Common Sense of the Exact Sciences*, v.
[94] Ibid.
[95] Nicholas Griffin, *Russell's Idealist Arenticeship* (Oxford: Clarendon Press, 1991), 11.
[96] Bertrand Russell, "The Victorian Age" in *Ideas and Beliefs of the Victorians* (London: Sylvan Press, 1949), 56.

Russell came from a strong rationalist tradition. His godfather was none other than John Stuart Mill, and both his parents were noted freethinkers. However, none of them had a direct influence upon Russell. Mill died when Russell was still an infant and he was only two when his mother died. His father, Viscount John Amberley, was active in freethought circles, and authored an influential book entitled *An Analysis of Religious Belief*. The work would have a profound effect upon his son, who was to write in a 1949 essay: "I speak as one who was intended by my father to be brought up as a Rationalist. He was quite as much of a Rationalist as I am, but he died when I was three years old, and the Court of Chancery decided that I should have the benefits of a Christian education."[97]

Russell's paternal grandfather, the former British Prime Minister Lord John Russell, became young Bertrand's guardian. But John Russell too was to die before his grandson was to know him. The chief influence on Bertrand's life was to be his grandmother, Lady Frances Russell. An austere and rather forbidding woman, she saw to it that he received a thorough Christian upbringing, although her own leanings were toward Unitarianism. Russell was later to credit much of his own independent way of thinking to her own example.

From an early age, Russell showed a capacity for mathematics. He found a satisfying certitude in this field which was lacking in the theological realm. As Ray Monk, in his 1996 biography of Russell, points out, the field of geometry was particularly appealing to him: "The beauty of geometry was that the truth of a proposition was not just asserted, it was *proved* . . . The idea that something - anything - could be known with certainty in this way was delightful, intoxicating, especially when, as Russell was quick to realise, it opened up the possibility that other things too might be amenable to strict, mathematical proof."[98]

Yet, during private studies in geometry taught to him by his older brother Frank, the precocious Russell came to see a problem with Euclidean geometry: Why should one *believe* the axioms? Frank told him that unless one assumed the axioms to be true, there could be no further progress in the lessons. Such a belief was not one which young Bertrand could accept.

---

[97] Bertrand Russell, "Am I an Atheist or An Agnostic?" in *Bertrand Russell on God and Religion* (Amherst, New York: Prometheus Books, 1986), 83.

[98] Ray Monk, *Bertrand Russell: The Spirit of Solitude* (London: Jonathan Cape, 1996), 27.

When Russell was fifteen, a later private tutor was to introduce him to the still rather esoteric subject of non-Euclidean geometry, especially the work of the recently deceased William Kingdon Clifford. In Monk's words:

> The importance of Clifford's book for Russell was that it crystallised the attitude he had been developing for years about the superiority of reason over intuition, tradition, authority and emotion as a means of arriving at the truth; the attitude that refuses to believe something unless there is some reason for doing so, not just in mathematics, or in science, but in all areas of life. . . . Clifford's book encouraged in Russell a faith that upheld reason as the foundation of all sound belief, and mathematics as the ideal to which all other knowledge should aspire. . . . "It is wrong always, everywhere, and for anyone", wrote Clifford, "to believe anything upon insufficient evidence." It was a view Russell was quick to adopt, and one that gave to his emotional delight in the possibility of demonstrative truth the force of a moral imperative. Not only was it "delicious" to be able to prove things, it was morally essential.[99]

That Russell's enthusiasm for Clifford continued well after his adolescence ended can be seen in a letter he wrote on March 10, 1910, to his mistress Lady Ottoline Morrell. He described Clifford as "an absolutely first-rate mathematician, [who] cared immensely about philosophy. . . . All his writing has the clearness and force that comes of white-hot intellectual passion."[100] In his examination of Russell's early years, Nicholas Griffin points out the many similarities between Clifford and his youthful admirer:

> There are many respects in which Clifford's thought would have been congenial to the young Russell, and even a number of enduring similarities between their work. Clifford, like Russell, was very much concerned with certainty in knowledge and expected advances in scientific knowledge to aid in the solution, or at least the clarification, of philosophical problems. Like Russell too, Clifford placed a moral emphasis on the use of reason in the pursuit of truth. . . . Both Clifford and Russell were systematic philosophers whose ideas and interests changed with such frequency that a final synthesis always eluded them. As a result positions were frequently abandoned before they could be worked out in explicit detail, and were often left in tantalizingly fragmentary form. . . . Both men advocated treating philosophical problems in scientific detail, yet usually confined

---

[99] Ibid., 27.
[100] Griffin, 10.

themselves to broad programmatic hints. . . . anyone who knows Russell's epistemology and style of argument and exposition will frequently be struck by an uncanny sense of familiarity in reading Clifford.[101]

This similarity of style is strikingly apparent in essays which Russell was to write throughout his long career. He shared with Clifford a strong desire to apply mathematical and scientific concepts to issues relating to social progress. In addition, he also continued to wage Clifford's battle against clericalism, religious cant, and theology. In a phrase that is almost vintage Clifford, Russell writes: "Clergymen almost necessarily fail in two ways as teachers of morals. They condemn acts which do no harm and they condone acts which do great harm."[102] Consider the following from Russell's 1930 essay "Has Religion Made Useful Contributions to Society?" (not surprisingly, his answer is a resounding "No!"):

> The knowledge exists by which universal happiness can be secured; the chief obstacle to its utilization is the teaching of religion. Religion prevents our children from having a rational education; religion prevents us from removing the fundamental causes of war; religion prevents us from teaching the ethic of scientific co-operation in place of the old fierce doctrines of sin and punishment. It is possible that mankind is on the threshold of a golden age: but, if so, it will be necessary first to slay the dragon that guards the door, and this dragon is religion.[103]

"Slaying the dragon of religion" - Clifford would have loved such a phrase!

That Russell was familiar with Clifford's essay "The Ethics of Belief" can be seen from the opening sentences of his own essay, "On the Value of Scepticism", which was initially delivered as an address to the Emerson Club in London in 1923: "I wish to propose for the reader's favourable consideration a doctrine which may, I fear, appear wildly paradoxical and subversive. The doctrine in question is this: that it is undesirable to believe a proposition when there is no ground whatever for supposing it true."[104] In the essay, which was published in 1928, Russell admitted that many ordinary beliefs of common sense need not, in ordinary practice, be

---

[101] Ibid., 11.
[102] Ibid., 68.
[103] Bertrand Russell, *Why I Am Not A Christian and Other Essays,* edited by Paul Edwards (New York: Simon and Schuster, 1957), 47.
[104] Bertrand Russell, "On the Value of Scepticism" in *The Collected Papers of Bertrand Russell, Volume 10* (New York: Routledge, 1997), 279.

questioned. In addition, he conceded that many scientific propositions were sufficiently probable rather than certain. To question *everything* would be a sort of heroic skepticism beyond the capability of most, if not all, humans. What he advocated was a type of skepticism involving three points: (1) when experts are agreed, the opposite opinion cannot held to be certain; (2) that when they are not agreed, no opinion can be regarded as certain by a non-expert; and (3) that when they all hold that no sufficient grounds for a positive opinion exist, the ordinary man would do well to suspend his judgment. If people got into the habit of following such guidelines, he felt, then it would revolutionize the world.

Like Clifford, then, Russell urged all people, regardless of their walk of life, to get into such a habit, for their own good and for the good of society as a whole. Later in his life he would cease to call this quality "skepticism", "but rather the attitude of scientific inquiry. Scientific inquiry begins with uncertainty, but aims at securing evidence sufficient for reasonable belief."[105]

The principle opponent of such good habits, Russell declared, were religious teachings and institutions. The philosopher Paul Edwards was to collect many of Russell's essays critical of religion, including his classic 1927 lecture "Why I Am Not A Christian", and published them in 1957. Russell, then aged 85, made it a point to reiterate in his introduction the fact that he had not changed his view:

> There has been a rumor in recent years to the effect that I have become less opposed to religious orthodoxy than I formerly was. This rumor is totally without foundation. I think all the great religions of the world - Buddhism, Hinduism, Christianity, Islam, and Communism - both untrue and harmful. . . . The harm that is done by religion is of two sorts, the one depending on the kind of belief which it is thought ought to be given to it, and the other upon the particular tenets believed. As regards the kind of belief: it is thought virtuous to have Faith - that is to say, to have a conviction which cannot be shaken by contrary evidence. Or, if contrary evidence might induce doubt, it is held that contrary evidence must be suppressed. . . . The conviction that it is important to believe this or that, even if a free inquiry would not support the belief, is one which is common to almost all religions and which inspires all systems of state education. The consequence is that the minds of the young are stunted and are filled with fanatical hostility both to those who have other fanaticisms and, even more virulently, to those who object to all fanaticisms. A habit of basing convictions upon evidence, and of giving to them only that degree of

---

[105] Bertrand Russell, "The Spirit of Inquiry" in *The Collected Papers of Bertrand Russell, Volume 11*, (New York: Routledge, 1997) 30.

certainty which the evidence warrants, would, if it became general, cure most of the ills from which this world is suffering.[106]

Here again one can see a similarity with Clifford's urging people to get into the habit of basing beliefs upon evidence.

For Russell, the chief motivating factor of religion is fear. It is an attempt to escape from reality. "Religion," he wrote, "since it has its source in terror, has dignified certain kinds of fear and made people think them not disgraceful. In this it has done mankind a great disservice: *all fear is bad*."[107] He felt that there are two objections to religion: intellectual and moral.

For Russell, as for Clifford, intellectual integrity was a virtue that is too often overlooked. In 1954, in an article entitled "Can Religion Cure Our Troubles?", which he wrote for a Stockholm newspaper, Russell asserted the following:

> I do not myself think that the dependence of morals upon religion is nearly as close as religious people believe it to be. I even think that some very important virtues are more likely to be found among those who reject religious dogmas than among those who accept them. I think this applies especially to the virtue of truthfulness or intellectual integrity. I mean by intellectual integrity the habit of deciding vexed questions in accordance with the evidence, or of leaving them undecided where the evidence is inconclusive. This virtue, though it is underestimated by almost all adherents of any system of dogma, is to my mind of the very greatest social importance and far more likely to benefit the world than Christianity or any other system of organized beliefs.[108]

Russell was not always as hopeful as Clifford. For Russell, seeking the truth might not involve happiness, but it was a duty nonetheless.

In his book *Bertrand Russell: A Political Life,* Alan Ryan points out a characteristic of Russell's that was also shared by Clifford: using religious rhetoric to denounce religion. "Russell," Ryan notes, "emulated the traditional preacher in one way at least; he invariably painted the existing world in the blackest possible colours in order to contrast it with the

---

[106] Ibid.,. vi-vii.
[107] Ibid., 54.
[108] Ibid., 194.

heaven to which we might aspire if only we cast off sin - or, in Russell's version, if we cast away fear and superstition."[109]

In 1946, Russell was asked to write the preface for the reprint of Clifford's *The Common Sense of the Exact Sciences*. He points out the continuing relevance of Clifford's work in mathematics, and then talks about Clifford's more philosophical speculations. There is a wistful tone to Russell's remembrance of things past:

> ... he saw all knowledge, even the most abstract, as part of the general life of mankind, and as concerned in the endeavour to make human existence less petty, less superstitious, and less miserable. He lived at a time when optimism was not so difficult as it has become, and when hope for the future seemed justified by the history of the previous two hundred years. It was possible, without any blind act of faith, to believe that the human species would become progressively more humane, more tolerant, and more enlightened, with the consequences that war and disease and poverty, and the other major evils of our existence, would continually diminish. In this beneficent process rational knowledge was to be the chief agent, and mathematics, as the most completely rational kind of knowledge, was to be in the van. This faith was Clifford's, and it was mine when I first read his book; in turning over its pages again, the ghosts of old hopes rise up to mock me.[110]

Still, Russell added that, if men of the past like Clifford had been perhaps too optimistic, one should not use present-day adversities to justify pessimism. Right up to the end of his long and distinguished life, Russell continued to battle for the issues which Clifford had championed a century before.

---

[109] Alan Ryan, *Bertrand Russell: A Political Life* (New York: Hill and Wang, 1988), 51.

[110] Bertrand Russell, preface to *The Common Sense of the Exact Sciences,* ix.

CHAPTER FIVE

CLIFFORD'S MODERN CRITICS

From the turn of the century up until the mid-1970s, discussion of "The Ethics of Belief" tended to focus upon the Clifford/James "debate". In this chapter, a critical overview will be given of the ways in which such philosophers as C. S. Lewis, Walter Kaufmann, J. L. Mackie, and Richard Double have continued to find this debate to be fruitful.

Since the mid-1970s, especially with the rise of the so-called "Reformed Epistemology" school of philosophy, Clifford's epistemic position become more of a focal point in-and-of-itself. The second part of the chapter will therefore examine how this has been addressed by such philosophers as Michael Martin, Peter van Inwagen, and Alvin Plantinga.

While the above individuals address the epistemological questions raised by Clifford, other philosophers have focused on the ethical aspects of his writings. Therefore, next will follow a further examination of the recent writings of Richard Gale and Richard Rorty, both of whom address what they see as the primarily ethical thrust of Clifford's arguments.

Finally, there will be an examination of the work of three individuals who have once again brought together the epistemic and ethical dimensions in their discussions of Clifford's "ethics of belief": Susan Haack, Anthony Quinton, and Lorraine Code.

I. Clifford/James Debate Continued

1. C. S. Lewis

C. S. Lewis (1898-1963) was a Christian apologist and literary critic who taught at both Oxford and Cambridge. His writings on Christian apologetics have become increasingly popular since his death. Lewis revisited the Clifford/James debate in his own essay entitled "On Obstinacy in Belief" (1934). In it, he takes Clifford to task for making a distinction between a Christian attitude and a scientific attitude to belief. Lewis writes:

> We have been told that the scientist thinks it his duty to proportion the strength of his belief exactly to the evidence; to believe less as there is less evidence and to withdraw belief altogether when reliable adverse evidence turns up. We have been told that, on the contrary, the Christian regards it as positively praiseworthy to believe without evidence, or in excess of the evidence, or to maintain his belief unmodified in the teeth of steadily increasing evidence against it.[1]

This view sounds like vintage Clifford! Surely, Lewis was familiar with "The Ethics of Belief" – his essay's title even seems to be a reference to Clifford's essay. Lewis makes the point that scientists and rationalists are closely related to Christians in the matter of belief. Both groups are concerned with "finding things out", i. e., coming to terms with the truth. The word "belief", in modern English, has come to mean a mild degree of opinion. Yet in some cases, "belief" also means to assent to a proposition which we think so overwhelmingly probable that there is a psychological exclusion of doubt. Theological beliefs are closest to this sense, but Lewis adds that many other beliefs about the world share this strong case of assent. He is making a point similar to that made by Clifford's own contemporaries Ward and Hutton, discussed in the previous chapter.

Lewis then makes a careful distinction between the *initial* assent given to a proposition and the adherence to its truthfulness which follows. Such initial assent should not be done without evidence. Lewis stresses that authority (as Clifford himself recognized) *is* a type of evidence. "All of our historical beliefs," Lewis writes, "most of our geographical beliefs, many of our beliefs about matters that concern us in daily life, are accepted on the authority of other human beings, whether they are Christians, Atheists, Scientists, or Men-in-the-Street."[2]

Lewis further adds that evidence of the senses shows that believers can not be differentiated from unbelievers by their lack of intelligence or by a perverse refusal to think. Indeed, many of them are themselves scientists. Their manner of belief-formation does not differ in kind from those who do not accept religious arguments. While "wish fulfillment" may be a factor in accepting Christian teachings or a belief in God, it can also be a factor in denying Christian teachings or not believing in God.

With perhaps another oblique reference to Clifford the mathematician, Lewis writes that mathematicians, scientists, and historians have different techniques for arriving at truth – reasoning, experiment, and documents –

---

[1] C. S. Lewis, "On Obstinacy in Belief" in *The World's Last Stand and Other Essays* (New York: Harcourt Brace Jovanovich, 1960), 115.
[2] Ibid.. 117.

but when not engaged in their own disciplines they are equally likely to hold to positions the evidence for which does not meet the standards of their own professions. There is no reason to assume that this is due to stark unreason. All of them consider themselves to have some good support for their views.

Lack of evidence, then, is usually not an issue during the formation of beliefs, but it does become so with the continued adherence to such beliefs, especially in the case of religious beliefs. Lewis writes:

> It is here that the charge of irrationality and resistance to evidence becomes really important. For it must be admitted at once that Christians do praise such an adherence as if it were meritorious; and even, in a sense, more meritorious the stronger the apparent evidence against their faith becomes. They even warn one another that such apparent contrary evidence – such "trials to faith" or "temptations to doubt" – may be expected to occur, and determine in advance to resist them.[3]

To Clifford, this would be an example of a "sin". But Lewis states that, while such a procedure would indeed be shocking to a scientist or historian, qua scientist or historian, in ordinary life it is not foolhardy or shocking at all.

Much like William James, Lewis describes the nature of religious belief as involving a sort of trust-relationshi Just as, by believing in the good intentions of a stranger when the evidence might not support this, one can thereby create the possibility of a friendship, so also by *believing* in God's existence even in the face of contrary evidence, one can strengthen one's relationship with the Almighty. Lewis gives as examples of inculcating a sense of trust: the condition of getting a dog out of a trap, removing a thorn from a child's finger, and getting a beginner out of a difficult condition in mountain climbing. These all involve getting them to accept incredible information – moving the paw further into the trap is the way to get it out; increasing the pain temporarily will end the pain from the thorn; going up to a further and more exposed ledge is the way not to fall. Lewis writes:

> Sometimes, because of their unbelief, we can do no mighty works. But if we succeed, we do so because they have maintained their faith in us against apparent contrary evidence. No one blames us for demanding such faith. No one blames them for giving it. No one says afterwards what an unintelligent dog or child or boy that must have been to trust us. If the young mountaineer were a scientist, it would not be held against him, when

---

[3] Ibid., 118.

he came up for a fellowship, that he had once departed from Clifford's rule of evidence by entertaining a belief with strength greater than the evidence logically obliged him to.[4]

Accepting the propositions of Christianity means exactly to accept that we are in the same position as the dog, child and mountaineer. While the initial acceptance of Christianity should not involve such a leap of faith, once one does accept that there is a creator who has infinite love for his creations, it is perfectly logical to put complete trust in his teachings. "This expectation", Lewis adds, "is increased by the fact that when we accept Christianity we are warned that apparent evidence against it will occur. . . ."[5] Fortunately, there is evidence to contradict this – external evidence, such as having one's prayers answered, as well as internal evidence, akin to knowledge-by-acquaintance. Christianity emphasizes a personal relationship with the creator. For those who do not initially accept this proposition, it is near-impossible to get them to see how this acceptance *leads* to such a relationshi Complete trust is an ingredient in this relationshi "To love involves trusting the beloved beyond the evidence, even against much evidence."[6]

People like Clifford cannot grasp this relationship, because they come across arguments for it primarily through apologetic works. It is still only speculative to them, rather than personally experienced. This, by the way, is not a telling point, since Clifford, and indeed most of his fellow rationalists, had once been fervent believers in Christianity.

Lewis next addresses the danger of granting such complete confidence, admitting that "the dog may lick the face of the man who comes to take it out of the trap; but the man may only mean to vivisect it in South Parks Road when he has done so."[7] Yet the entire concept of "trust" is based on the presumption that demonstrative certainty is not possible.

In regards to the story of "Doubting Thomas", the apostle who refused to believe the information given by his fellow apostles that Christ had risen from the dead, until such a time as *he* could actually see and touch the wounds Christ had suffered on the cross, Lewis points out:

> The saying "Blessed are those that have not seen and have believed" has nothing to do with our original assent to the Christian propositions. It was not addressed to a philosopher inquiring whether God exists. It was addressed to a man who already believed that, who already had long

---

[4] Ibid., 119.
[5] Ibid.
[6] Ibid., 120.
[7] Ibid.,121.

acquaintance with a particular Person, and evidence that that person could do very odd things, and who then refused to believe one odd thing more, often predicted by that Person and vouched for by all his closest friends.[8]

It is more a question of psychology than philosophy – "you should have known me better than that." It is a move from the logic of speculative thought to the logic of personal relations.

C. S. Lewis, in this article, further develops the theme which James' had argued in "The Will to Believe" – that our passional natures have an impact on the legitimacy of our beliefs. This view would itself be strenuously objected to by the next philosopher to be examined.

2. Walter Kaufmann

The Princeton philosopher Walter Kaufmann (1921-1980) had a fondness for W. K. Clifford's work. He reprinted "The Ethics of Belief" in his popular textbook *Religion From Tolstoy to Camus* (1961), placing it before a selection from James' "The Will to Believe". In his introduction to "The Ethics of Belief", Kaufmann noted: "James' essay has often been reprinted; but though he explicitly refers to Clifford's piece, few indeed have read that; and it is not easy to find unless one has ready access to a large library. Here, for once, the two essays are offered together."[9]

One reason for Kaufmann's fondness for Clifford was his own acceptance of an "ethics of belief", as can be seen in the following excerpt from Kaufmann's *Critique of Religion and Philosophy* (1958):

> Asked whether a statement is true, we consider it as a hypothesis which is subject to investigation and must eventually be judged in the light of the relevant evidence. It is by no means immoral for a scientist, historian, or philosopher to hope that some proposition may be proved true, or to feel strongly about it. But it is considered immoral for him to be partial to the point of suppressing relevant evidence, and it is a sign of incompetence, if not a violation of professional ethics, if he fails to undertake a relevant investigation for fear that its results might be fatal for a belief he cherishes.[10]

---

[8] Ibid. 122.
[9] Walter Kaufmann, *Religion from Tolstoy to Camus* (New Brunswick: Transaction Publishers,1994), p. 18.
[10] Walter Kaufmann, *Critique of Religion and Philosophy* (New York: Anchor Books, 1961), 104.

One sees here a defense of an ethics of investigation akin to that of Clifford's. Kaufmann goes on to point out, again *a la* Clifford, that religious believers tend to feel that their own special beliefs are not privy to such investigation, and indeed that there is something suspect about even suggesting they should be so examined. In the following passage from *Critique of Religion and Philosophy,* Kaufmann begs to differ with Lewis' claim that the religious believer and the natural scientist have exactly the same attitude toward belief:

> The attitude of religious people toward religious propositions is quite different from all this. If a man accepts a religious proposition as true, it is hardly ever after having first considered it as a hypothesis and found compelling evidence through an impartial inquiry. Few religious people have studied comparative religion, and hardly any have attained their beliefs as a result of such a study: yet this would be *de rigeur* if the religious person's attitude toward the religious propositions he believes were at all similar to the historian's or the scientist's attitude toward the propositions with which they concern themselves. The fact that the religious person frequently considers his religious propositions ever so much more important only aggravates the problem. *The more important the issue at hand, the more it demands careful scrutiny.* This is a simple but important point which most religious people overlook.[11]

And in his later book *The Faith of a Heretic* (1961), Kaufmann goes on to argue that religion remains a privileged field, along with politics and advertising. One is taught from an early age to accept without question the claims of these three areas (Clifford, living in an earlier age, would perhaps not have thought of public relations in his development of the ethics of belief). "It is considered perfectly all right for men of the cloth to make a business of pretending they believe what they really do not believe" Kaufmann writes; "to give the impression, speaking from the pulpit, that they are convinced of things that, talking to philosophers, they are quick to disown; and to feign complete assurance about matters that, in private, trouble them and cause them endless doubts."[12] These were some of the issues which most troubled the Stephen brothers, Thomas Huxley and W. K. Clifford during the Victorian Crisis of Faith.

In many ways, Kaufmann's *Critique of Religion and Philosophy* provides a sort of posthumous answer from Clifford to William James' "The Will to Believe". His chapter entitled "Religion, Faith, and

---

[11] Ibid. 104-105.
[12] Walter Kaufmann, *The Faith of a Heretic* (New York: Anchor Books, 1963), p. 27.

Evidence" looks at the definitions of these terms, as well as "belief." Contrary to Plato and J. L. Austin, Kaufmann claims that "I believe" is not always a statement of lesser force than "I know", for in many cases it is synonymous with "I am certain". He discusses the role which evidence plays in support of knowledge:

> The close connection between knowledge and evidence becomes particularly clear when we move from one field to another in which different standards of evidence obtain. A man may say that he knows something to be true; but if informed that his assertion, if repeated under oath, would send another person to the gallows, he might say on second thought he did not know. The other way around, we should consider a man rather strange if, asked whether he knew that it rained in New York yesterday, he should apply the rules of evidence employed in the preceding case and say he did not know, because his belief was based on circumstantial evidence.[13]

Kaufmann delineates two senses of "belief". In the first, belief includes knowledge; in the second, it is contrasted with knowledge. In this second sense, "belief" is distinguished by the lack of evidence which would be sufficient to compel any reasonable person to accept a proposition as true. "Faith", he adds, is a kind of belief of the second sense which is passionately held, and which would involve emotional disappointment if found to be wrong. "Faith" is likely to keep people from engaging in impartial investigations.

Kaufmann is scathing in his criticism of William James for arguing in favor of a type of faith. Calling "The Will to Believe" a "slipshod but celebrated essay", he writes: "James' appeal depends entirely on blurring the distinction between those who hold out for 100 percent proof in a matter in which any reasonable person rests content with, let us say, 90 per cent, and those who refuse to indulge in a belief which is supported only by the argument that after all it could conceivably be true."[14] James, he charges, makes a virtue out of wishful thinking, and commits the fallacy of false dilemma: it is not the case that the alternative to firm faith is weak indecision. One can act with vigor, while still realizing one might be wrong:

> James' essay on "The Will to Believe" is an unwitting compendium of common fallacies and a manual of self-deception. Two errors remain to be noted. First, he blurs the distinction between facts which my belief could at

---

[13] Kaufmann, *Critique of Religion and Philosophy*, 112.
[14] Ibid., 116.

least conceivably help to bring about – e.g., that a girl reciprocates my love – and facts which no belief could help to bring about if they were not facts to begin with – e.g., that God exists or that Jesus was resurrected on the third day. Secondly, he assumes without argument that religion in general offers us some kind of hypothesis, which he himself calls, using italics, "the religious hypothesis." In fact, religion in general is an abstraction while there really are a number of historical religions which are characterized among other things by many utterly heterogeneous beliefs which cannot by any means be dealt with in like fashion.[15]

Later, Kaufmann sounds almost exactly like Clifford, when he writes: "James' apology for eccentric beliefs on the ground that after all they might conceivably be right, strikes at the roots of all intellectual discipline and the foundations of our civilization."[16] Kaufmann adds that James fails to grasp the distinction between a legal right and an intellectual right. One can certainly defend the *legal* right to believe on insufficient evidence – the government or other powerful forces should not set up a type of thought-police. But *intellectually* no one has a right to hold a belief on insufficient evidence. It is disreputable. "And while a great deal can be said for tolerance of irrationality by the state" Kaufmann adds, "no less can be said against tolerance of irrationality by philosophers."[17]

Kaufmann then neatly turns the table on James, with an oblique reference to Clifford:

> Beliefs are legion, and we cannot give equal consideration to all. If a belief is based on badly insufficient evidence or faulty arguments or both, then we are generous indeed if we still stop to ask: What causes those who maintain this belief to cling to it? Heuristically, this question is worth while in many cases: we may discover sufficient evidence for a belief a little different from the one maintained. But if we find instead that a belief backed by flimsy evidence and poor reasoning can be readily accounted for when we look at the causes that have led to its adoption, then we need not fear the outside chance that after all it could conceivably be true. Of course, it could be. But if we are worried about that, then we deserve the stricture that James would apply unjustly to those who insist on evidence: we are guilty of "excessive nervousness."[18]

It is James rather than Clifford who would keep his troops out of battle. One later jibe at James makes a point about the possible roots of religious

---

[15] Ibid., 120.
[16] Ibid., 131.
[17] Ibid.
[18] Ibid., 132.

belief: "William James turned to religion because he wanted to feel at home in the universe. But *the greatest accomplishment of religion has been that it did not allow man to feel at home in the universe,* that it raised a hope in man's heart which the world could not quench, and that instead of telling man to abandon such a foolish hope, religion staked its life on it."[19]

3. J. L. Mackie

In his noted book *The Miracle of Theism: Arguments for and Against the Existence of God* (1982), the philosopher J. L. Mackie makes reference to Clifford in his discussion of "Belief without Reason". Earlier in the book, he attempts to prove that theistic arguments cannot be rationally defended. However, many would claim that this does not matter. Their beliefs are justified by *faith*, not by argumentation. This leads to the paradoxical question of whether or not belief without reason may be intellectually respectable – a position which Mackie ascribes to James.

Three key points are stressed by Mackie: 1. James had argued that most of what anyone believes is based on authority; 2. A distinction must be made between absolutism and empiricism; 3. One must distinguish between knowing the truth and avoiding error:

> Almost all of these initial steps in James' argument are not only eloquently expressed but also correct and important. Most of our beliefs do rest on authority, and our "passional nature" does play some part in many, perhaps all, of them. In almost all areas judgements are fallible in varying degrees, and while we aim at truth we can claim at most that tested and confirmed hypotheses are likely to come close to the truth. In science it is reasonable not only to make enterprising guesses but also to combine critical testing of them with the hope and tentative belief that they are not too far from truth. In social and political affairs it is reasonable – since it is a necessary condition for co-operation – to trust others in advance of any certainty that they are trustworthy. Moral judgements of some central sorts are not capable of being true, and *a fortiori* cannot be shown to be true; but it is not contrary to reason to make them, and the sentiments and ways of thinking that they express are essential to any tolerable human and especially social life. In all these ways we must at least qualify Clifford's dictum; but the crucial question is, How do these principles relate to religion and in particular to theistic belief?[20]

---

[19] Ibid., 355.
[20] J. L. Mackie, *The Miracle of Theism: Arguments for and against the Existence of God* (Oxford: Clarendon Press, 1986), 206-207.

Mackie argues that James' presentation of religious belief conflates three different elements. One concerns moral choices. "These are, indeed, free in the sense that they need not and cannot wait for the intellect to determine them. They escape Clifford's rigid agnosticism."[21] However, the *fact* that one must choose does not provide any guidance for *which* moral acts to choose.

The second element is that passion is a tie-breaker. James is wrong to imply that the many beliefs based on authority fall under the category of "passion." Often, as Clifford noted, we have quite good reasons to accept authorities' truth claims, because we have knowledge of why they are authorities.

The third strand in James' argument, Mackie writes:

> . . . is the most important. Given that there is, inevitably, a "passional" component in thought, and, equally inevitably, a great and constant risk of error, and given also that, about many matters, the chance of being right has a value not outweighed by the disvalue of the chance of being wrong, we must reject Clifford's principle of never believing anything on insufficient evidence. We must be willing not only to frame hypotheses and test them, but also to give a tentative acceptance to hypotheses which have some plausibility and have received some confirmation through testing. This is a principle which an atheist can endorse as readily and whole-heartedly as any theist.[22]

It is the next step in James' argument that Mackie finds fault with. It is not necessarily the case that James' "live option" of meeting god halfway (or as Lewis would hold, having a personal relationship with god) should be a live option at all. To hold that there is a certain kind of truth (religious truth) which can only be known by "playing along with it" is fraught with problems, precisely because our "passional" natures are intimately involved. Mackie writes:

> An experiment whose aim is to ascertain the truth must be so conducted as to allow the hypothesis in question to be falsified or at least disconfirmed. A hypothesis is confirmed only by surviving severe tests, that is, tests which, if it is false, are likely to show that it is false. While we must, as James says, reject as irrational a rule of thinking which would prevent us from acknowledging certain kinds of truth even if they were really here, we must equally reject as irrational a rule of thinking which would prevent us from denying such supposed truths even if they were really not there. And this is not only in order to avoid error: it is an essential part of the

---

[21] Ibid., 207.
[22] Ibid., 208-209.

method of confirming truth. If faith is to be defended as an experiment, it must conform to the general principles of experimental inquiry.[23]

Therefore, it is Clifford's position which is closest to adhering to the general rules of truth-confirmation. Experiments to confirm a proposition must be able to resist psychological explanations.

4. Richard Double

Richard Double, a professor of philosophy at Edinboro University of Pennsylvania, adds an important point to understanding the Clifford/James debate. In his 1996 book *Metaphilosophy and Free Will,* Double argues that it is only by examining the meta-level of discourse that one can appraise differing arguments, and that the most philosophers can do to convince others of their propositions is to appeal to a desire-based case. He uses the Clifford/James debate to help support his case that metaphilosophies are not provable. Double writes:

> My . . . reason for thinking that metaphilosophies are not provable is an inductive one: How could we hope to settle disagreements between familiar disputants about the proper role of philosophy? Consider the "Will to Believe" dispute. W. K. Clifford and Bertrand Russell viewed the avoidance of unwarranted beliefs as a *moral* obligation. In my terms, they saw philosophy's role as Worldview Construction and adopted the concomitant view that we should resist the temptation to trade the truth-tracking abilities of the intellect for any amount of psychological benefits. William James thought that if the answer to a question is neither provable nor disprovable, we ought to choose the option that is most valuable to us as *persons* when the choice is *live, momentous,* and *forced.* This shows a Praxis motivation, although he does not exemplify pure Praxis. If he did, he would not have included the various qualifications but would have recommended complete license.[24]

The differing strategies of avoiding false beliefs versus gaining valuable new beliefs is tied up with an overall metaphilosophical perspective.

Double demonstrates his own metaphilosophical vision of the philosopher as a courageous truth-seeker when he writes: "For me, the persona of W. K. Clifford I derived from reading 'The Ethics of Belief'

---

[23] Ibid., 209.
[24] Richard Double, *Metaphilosophy and Free Will* (New York: Oxford University Press, 1996), 36.

was very moving, although I think Clifford's argument is hyperbolic and philosophically weak."[25] It is unfortunate that he does not elaborate in what ways he finds Clifford's argument to be weak. The critics to be examined in the following section are not hesitant in doing so.

II. Epistemic Duties

1. Michael Martin

Some critics attempt to defend an evidentialism divorced from ethics. Michael Martin, in *Atheism: A Philosophical Justification,* argues:

> Although basing your belief on what is beneficial to you and others is not necessarily morally wrong, as apparently Clifford thinks, there are certainly moral dangers in doing so, and as a general social policy it should be avoided. Moreover, Clifford overlooks an important point. His argument for using purely epistemic reasons is itself a moral one. Thus, ironically, his reason for not using beneficial reasons in justifying belief is apparently based on one type of beneficial reason: the undesirable *moral* consequences of doing so.[26]

Clifford, Martin argues, should have argued that there is an independent *epistemological* duty to base one's beliefs on purely epistemic reasons. If one does not base one's beliefs on purely epistemic reasons, one is epistemically irresponsible. This epistemic duty need not be conflated with an ethical duty as well. Roderick Chisholm, in Martin's view, had made a similar error:

> Roderick Chisholm . . . in arguing against Clifford, maintains that a proposition is innocent until proven guilty; that is, it is unreasonable for us to believe a proposition only when we have adequate evidence for the contradictory of the proposition. Chisholm's view is compatible with the thesis that it is not unreasonable to believe a proposition on the basis of beneficial reasons if there is no adequate evidence for the contradictory. . . . However, it is unclear if Chisholm recognizes an independent epistemological obligation to believe on the basis of purely epistemic reasons. Is he saying that it is *epistemically* or *morally* permissible for someone to believe p if there is no adequate evidence for ~ p? On one plausible interpretation he could be saying that although there is an *epistemological* duty to believe that p on the basis of purely epistemic

---

[25] Ibid., 54.
[26] Michael Martin, *Atheism: A Philosophical Justification* (Philadelphia: Temple University Press, 1990),31.

reasons, it is *morally* permissible to believe p on beneficial grounds only if there is no epistemic reason to believe ~ [27]

Martin states that Clifford was at least partly correct in arguing for the presumption of the primacy of epistemic reasons. While he feels it is appropriate to speak of "epistemic obligations", the word obligation should not be taken in a moral sense.

2. Peter van Inwagen

The philosopher Peter van Inwagen, in his own examination of "The Ethics of Belief", states that Clifford's evidentialism, although theoretically pertinent to *any* human belief, is almost always applied to *religious* beliefs rather than to philosophical or political beliefs. He writes:

> It is an extremely popular position that religion is different. Or, at least, it must be that many antireligious philosophers and other writers hostile to religious belief hold this position, for it seems to be presupposed by almost every aspect of their approach to the subject of religious belief. And yet, this position seems never to have been explicitly stated, much less argued for. Let us call it the Difference Thesis. A good example of the Difference Thesis at work is provided by W. K. Clifford's famous essay "The Ethics of Belief." One of the most interesting facts about "The Ethics of Belief" is that nowhere in it is religious belief explicitly mentioned. It would, however, be disingenuous in the extreme to say that this essay is simply about the ethics of belief in general and is no more directed at religious belief than at any other kind of belief. "Everyone knows," as the phrase goes, that Clifford's target is religious belief. (Certainly the editors of anthologies know this. "The Ethics of Belief" appears in just about every anthology devoted to the philosophy of religion. It has never appeared in an anthology devoted to epistemology.)[28]

The evidence actually disproves this last assertion. For instance, "The Ethics of Belief" appears in the popular anthology *Belief, Knowledge, and Truth: Readings in the Theory of Knowledge,* edited by Robert Ammerman and Marcus Singer – a textbook explicitly devoted to epistemology per se.[29]

---

[27] Ibid. , 32.
[28] Peter van Inwagen, "Quam Dilecta" in *God and the Philosophers* (New York: Oxford University Press, 1994), 44.
[29] W. K. Clifford, "The Ethics of Belief" in *Belief, Knowledge, and Truth: Readings in the Theory of Knowledge,* edited by Robert R. Ammerman and Marcus G. Singer (New York: Charles Scribner's Sons, 1970), 39-45.

Still, it is true that "The Ethics of Belief" is usually presented in anthologies discussing religious beliefs specifically. Van Inwagen goes on to note that "Clifford's Principle" is almost never mentioned except in hostile examinations of religious belief, even though Clifford himself gives several nonreligious examples, such as that of the shipowner, in "The Ethics of Belief." He adds: "It is this that provides the primary evidence for my contention that many antireligious philosophers and other writers against religion tacitly accept the Difference Thesis."[30]

Clifford might well have appreciated van Inwagen's pugnacious and sarcastic prose style, which is so close to his own. For instance, van Inwagen creates an "Enlightenment Creed", to which he considers himself an "apostate." He turns Clifford on his head, by using *religious* language to describe the non-religious stance that Clifford advocated:

> When I look back on the days of my allegiance to the Enlightenment, I discover that this allegiance was primarily a device to assist me in admiring myself. I still admire myself, I'm afraid, but at least I have silenced the voice of one flatterer. ("How intelligent you are," the Enlightenment would whisper in my ear, "how progressive, how, well, *enlightened*.") It may well be that not every adherent of the Enlightenment has used it that way; I do not claim to be able to look into the souls of the living, much less the long dead. But to read such Enlightenment figures as Hume or Voltaire with Christian eyes is to see every possible opportunity for self-admiration taken; and Voltaire and Hume, like me in my own Enlightenment days, do not seem even to be able to get on with the business of self-admiration without perpetual sneers at "milkmaids" (Voltaire) – that is, at the great mass of people who keep the wheels turning while the Enlightenment sips its chocolate and peers at them through its quizzing glass.[31]

Whatever one might say of Clifford, he for one never sneered at "milkmaids" or other "common folks". His strongest barbs were aimed at authority figures such as priests, whom he felt were guilty of dissuading the common people from investigating their beliefs.

Why is it that Clifford's Principle is so often applied to religious beliefs in particular? It is because these are the types of beliefs that tend to have the greatest amount of repercussions for society as a whole. Perhaps in a society less religious, Clifford would focus more on political and scientific beliefs, or even – as Kaufmann proposed – beliefs fostered by professional advertisers. Clifford was fighting against the hegemony of organized

---

[30] Ibid, 45.
[31] Ibid., 55.

religion. If alive today, he might well join van Inwagen in the latter's campaign against authoritarian voices in science. But he would first make sure that the Enlightenment project itself continued to be defended. Certainly he would have enjoyed a good debate with van Inwagen, whose style of argumentation is close to that of Clifford's old intellectual opponent in the Metaphysical Society, G. H. Ward.

3. Alvin Plantinga

No doubt the most prominent contemporary Christian writer to criticize Clifford is the Notre Dame Professor Alvin Plantinga. A self-professed "Reformed Epistemologist", tracing his intellectual sympathies back to John Calvin, Plantinga has long argued that it is rational to believe in God despite not having any evidence whatsoever, and that evidentialists like Clifford fail to make a good counterargument. Plantinga writes:

> In *God and Other Minds,* I assumed that the proper way to approach the question of the rationality of theistic belief is in terms of argument for and against the existence of God. Once it was clear that this approach is inconclusive – because there aren't any really cogent arguments either for or against the existence of God – I began to consider explicitly the evidentialist objection to theistic belief: the objection that theistic belief is irrational just because there is no evidence or at any rate insufficient evidence for it.[32]

In his article "Rationality and Religious Belief", Plantinga states: "The nineteenth-century philosopher W. K. Clifford provides a splendid if somewhat strident example of the view that the believer in God must have evidence if he is not to be irrational"; Plantinga is a bit more charitable toward Clifford than van Inwagen, for he adds: "Here he does not discriminate against religious belief: he apparently holds that a belief of any sort at all is rationally acceptable only if there is sufficient evidence for it."[33]

Plantinga claims that this is a foundationalist view. "And from the foundationalist point of view," he writes, "our question must be restated: Is belief in God evident with respect to the foundations of my noetic structure? Clifford, as I say, takes it to be obvious that the answer is no.

---

[32] Alvin Plantinga, "Self-Profile" in *Alvin Plantinga,* edited by James E. Tomberlin and Peter van Inwagen (Boston: D. Reidel, 1985),.56.
[33] Alvin Plantinga, "Rationality and Religious Belief" in *Contemporary Philosophy of Religion,* edited by Stephen M. Cahn and David Schutz (Oxford: Oxford University Press, 1982), 257.

But is this obvious? To restate my earlier question: Might it not be that belief in God is itself in the foundations of my noetic structure?[34]

Plantinga says that one can either claim that theists believing without evidence have violated a duty, or that their noetic structure is defective:

> For example, suppose I seem to see a tree: I have that characteristic sort of experience that as a matter of fact goes with seeing a tree. I may then form the belief that I see a tree. In the typical case that belief will be basic for me; in the typical case I will not believe the proposition that I see a tree on the basis of other beliefs I hold.[35]

Another example of a basic belief he gives is the belief that I had breakfast this morning. "I will simply believe that I had breakfast, not believing it on the evidentialist basis of any other proposition; I take it as basic."[36]

All of this is somewhat reminiscent of a remark Wittgenstein makes in his work *On Certainty:*

> I am sitting with a philosopher in the garden; he says again and again "I know that that's a tree", pointing to a tree that is near us. Someone else arrives and hears this, and I tell him: "This fellow isn't insane. We are only doing philosophy."[37]

In this work, Wittgenstein seems to be dealing with something akin to Plantinga's basic belief notion. There are beliefs which must be taken to be certain, else we can have no knowledge at all. Certainty is, in a sense, the grounds for knowledge, the hinge upon which our language games swing. "One might say: 'I know' expresses *comfortable* certainty, not the certainty that is still struggling."[38]

Plantinga's criticizes foundationalism for holding to the view that propositions obtain warrant in only one of two ways: either through being a basic belief, or else through acquiring warrant by virtue of being believed on the basis of some other proposition that already has warrant. But this being the case, a proposition like "I believe in God" can be treated in the same manner as a proposition like "I believe I had 'Rice Crispies' for breakfast this morning." Why do foundationalists demand evidence for

---

[34] Ibid., 260.
[35] Alvin Plantinga, 114.
[36] Ibid.
[37] Ludwig Wittgenstein, *On Certainty* (New York: Harper and Row, 1969), 61e.
[38] Ibid., 46e.

the former and not the latter? Furthermore, members of a given noetic community need not justify their basic beliefs to others. He writes:

> The Christian or Jew will of course suppose that belief in God is entirely proper and rational; if he doesn't accept this belief on the basis of other propositions, he will conclude that it is properly basic for him and quite properly so. Followers of Bertrand Russell and Madelyn [sic] Murray O'Hare may disagree, but how is that relevant? Must my criteria, or those of the believing community, conform to their examples? Surely not. The theistic community is responsible to *its* set of examples, not to theirs.[39]

While faulting Clifford for his strident and simplistic tone, Plantinga is equally guilty of presenting the evidentialist view in an overly-simplistic manner. As his fellow Christian philosopher William Alston points out: "Plantinga presents no textual support for the claim that the evidentialists he cites, W. K. Clifford, Bertrand Russell, A.G.N. Flew, and Michael Scriven, adhere to any form of classical foundationalism."[40] Plantinga treats Clifford as a "stock" or "paradigm" figure, without necessarily carefully examining what Clifford himself really meant. Plantinga responds to this in an interesting way:

> Alston observes that I offer no evidence for my claim that the evidentialist objection to theistic belief typically finds its basis in classical foundationalism. Of course he's right: I *don't* offer any such evidence. I do believe, however, that classical foundationalism typically underlies the evidentialist objection, and I believe this is a plausible belief.[41]

Plantinga thereby rather willfully violates "Clifford's Principle", in that he chooses not to look for evidence to support his belief that Clifford was a foundationalist.

In his essay "Direct Justification, Evidential Dependence, and Theistic Belief" Robert Audi raises some major problems with Plantinga's assertion that theistic beliefs may be *properly basic*, that is rational yet not held on the basis of any other beliefs or propositions at all. He lays down three examples of beliefs which may be held to be properly basic:
1. I see a tree.
2. I had breakfast this morning.
3. That person is angry.

---

[39] Plantinga, "Rationality and Religious Belief", 276.
[40] William Alston, "Epistemology of Religious Belief" in *Alvin Plantinga,* edited by James E. Tomberlin and Peter van Inwagen (Boston: D. Reidel, 1985), 295.
[41] Alvin Plantinga, "Replies" in *Alvin Plantinga* 389.

Audi accepts Plantinga's justifications for asserting that these are properly basic: they are believed other than on the basis of previous beliefs, yet are not groundless. However, he further states that one can accept these claims yet still wonder how the belief in God can be properly basic. Plantinga's justification for this is rather tentative. Quoting John Calvin with approval, Plantinga suggests that "God has so created us that we have a tendency or disposition to see his hand in the world about us. More precisely, there is in us a disposition to believe propositions of the sort *this flower was created by God* or *this vast and intricate universe was created by God* when we contemplate the flower or behold the starry heavens."[42]

Interestingly enough, this seems to be somewhat similar to the justification Charles Peirce gave, in his essay "The Concept of God," for belief in God's existence, where contemplation of the order and predictability in the universe leads one to see a guiding hand behind it. However, many equally brilliant philosophers and scientists, examining the same evidence, fail to see this guiding hand behind the flower or starry heavens. It is by no means obvious to them, whereas the proposition "I see a tree before me" presents no such difficulty at all. In the words of Audi:

> ... if we ask Jill, a normal adult innocent of philosophy, who sees a tree in front of her, why she believes she sees a tree in front of her, she is likely to be puzzled, and, if she tolerates our query, to say something to the effect that she sees it quite clearly. She is unlikely to cite, and indeed there may well not be, a proposition she believes such that we can plausibly suppose her belief that she sees a tree is based on her believing that proposition.[43]

Jill is much like the puzzled observer in Wittgenstein's *On Certainty*. But would Jill be as self-possessed if asked to justify her belief in God? It is not at all clear that the latter is a basic belief: there are far too many counterexamples of people who do not possess such self-assurance, self-assurance they *do* possess in regards to seeing a tree before them.

In cases where it is not clear that one is dealing with basic beliefs, Audi adds, one may justifiably ask for further evidence. Basic belief in God's existence differs from culture to culture. A Hindu's basic belief in the creative force behind the universe is by no means synonymous with that of a Christian's, such as Plantinga. Nor is it likely that all *Christians* have an identical basic belief on this. To clarify the circumstantial nature of such

---

[42] Robert Audi, "Direct Justification, Evidential Dependence, and Theistic Belief" in *Rationality, Religious Belief, and Moral Commitment,* 142.
[43] Ibid. 145.

beliefs, Audi gives the example of a bowl of fruit. Ann is standing 12 feet away from this, and has a basic belief that the fruit in the bowl is edible.

> Before artificial fruit was invented, this basic belief might have been perfectly rational; but after she discovers that many people use artificial fruit, which at that distance she cannot distinguish from real fruit, she is less likely to form the basic belief, at that distance, that there are apples in a fruit bowl she sees . . .[44]

In other words, Ann will now require further evidence before she tells a friend to go over and take a bite from the apple in question: imagine the *faux pas* of encouraging someone to eat a wax fruit!

Audi speculates that the mature, reflective theist of today, taking into consideration the criticisms that have been leveled against traditional beliefs in God, will hesitate before blithely asserting that this is a basic belief. For example, the problem of evil has led many rational people to seriously doubt that God, or at least the traditional theistic conception of God, exists in reality. Like Ann, they wish for further justification before they will accept this. They have learned too much to merely accept the Calvinist non-evidential viewpoint. One may assail them for being Doubting Thomases, but their doubts will not be alleviated without some convincing evidence presented to them.

To hold that belief in God is properly basic, and to hold that those who see it differently can be ignored, is to commit a kind of ghettoization. Why do some people not accept such beliefs? Plantinga implies that the nonbelievers have either an improperly functioning noetic system, or they are guilty of committing willful sin. In his article "On Reformed Epistemology", Plantinga asserts that it is sin that prevents individuals from accepting properly basic beliefs, and that sin is the cause of "error, confusion, fundamental wrong-headedness, and all the other epistemic ills to which humanity is heir."[45] But this precludes any further debate. In addition, it is hard to see how this avoids begging the question. Here we have a return to the same sort of conversation-stopper which G. H. Ward used in his own criticism of Clifford. When sin rears its ugly head, how can one continue the discussion?

It may be perfectly understandable why certain people hold certain beliefs which they have been taught from an earliest age – the question remains, do these beliefs express true propositions? Evidentialism presents

---

[44] Ibid., p. 156.
[45] Alvin Plantinga, "On Reformed Epistemology", in *The Reformed Journal* 32, No. 1 (January 1982), 14.

a method for testing these beliefs. Even Clifford was by no means completely dismissive of people's personal beliefs. He held that these beliefs should adhere to the objective facts of the universe. He writes in "The Ethics of Belief":

> It is the sense of power attached to a sense of knowledge that makes men desirous of believing, and afraid of doubting. This sense of power is the highest and best of pleasures when the belief on which it is founded is a true belief, and has been fairly earned by investigation. For then we may justly feel that it is common property, and holds good for others as well as for ourselves. Then we may be glad, not that *I* have learned secrets by which I am safer and stronger, but that *we men* have got mastery over more of the world; and we shall be strong, not for ourselves, but in the name of Man and in his strength. But if the belief has been accepted on insufficient evidence, the pleasure is a stolen one.[46]

Locke and Clifford present a formula by which knowledge may be advanced on an objective basis. Audi rightly points out that abandoning evidentialism can lead to some strange consequences. Plantinga and his fellow Reform Epistemologists, for all their erudition, come rather close to following the very enthusiastic line which Locke had critiqued at the very beginning of the evidentialist debate.

III. Ethical Duties

1. Richard Gale

While the above discussion has focused on epistemology per se, there have been several recent philosophers who have attempted to define the *ethical* aspects of Clifford's "Ethics of Belief" argument.

In his 1993 book *On the Nature and Existence of God,* University of Pittsburgh philosopher Richard Gale takes Clifford to task along teleological lines. He considers Clifford's argument to be a version of act utilitarianism. He calls Clifford's position "'the plague theory' of epistemically unwarranted belief," and writes that "his basic contention is that while such a belief might maximize utility in the short run, in the long run its overall consequences are horrendous."[47] He adds:

---

[46] W. K.Clifford, "The Ethics of Belief" in *Lectures and Essays* (London: Macmillan, 1886), 343.
[47] Richard Gale, *On the Nature and Existence of God* (New York: Cambridge University Press, 1993), 355.

Like many an act-utilitarian trying to fend off a desert-island unkept-promise counterexample, Clifford has greatly exaggerated the deleterious consequences of allowing ourselves even a single epistemically unwarranted belief, however trivial and disconnected from the workaday world. To put it mildly, his plague theory has very dubious empirical credentials.[48]

Gale also cannot resist remarking upon Clifford's writing style. Before giving several flamboyant passages from "The Ethics of Belief", he puckishly says that "Pomp and Circumstance" should be played in the background for maximum effect while they are read aloud, then adds: "I assume that ten minutes have passed and that the reader has just begun to pull back together again after rolling around on the floor in hysterical convulsions."[49]

Gale admits that the mere fact that Clifford's principle is unsupported by an act utilitarian argument does not prove it false. But counterexamples based upon trust relationships can be provided, which show that people have a moral duty to believe certain things about others for which they have no adequate evidence. Gale holds that there may be a moral requirement *not* to perform such an inquiry.

However, as seen in chapter t hree, it is also by no means evident that Clifford was primarily a utilitarian of any sort, or at least that he relied solely upon such argumentation to support his ethics of belief. Let us now turn to an argument which looks at Clifford from a more Kantian perspective, as one who argues that the duty to the seek the truth outweighs any potential unhappiness such a pursuit might bring about.

2. Richard Rorty

The late Stanford philosopher Richard Rorty offers another perspective on Clifford's ethical stance, looking at his argument as a type of deontology. In the article "Religious Faith, Intellectual Responsibility, and Romance" (written in 1997 for *The Cambridge Companion to William James*), Rorty writes that Clifford's chief mistake was to hold that humans have a duty to seek the truth distinct from their duty to seek happiness. "His way of describing this duty is not as a duty to get reality right but

---

[48] Ibid., 356.
[49] Ibid., 355.

rather as a duty not to believe without evidence."⁵⁰ It is unlikely that Clifford would have seen this distinction. For him, the purpose of beliefs *is* to get us in touch with reality. Likewise, Clifford did not differentiate pursuing the truth and pursuing happiness. The latter is entailed by the former. Happiness based upon illusions or avoiding reality is not genuine.

Rorty summarizes the Clifford-James debate in the following way:

> Clifford asks us to be responsive to "evidence," as well as to human needs. So the question between James and Clifford comes down to this: is evidence something which floats free of human projects or is the demand for evidence simply a demand from other human beings for cooperation on such projects?⁵¹

Why is "evidence" in quotes? It is precisely to encourage human cooperation that Clifford developed his evidentialist position. Even Rorty recognizes this, when he states that Clifford's demand can be put in a "minimalistic" form, "which concedes to James that intellectual responsibility is no more and no less than responsibility to people with whom one is joined in shared endeavor."⁵² In this regard, the wrongness of believing without evidence means that one is only pretending to join in a common project of truth-seeking:

> Even if we drop the foundationalist notion of "evidence," Clifford's point can still be restated in terms of the responsibility to *argue*. A minimal Clifford-like view can be summed up in the claim that, although your emotions are your own business, your beliefs are everybody's business. There is no way in which the religious person can claim a right to believe as part of an overall right to privacy. For believing is inherently a public project: all we language users are in it together. We all have a responsibility to each other not to believe anything which cannot be justified to the rest of us. To be rational is to submit one's beliefs – all one's beliefs – to the judgment of one's peers.⁵³

Intellectual responsibility means that, where evidence and arguments are unavailable, options must cease to be live or forced. According to Rorty, it is James who gives a utilitarian ethics of belief argument. "Such

---

⁵⁰ Richard Rorty, "Religious Faith, Intellectual Responsibility, and Romance" in *The Cambridge Companion to William James,* edited by Ruth Anna Putnam (New York: Cambridge University Press, 1997), 84.
⁵¹ Ibid., 86.
⁵² Ibid., 87.
⁵³ Ibid., 88.

an ethics," he writes, "will defend religious belief by saying, with Mill, that our right to happiness is limited only by others' rights not to have their own happiness interfered with."[54] Rorty makes a crucial distinction between private and public beliefs. He further argues that it is a false (because useless) belief that the quest for truth and the quest for happiness are separate and distinct. (It is strange that Rorty, who refers to himself as a "Deweyan", would commit the cardinal sin of making a dualism.)

To be fair to Clifford, Rorty points out that Clifford's "rage" was really against the moral irresponsibility of religious fundamentalists. He adds:

> The kind of religious faith which seems to me to lie behind the attractions of both utilitarianism and pragmatism is, instead, a faith in the future possibilities of mortal humans, a faith which is hard to distinguish from love for, and hope for, the human community. I shall call this fuzzy overlap of faith, hope and love "romance."[55]

Rorty touches on a central problem – the ambiguity of the word "belief." "The stark Cliffordian position," he writes, "says: no beliefs, only hopes, desires, yearnings, and the like."[56] One can consider Clifford a romantic, in Rorty's terms, for his own hopes for humanity were tied up with an urge to overcome ill-supported beliefs.

IV. The Ethics of Belief Revisited

1. Susan Haack

University of Miami philosopher Susan Haack's "'The Ethics of Belief' Reconsidered" gives a careful exploration of the possible relationships between ethical and epistemic appraisals. Returning to Clifford's first example in "The Ethics of Belief", Haack agrees that the shipowner *is* morally culpable, for his ignorance is the equivalent of a failure to pursue inquiry. "But," Haack adds, "the case has a number of features which are not invariably found whenever someone believes unjustifiably, and some of which are essential to the unfavorable moral appraisal appropriate here."[57] Clifford, she writes:

---

[54] Ibid., 89-90.
[55] Ibid., 96.
[56] Ibid., 91.
[57] Susan Haack, "'The Ethics of Belief' Revisited" in *The Philosophy of Roderick Chisholm,* edited by Lewis Hahn (Chicago: Open Court, 1997), 135.

... first remarks that the shipowner would still be morally responsible even if his belief that the vessel was seaworthy was true, because "he had no right to believe on such evidence as was before him." Later, however, Clifford comes up with a better argument: by failing to investigate properly, and inducing himself to believe on inadequate evidence, the shipowner would have taken an unacceptable risk of harmful upshot.[58]

If the proposition were not a consequential one, Haack says, then the immorality is far less clear. Clifford offers two arguments about apparently harmless unjustified beliefs. First, no belief is *really* inconsequential, since there is always the potential that an action which might prove harmful could be based upon it; and second, that unjustified beliefs encourage intellectual laxity, which has a risk of harm. Haack adds:

> Clifford's responses depend on two false assumptions: that mere potential for harm, however remote, is sufficient (provided the subject is responsible for the unjustified belief) for unfavorable moral appraisal; and that a subject is always responsible for unjustified believing. But remote potential for harm is not sufficient; if it were, not only drunken driving, but owning a car, would be morally culpable. And a subject is not always responsible for believing unjustifiably; the cause, sometimes, is cognitive inadequacy.[59]

Clifford confuses the issue by combining these two potentialities into one argument against "credulity." There are bad epistemic habits, such as sloppy inquiry, jumping to conclusions, wishful thinking, which, if unchecked, can have harmful effects (although, she adds, Clifford may not be right to suggest that giving into such bad habits necessarily encourages such vices in others). But he ignores unjustified beliefs that are not based upon such self-deception or negligence.

Haack is quick to add that these criticisms of Clifford do not provide support for James' counterargument. If James had been arguing that it is not *morally* wrong to hold beliefs on insufficient grounds, then he would be correct. But James, like Clifford, conflates the ethical and the epistemic:

> Some of the arguments in "The Will to Believe" seem to be intended as epistemological: that knowing the truth is no less valuable than avoiding error; that believing that p sometimes contributes to bringing it about that p is true. But others seem to be of an ethical character: that we should not condemn those who have faith for believing without adequate evidence, but should "respect one another's mental freedom"; and the quotation from

---

[58] Ibid.
[59] Ibid. 137.

FitzJames Stephens at the close of the paper, urging that we have faith because "if death ends all, we cannot meet death better". This suggests that the best way to read James is as holding that it is not always wrong *either* epistemologically *or* morally to believe on insufficient evidence.[60]

James allows for the weakening of epistemic standards. Haack summarizes thusly:

> Unlike both James and Clifford, I distinguish epistemological from ethical appraisals. Like James and unlike Clifford, I do not think it always morally-wrong to believe on insufficient evidence. Clifford's position is over-demanding morally. Like Clifford and unlike James, however, I think it is always epistemologically-wrong to believe on insufficient evidence – that believing without sufficient evidence is always epistemologically-unjustified belief. James' position is over-permissive epistemologically.[61]

Haack offers what she calls "a friendly, if revisionary, reinterpretation" of what is plausible in Clifford's "the ethics of belief".[62]

2. Anthony Quinton

Oxford philosopher Anthony Quinton has had a long-standing interest in Clifford's work. In the article on "British Philosophy" which he wrote for *The Encyclopedia of Philosophy* (1967), Quinton devotes a section to Clifford and Pearson and their attempt to apply evolutionary theories to ethics. "Much the most interesting philosophically of these Victorian naturalists," he writes, "with their evolutionary theories of morality and their half-materialist, half-skeptical view of natural knowledge, were W. K. Clifford and the statistician Karl Pearson . . ."[63] Quinton continues:

> Clifford's ethics turn on the conception of the "tribal self," seen as an evolutionarily developed system of impulses mitigating the demands of private interest for the sake of the welfare of the group in the struggle for existence. Clifford was a passionate opponent of ordinary religious belief but was prepared to endorse some kind of religion of humanity inspired by cosmic emotion.[64]

---

[60] Ibid., 138.
[61] Ibid.
[62] Ibid. 136.
[63] Anthony Quinton, "British Philosophy" in *The Encyclopedia of Philosophy, Volume 1* (New York: Macmillan, 1967), 388-389.
[64] Ibid., 389.

In his later entry on "Knowledge and Belief", Quinton demonstrates his sympathy with Clifford's evidentialism, and makes a further criticism of James' defense of faith:

> There is some point to the malicious definition of faith as firm belief in something for which there is no evidence, for faith does involve a measure of risk, a voluntary decision to repose more confidence in a proposition, person, or institution than the statable grounds for doing so would, if neutrally considered, justify.... It is often said that science rests on faith in the uniformity and intelligibility of nature as much as religion does on an undemonstrable conviction that the world is under the direction of a wise and benevolent intelligence. Certainly, science would be wholly sterilized if men were not prepared to consider adventurous and unjustified hypotheses. But it is not obvious that these adventurous conjectures have to be believed by their propounders. The austere maxim of W. K. Clifford – "It is wrong, everywhere and for anyone, to believe anything upon insufficient evidence" – is not strictly incompatible with intellectual enterprise.[65]

Quinton goes on to add that even so rigorous a theorist of knowledge as Karl Popper allows for the importance of unscientific faith in regularities of nature to guide hypotheses, but the question remains as to whether "faith" is the proper word to use. Is it really being used in the same sense as in discussions of religious faith?

In 1985, Quinton returned to this theme in his Richard Peters Lecture. Entitled "On the Ethics of Belief", it was delivered at the University of London Institute of Education. Using Clifford's "The Ethics of Belief" essay as a beginning point, Quinton notes: "In its original coinage by W. K. Clifford the phrase 'ethics of belief' was in no way metaphorical or figurative and it introduced a highly moralistic, and indeed indignant, discussion of the right ordering of our beliefs."[66] Clifford had distinguished two ways in which belief has a public influence: 1. Through public expression – having a belief means that one is ready to profess it. 2. To be disposed to act in a certain way. Quinton writes:

> Clifford points out that there are two ways in which our ostensible expressions of belief may be deficient. The belief-expression may be insincere. It may, on the other hand, be cognitively rather than morally defective, be, as he puts it, a failure in knowledge and judgement rather

---

[65] Anthony Quinton, "Knowledge and Belief" in *The Encyclopedia of Philosophy, Volume 4* (New York: Macmillan Publishing Co., 1967), 344.
[66] Anthony Quinton, "On the Ethics of Belief" in *From Wodehouse to Wittgenstein* (New York: St. Martin's Press, 1998), 79.

than veracity. If we are dishonest we act so as to inspire beliefs that we suppose to be false or unreasonable. If we are mistaken or unreasonable we inspire beliefs that actually are false or unjustified.[67]

The assumption here is that it is disadvantageous to believe what is not true. Quinton recognizes that evidence must be given to support such a claim. Surely, it is not universally the case. For instance, one can argue that it is an advantage that most of us do not know the precise date and details of our deaths. It is also probably best that we do not know the precise knowledge about what everyone we encounter thinks of us. Yet even here, one can make the opposite case. It can be advantageous, when planning one's retirement and finances, to have some rough knowledge of one's life expectancy. Similarly, having some rough knowledge of others' thoughts about you can be advantageous in knowing whom to associate with.

The general rule that it is advantageous to have true beliefs is primarily based on the fact that we are goal-oriented creatures. Without correct information, it is unlikely that we will achieve the goals we value, except perhaps out of pure luck. In Quinton's words:

... the usual case when we act on a false belief is that we fail to get what we want and commonly get in its place, not just something that, as an alternative to what we are aiming at, we are indifferent to, but something we should much rather not have, something that we do not want.[68]

Unreasonable beliefs are not necessarily the same as false beliefs, but the consequences are also likely to prevent one from achieving one's aim. In this regard, Clifford's maxim is still relevant.

Quinton recognizes a flaw in Clifford's own presentation. Clifford's maxim can, on one level, be seen as a truism, since it can be taken to mean that one is not justified to believe anything one is not justified to believe. But more to the point, Clifford's maxim fails to take into account the fact that evidence and justification for beliefs can vary in strength. "Like many others, notably Chisholm, Clifford adopts an exceedingly constricted view of possible belief-attitudes – namely that one can believe or disbelieve or suspend judgements altogether, that is neither believe nor disbelieve. That attenuated repertoire is, I think, demonstrably inadequate to our actual needs and circumstances."[69]

---

[67] Ibid., 80-81.
[68] Ibid., 81-82.
[69] Ibid., 87.

The problem lies in the fact that, to guide action, all practical beliefs must relate to the future. Yet, no belief about the future can itself be certain. There can only be a selection from a range of possible unperformed actions. Some beliefs about the future are stronger than others. For instance, the belief that the sun will rise tomorrow is not cause for reasonable doubt. Such an empirical generalization is established beyond a reasonable doubt, and evidence for it need not be constantly acquired. But most of the beliefs we consider to be crucial are not supported by such near-certainties. We must act out of probabilities, and the assent we give them if often qualified. Clifford has failed to take into consideration the variable degrees of belief that guide us. He is guilty of what Quinton calls "intellectual intemperance":

> The binary obsession of theorists of belief which I have been criticising corresponds to an ethical deficiency in the management of beliefs which is exceedingly widespread and to which we are all, no doubt, liable. This is the vice of intellectual intemperance, of asserting beliefs without qualification when some measure of qualification is rationally in order, when we have some reason, but not conclusive reason for taking them to be true.[70]

It is this sort of "intellectual intemperance" which makes Clifford's writings seem so ferocious. To some extent, this is merely a habit of fanciful exaggeration for effect. Clifford's virtues are overpowered by this vice. Yet, in Quinton's view, the cause of this vice is the uncomfortable nature of being in a state of doubt – a characteristic which Peirce had addressed in *The Fixation of Belief.* It is difficult for most people to remain in a half-state of belief.

Ironically, Clifford's maxim seems aimed at encouraging such a tentative state, while using intemperate language to get its point across. He is challenging all dogmatic faith claims, which are themselves often intemperately expressed. This may be due to the fact that temperance seems a rather dispirited sort of virtue – overly cautious, as James might have phrased it. But Quinton adds:

> It is, however, perfectly consistent and combinable with another intellectual virtue of a more positive and colourful kind, that of intellectual courage. That does not consist in bravely risking the danger of acting on beliefs which there is not much reason to suppose are true. Rather, it is a matter of incurring the risk of lost time and effort that is involved in trying to find out if reasonable grounds exist for new and adventurous thoughts

---

[70] Ibid., 90.

and, in particular, in the serious and effortful business of questioning the credentials of things it is customary to believe.[71]

Courage need not be intemperate. Other related intellectual virtues include fairness (the willingness to consider beliefs that are inconsistent or count against one's own) and charity (couching one's expressions of belief in such a way as to minimize the pain they may cause others). He concludes with the following:

> It is an analytic truth that we ought to believe what is epistemologically right to believe, in other words, what there is good reason to believe. And from that it follows that we ought morally to believe only what there is good reason to believe (and we ought prudentially to believe only that as well). But the implication is not rigidly deductive. It is morally desirable for my beliefs to be reasonable to the extent that if I have them I will have a tendency to express them, whose indulgence is on the whole more calculated to influence other people to accept those beliefs than, perhaps because of obstinate counter-suggestibility, to reject them. Since beliefs may remain unexpressed and may be resisted when they are expressed there is a twofold weakening of the connection between the epistemic improvement of one person's beliefs and the advantage to others which we can rationally expect to accrue from the possibly consequential improvement of their beliefs. But so long as it has some tendency that way and none to speak of in the other – which it is also reasonable to suppose – it is clearly morally desirable.[72]

Clifford's argument may be lacking the virtue of charity, yet there are hazards in being *too* charitable. As Quinton points out, this can veer dangerously close to wishful thinking. It is related to a sense of hope – and hope has a traditional association not only with charity, but "more disconcertingly for anyone concerned with the rationality of belief, with faith."[73] Quinton's distrust of faith continues unabated.

3. Lorraine Code

York University philosopher Lorraine Code, in her 1987 book *Epistemic Responsibility,* gives a much more sustained critique of Clifford's conflation of ethics and epistemology than any previous

---

[71] Ibid., 92.
[72] Ibid., 94.
[73] Ibid.,.93.

philosopher, and the dangers inherent in using moral terms to describe epistemological states. In "The Ethics of Belief", she writes, epistemic and ethical considerations are tightly entangled:

> Clifford goes on to argue that the shipowner would, in fact, have been blameworthy even if the ship had arrived safely, claiming that "the question of right and wrong has to do with the origin of his belief, not the matter of it." The shipowner had no basis for believing the evidence he chose to believe, whatever the outcome of his actions based upon it. This argument seems to be a move in the direction of separating the epistemic and the ethical strands of the situation so that each can be evaluated on its own terms. It would then be possible to judge the epistemic aspects on their own merits, separated from their ethical implications. But, in fact, Clifford believes himself to be making a strictly moral judgment here, thus glossing over the extent to which prior, unwarranted epistemic moves *produce* the condemnable action. This probably occurs because the magnitude of the moral wrong in the actual case is such that it is easy to allow its moral import to eclipse its underlying epistemic significance.[74]

There are two *separate* judgments to be made here. The shipowner is open to criticism not only because of his action, but also because of his *method* of belief- formation. The former is, primarily, moral censure, the latter, primarily epistemic. These judgments are however connected, in that the shipowner is morally blameworthy largely *because* he has been epistemically irresponsible. He is epistemically blameworthy because he has acted irresponsibly through ignoring evidence that might have led him to cancel the sea voyage. "But the irresponsibility attaches primarily to the epistemic maneuvers" she writes. "Had his knowing been responsible, it is possible that his action might have been different."[75]

Codes argues that the traditional "ethics of belief" arguments are not very helpful in delineating epistemic responsibility. There are cases in which moral considerations outweigh epistemic ones. The ways in which evidence is considered may vary depending on whether one is more concerned with ethics or epistemology. Thus:

> ... the point seems to be that evidence about the behavior and character of other persons is significantly different, epistemically, from evidence, for example, about the moons of Jupiter. A different juxtaposition of ethical and epistemic criteria is appropriate in evaluating each kind of case. Yet this does not conflate epistemic and moral criteria, nor does it imply that

---

[74] Lorraine Code, *Epistemic Responsibility* (Hanover, New Hampshire: Brown University Press,1987), 72-73.
[75] Ibid. 73.

similar epistemic contortions are in order where historical, geographical, or scientific knowledge and/or beliefs are at stake. Neither does it warrant the conclusion that epistemic considerations, in the quest for knowledge in general, can always (or even usually) be overridden by moral considerations of this nature.[76]

Yet, Code also provides a possible approach toward defending Clifford himself, by developing a model of what she calls "an intellectually virtuous character." This is a person who maintains "a matter of orientation toward the world and toward oneself as a knowledge-seeker in the world. . . . Intellectually virtuous persons value knowing and understanding how things really are. They resist the temptations to live with partial explanations where fuller ones are attainable; they resist the temptation to live in fantasy or in a world of dream or illusion, considering it better to know, despite the tempting comfort and complacency a life of fantasy or illusion (or one well tinged with fantasy or illusion) can offer."[77]

In the next and final chapter, I will argue that Clifford fits such a model, and will attempt to defend his "The Ethics of Belief" not along epistemic lines nor on teleological or deontological lines. "The Ethics of Belief", I will argue, can best be understood as a type of virtue ethics, and it remains relevant.

---

[76] Ibid, 82.
[77] Lorraine Code, *Epistemic Responsibility* (Hanover and London: University Press of New England, 1987), 58-59.

CHAPTER SIX

THE VIRTUES OF "THE ETHICS OF BELIEF"

I. "The Ethics of Belief"

1. Criticisms

As the previous chapters show, there is much about "The Ethics of Belief" which is open to criticism. It was delivered as an address to a debate society, and then published in a journal encouraging different points of view, so it is not surprising that, almost a century and a half after its initial appearance, "The Ethics of Belief" continues to be provocative. Let us look at the central criticisms of the essay, and then at possible responses. To what extent can "The Ethics of Belief" continue to be defended?

There seem to be three main problems with Clifford's evidentialism:

A. First, the basis claim—"It is wrong always, everywhere, and for any one, to believe anything upon insufficient evidence"—is untenable. No one can live up to such a standard. William James argued that this claim would lead to complete inaction, since the avid pursuit of evidence would preclude—somewhat like Zeno's paradox—any movement at all before one was satisfied with a belief's sufficiency. The world cannot wait for such evidence-gatherers. Things move too quickly. Charles Peirce, much more carefully than Clifford, examined the nature of belief itself, and argued that it is only when genuine doubts arise that one seriously searches for such evidence. For the most part, we freely accept a multitude of beliefs for which we lack sufficient evidence.

B. Second, the basic terms used by Clifford are ill-defined. While making the normative claim that we must apportion beliefs to evidence, nowhere in the essay does Clifford define what he means by "sufficient evidence." His use of the word "belief" is itself unclear. Does he hold a view similar to that of Peirce's? Or, as Peter van Inwagen argues, does Clifford deliberately hide the fact that his essay is specifically criticizing *religious* beliefs, and not just beliefs in general? Furthermore, as modern-day critics like Michael Martin, Susan Haack, and Lorraine Code have pointed out, Clifford conflates issues of epistemology and ethics. It is difficult, when reading "The Ethics of Belief", to be sure when Clifford is claiming one has made a moral transgression or an epistemic blunder, and he himself did not seem to feel there was any significant difference between the two.

C. Third, it is also unclear what kind of normative argument Clifford is making. Is he essentially a deontologist, a teleologist, or some other sort of ethical theorist? For instance, his ship owner example first appears to be consequential—by not examining his belief that the ship was sound, the owner was responsible when it if fact sank because of its unseaworthiness. Yet Clifford then states that, even if the ship had not sunk, the owner would be culpable, since he had no *right* to believe in its seaworthiness. Is the ship owner then being judged for his actions or his intent? Neither teleology nor deontology on their own terms seems to capture the moral stricture which Clifford is leveling here.

2. Response to Criticisms

A. As seen in chapter four, Charles Peirce's essays "The Fixation of Belief" and "How to Make Our Ideas Clear" give a much richer analysis than does Clifford's "The Ethics of Belief" regarding the different ways in which people arrive at their beliefs, and the methods they use to preserve them from doubt. Peirce had argued that there are three universal classes of believers: the aesthete, the practical person, and the scientist. Only the latter relishes uncertainty and tentative beliefs. Without necessarily having to accept Peirce's idiosyncratic tripartite division, one can still better understand "The Ethics of Belief" by viewing Clifford himself as a prime example of the third type of believer. Clifford's error was to assume that *all* individuals within a community of inquirers could follow his same approach. He made no attempt to categorize believers by the strategies they use in forming their beliefs.

As Peirce and many other philosophers have argued, it is impossible to question all of one's beliefs. Such different thinkers as W. V. Quine, Michael Polyani, and Ludwig Wittgenstein have developed this critique. Most of our beliefs, they argue, are not acquired through careful consideration, but rather as part of a general culture, a body of accepted wisdom. It is only by understanding that an infinite number of loosely connected propositions lay behind our conscious beliefs, and by seeing that most of them are relatively fixed and exempt from doubt, that we can really understand the entire issue of belief-formation and preservation. To claim that such non-examined beliefs are held immorally seems to completely misunderstand the very nature of belief itself.

Even in Clifford's own times, his philosophical opponents in the Metaphysical Society raised questions about the beliefs of evidentialists. Where, they asked, was the conclusive evidence for the uniformity of nature, the reliability of memory, and the assurance that the future will be like the past? The intuitionists like Ward and Hutton cleverly made use of the skeptical arguments of the empiricists' hero David Hume, much as the empiricists (as seen by Clifford's usage of Milton and Coleridge in "The Ethics of Belief") delighted in referring to religious authorities to support their irreligious claims.

But the duty to examine beliefs and seek sufficient evidence for them remains a central issue in epistemology. Van Harvey, in his essay "The Ethics of Belief Reconsidered", concedes that Clifford's discussion of belief is, by modern standards, naïve and out-of-step. We cannot really follow his moral imperative to question all of our beliefs until we have sufficient evidence for them. Harvey writes:

> Since Clifford assumes that this universal moral imperative is the essence of the matter, to reject it seems to commit us to rejecting his entire argument. But, before we do this, we might ask whether there is anything to be salvaged from it that would enable us to talk meaningfully about an ethics of belief.[1]

Harvey feels that there is. He argues that, while Clifford's *epistemological* assumption that it is possible to justify all of our beliefs may be unwarranted, the basic *ethical* assumption that we have a responsibility to gather evidence still can be feasibly defended. The legitimate elements of Clifford's ethics of belief tend to be obscured by focusing solely upon the moral imperative not to believe anything upon insufficient evidence. This is a tactic of which the Reformed Epistemologists like Alvin Plantinga are particularly guilty. Merely showing that Clifford's evidentialism is untenable does not address the specific charges which Clifford levels against the ways in which religious propositions tend to be shielded from examination.

Like other critics of "The Ethics of Belief", Harvey stresses the need to differentiate between the two models which Clifford is using, the epistemological and the ethical. But one should not lose sight of the overall point of the essay—the need for belief-accountability. Regarding

---

[1] Van Harvey, "The Ethics of Belief Reconsidered" in *The Ethics of Belief Debate,* edited by Gerald D. McCarthy (Atlanta: Scholars Press, 1986), 194.

the ship owner, for instance, Harvey says: "He is not being asked to hold all of his beliefs on the basis of inquiry. He is responsible only for arriving at a specific range of critical judgments, judgments which will, of course, be made against the background of beliefs he will probably hold acritically."[2] In other words, the ship owner had a special responsibility to examine those beliefs which pertain specifically to his profession and to his responsibility to his passengers. Not all of his beliefs are of the same importance (for instance, if he believed that the food being served on board was delicious, while the passengers found it to be disgusting, the matter would hardly be of the same caliber as his belief about the soundness of the ship itself). What is called into question here is the *character* of the ship owner—the sort of person he is, the way he acted towards those for whom he had definite duties, and the manner in which he attempted to justify his views. In other words, a kind of virtue ethics is at play here.

While Clifford himself might not have accepted Harvey's distinction about role-specific beliefs, it nonetheless helps to make the concerns Clifford expresses in "The Ethics of Belief" still tenable. This emphasis on character traits will be examined in more detail in the discussion below on virtue ethics. For the time being, it is sufficient to assert that denying the literal truth of Clifford's evidentialist claim does not obviate the concern he expresses for both ethical and epistemological responsibility.

B. How can one best deal with Clifford's lack of clarity on the key issues of "sufficient evidence", the meaning of "belief", and the merging together of ethical and epistemic matters?

It is important to remember that Clifford was not a professional philosopher, and also that the careful definition of terms was not at that time even one of the prime areas stressed *by* professional philosophers. It was many decades later that philosophers like Ralph Barton Perry, Roderick Chisholm, and most especially H. H. Price, began to give careful consideration to the meaning of the word "belief". To fault Clifford for not being more precise is to treat him a-historically. In his *own* field of mathematics, Clifford was as scrupulous in defining his terms as one could want, but in the less exacting discussions in the Metaphysical Society, he used a less rigorous standard of argumentation than he would have accepted from his mathematical colleagues.

Indeed, in Great Britain the profession of philosophy itself, like many other social sciences, was just beginning to break away from theological control, which added an experiential aspect to Clifford's discussion of

---

[2] Ibid., 196.

belief. As seen earlier, one reason for Clifford's ire against theology was due in no small part to the great political power which theologians still wielded. This is why examining "The Ethics of Belief" in its historical context is a fruitful exercise. Van Inwagen may be essentially correct that Clifford's evidentialism is usually mentioned in connection with religious beliefs rather than beliefs in general, but these were the very sorts of beliefs which Clifford thought most likely to be shielded from discussion. If he were alive today, I can well imagine that Clifford would wield his evidential lance against political and economic beliefs as strenuously as he would against lingering religious beliefs, for all of these have immense social consequences, and paid advocates who deliberately bamboozle the public and discourage close examination of their basic arguments. Walter Kaufmann was quite astute when he surmised that the advertising profession would also bear examination from a Cliffordian perspective.

Evaluating religious beliefs is a particularly difficult task, as there are many different types of such belief: anthropological, cosmological, ethical, historical, and theological (among others). The belief, for instance, that Jesus was born in Bethlehem is different from the belief that God loves all humans, as well as from the belief that the earth was created in six days. How to properly analyze these differences remains a challenge. Clifford was perhaps not sensitive to such nuances, but he would no doubt be amazed to learn that at the beginning of the twenty-first century, in the most industrialized country on earth, so-called "scientific creationists" are attempting to have their religious beliefs taught as scientific fact in the public schools.

Regarding the concept of "sufficient evidence", Clifford is also by no means the only thinker who does not give a proper accounting of what he means by the phrase. In their introduction to the 1994 book *Questions of Evidence: Proof, Practice, and Persuasion Across the Disciplines,* editors James Chandler, Arnold I. Davidson, and Harry Harootunian write: "The topic of evidence is so central for research and scholarship that it is extraordinary how little direct attention it has received."[3] In her article "Belief and Resistance: A Symmetrical Account" in the same volume, Barbara Herrnstein Smith adds:

> Questions of evidence – including the idea, still central to what could be called informal epistemology, that our beliefs and claims are duly corrected by our encounters with autonomously resistant objects (for

---

[3] James Chandler, Arnold I. Davidson, and Harry Harootunian, "Editors' Introduction" in *Questions of Evidence: Proof, Practice, and Persuasion across the Disciplines* (Chicago: University of Chicago Press, 1994), p. 1.

example, facts, rocks, bricks, and texts-themselves) – are inevitably caught up in view of how beliefs, generally, are produced, maintained, and transformed. In recent years, substantially new accounts of these cognitive dynamics – and, with them, more or less novel conceptions of what we might mean by "beliefs" – have been emerging from various nonphilosophical fields (for example, theoretical biology, cognitive science, and the sociology of knowledge) as well as from within disciplinary epistemology.[4]

In addition, Clifford *did* delineate different types of evidence in the sections of "The Ethics of Belief" devoted to inference and to arguments from authority. He cannot be faulted for evading this question, even if one does not feel his discussion is completely adequate.

Finally, what of the objection that Clifford conflates epistemic and ethical obligations, to the detriment of understanding either one? Susan Haack, in her essay "'The Ethics of Belief' Reconsidered", does a masterful job of laying out the possible strategies which Clifford never explicated:

1. Epistemic appraisal is a subspecies of ethical appraisal (the special-case thesis).
2. Epistemic appraisal is distinct from, but invariably associated with, ethical appraisal (the correlation thesis).
3. There is not invariable correlation, but partial overlap, where epistemic appraisal is associated with ethical appraisal (the overlap thesis).
4. There is no connection between epistemic appraisal and ethical appraisal (the independence thesis).
5. Epistemic appraisal is distinct from, but analogous to, ethical appraisal (the analogy thesis).[5]

This refinement of the positions is extremely helpful in understanding not only Clifford's essay, but the ethics of belief debate in general. Yet it is only in recent times that such a careful breakdown of the possible connections between the epistemic and the ethical has taken place in philosophical circles. Clifford's audience tended to share his assumption that the two areas were of a piece. It is true that Clifford never

---

[4] Barbara Herrnstein Smith, "Belief and Resistance" in *Questions of Evidence, Proof, Practice, and Persuasion across the Disciplines* (Chicago: University of Chicago Press, 1994), 139.

[5] Susan Haack, "'The Ethics of Belief' Revisited" in *The Philosophy of Roderick Chisholm,* edited by Lewis Hahn (Chicago: Open Court, 1997), 129.

distinguishes "it is epistemically wrong" from "it is morally wrong." It is not evident which, if any, of the five theses above he would subscribe to. So, the argument that he conflates two different philosophical areas is a telling one. But this does not destroy either the epistemic or the moral force of his ethics of belief. If one looks at his argument from a virtue approach, the conflation of the epistemic and the ethical can actually be helpful in understanding the type of character-formation which Clifford seems to be advocating. Regardless of the exact connection between these two areas, their interrelatedness plays an important role in determining the kind of a person one is discussing. Let us now turn to an examination of the virtue approach, and why "The Ethics of Belief" should be considered by *its* standards.

C. Both Richard Gale – by showing that most unsupported beliefs will not have deleterious consequences—and Richard Rorty—by showing that the duty to inquire can easily come into conflict with personal happiness—proved the inadequacies of "The Ethics of Belief" from, respectively, a consequential and a duty-based approach. In a sense, Clifford was a child of both Kant's and Mill's, in that he was greatly influenced by the former's stress on duty, and the latter's concern for human betterment. But he himself cannot be categorized as either a Kantian or a utilitarian. Rather, he borrows aspects from each in making his own moral arguments, which are closer to the approach of Aristotle and other ancient virtue thinkers.

"The Ethics of Belief" can best be defended along virtue ethics lines—as an attempt to motivate individuals to use their reasoning powers to the best of their abilities, for both their own good and for the good of society as a whole. It thus contains elements of both deontological and teleological argumentation, but these are aspects of the larger project, which has to do with character-formation.

Virtue ethics is concerned with cultivating proper habits, which will aid one in developing his/her inner talents. Moral evaluation here is concerned not with duties or consequences per se, but rather with the nature of the person involved, and his/her overall character.

Virtue ethics, in distinction from both Kantian duty-based ethics and the utilitarianism of Bentham and Mill, has three major components: 1) It is critical of rule-based ethical theories, all of which seem to miss the full significance of moral experiences; 2) It emphasizes character-appraisal rather than act-appraisal; and 3) It delineates a series of virtues which are appropriate for moral agents to cultivate.

While certainly influenced by Kant's stress upon moral obligations, and also by the consequential elements of Bentham and Mill's discussion of the good of society as a whole, Clifford seems closest to the Aristotelian model. The choices we make in forming our beliefs have an impact on what sort of a person we are, and this in turn affects those later choices we make. One can choose to be intellectually lazy, by using "the method of tenacity" to avoid having one's beliefs challenged, or by using "the method of authority" to allay any doubts. But this has a direct impact on one's character, and one can be judged accordingly. It also has an impact on the people around one, who are influenced by the virtues *and* the vices (the good habits and the bad habits) of their peers.

Perhaps Clifford's "rule" of evidentialism, if taken literally, would lead to the sort of inaction of which William James feared. But Clifford was concerned not so much with laying out a system of rules to follow, but rather with the sort of person one could most admire, and the type of society in which such persons could best thrive. Thus, character-development was a key part of his ethics of belief. And coupled with this were both epistemic and ethical virtues to be sought after, as well as epistemic and ethical vices to be avoided.

The modern philosopher who has done more than anyone else to reawaken interest in virtue ethics is Alasdair MacIntyre. He has stressed the importance of looking at the *narrative* of human lives, their connected histories, the way that people structure their lives as a whole. The piecemeal approach of both duty-based and utilitarian ethics miss out on this *lived* perspective. In his book *After Virtue,* MacIntyre argues that every society has its own role models, its own stock characters, who serve as guides for the types of social roles that are considered desirable.

In *Epistemic Responsibility,* Lorraine Code discusses this renewed interest in the virtue approach for both epistemology and for ethics: "Virtue, either intellectual or moral, is an attribute of character. One good action cannot make a virtuous person any more than, to paraphrase Aristotle, one swallow can make a summer. Aristotle's virtuous man is virtuous because of the connectedness of his life – his relations to himself and to his society are of a piece."[6] The virtuous, in this case, does not strongly differentiate between epistemic and ethical habits. There is a sort of *integrity,* a blending together of these attributes, to make a complete person. She gives an example of a possible intellectually virtuous "character":

---

[6] Lorraine Code, *Epistemic Responsibility* (Hanover and London: University Press of New England, 1987), pp. 27-28.

How then are we to delineate more precisely the nature of an intellectually virtuous character? I have maintained that intellectual virtue is, primarily, a matter of orientation toward the world and toward oneself as a knowledge-seeker in the world. Pursuing this point a little further, it is helpful to think of intellectual goodness as having a realistic orientation. It is only those who, in their knowing, strive to do justice to the *object* – to the *world* they want to know as well as possible – who can aspire to intellectual virtue. . . . Intellectually virtuous persons value knowing and understanding how things really are. They resist the temptations to live with partial explanations where fuller ones are attainable; they resist the temptation to live in fantasy or in a world of dream or illusion, considering it better to know, despite the tempting comfort and complacency a life of fantasy or illusion (or one well tinged with fantasy or illusion) can offer.[7]

As the previous chapters have demonstrated, Clifford himself fit this model, as well as encouraging others to pursue it. He wished to understand the world "as it really was", and tried to clear away outdated and oppressive beliefs which obscured this scientific understanding. He felt it to be immoral to accept dreams or illusions, no matter how comforting, when the means existed for grasping reality itself. And he advocated the position that all members of society, regardless of their station, should ceaselessly examine their beliefs, and should be willing to change them in light of new evidence or contradictory facts. In a way, Clifford was (to use MacIntyre's term) a Victorian "stock character": earnest, hard-working, adventurous (MacIntyre considers "the mountaineer" to be a Victorian stock character), and concerned with social betterment. While MacIntyre, whose personal views are closer to those of Clifford's old adversaries Ward and Hutton, might shudder at the possibility, I believe (with I hope good evidence) that Clifford is still a relevant "stock character" for the present time. His advocacy of good habits in belief-formation and his call for a lessening of belief-preservation is pertinent to the modern world, which—even more than in his own time—is faced with new challenges, and new possibilities, on a daily basis.

Yet Clifford's desire that all people should follow his evidential model can itself be criticized along virtue lines. There are limits to what people can achieve, and to encourage them to pursue goals which they are ill-equipped to handle is an improper act. While Aristotle argued that all people have a desire to know (perhaps an overbelief on Aristotle's part), he also recognized that they have different talents, and different abilities. Not everyone is capable of being a philosopher, just as not everyone is capable of being a mathematician, a mountain climber, a poet, or a good

---

[7] Ibid. 58-59.

public speaker. Clifford was rare indeed in combining these attributes, but he was mistaken in his belief that everyone could follow his own example.

Code feels that Clifford's standard is too exacting. She writes:

> To make epistemic responsibility dependent upon rational rejection of the irrationalities permeating an entire educational fabric would impose an impossibly rigorous standard. Rare individuals have the insight, understanding, and courage to resist the stronghold of tradition: such were the philosophers who were able to bear the pain and loneliness of turning their back on the images in Plato's cave and facing the light, however unbearable. These individuals can urge others to follow; hence the normative value of the ideal *character,* the genuine exemplar of intellectual virtue. But it would be unreasonable to demand that all human knowers, including all teachers, authorities, and experts, exhibit or strive to attain such extraordinary standards. Efforts in this direction – mindfulness on the part of each individual knower of his or her responsibility and fallibility both in seeking and in claiming knowledge – are to be urged and applauded. More cannot reasonably be asked.[8]

These are the sorts of individuals whom Nietzsche referred to as "The Free Spirits".

How then can one judge Clifford for his "irrational" urging of more? His own evidentialism could well be too extreme a model, at least on its own terms. But one can perhaps better understand Clifford's project by seeing it as an "as if" type of philosophy rather than a hard-and-fast system of rules which one is obliged to follow.

II. "The Ethics of Belief" and "The Philosophy of 'As If'"

1. "As If"

The question naturally arises—Did Clifford really believe what he said in "The Ethics of Belief"? Was he sincere in his evidentialism? William James, in his review of Clifford's posthumously published *Lectures and Essays,* perceptively states: "Professor Clifford's fine organ-music, like the bands and torches of our political campaigns, must be meant for our nerves rather than for our reason."[9] In other words, Clifford's language appeals more to our emotions that to our critical faculties. Furthermore,

---

[8] Ibid., 251.
[9] William James, *Collected Essays and Reviews* (New York: Longmans, Green and Col., 1920), 143.

James complains, he uses the terms "Science" and "Reverence for Truth" almost like conjuring tricks, as a means of unsettling the minds of simple listeners, to get them to question their cherished beliefs. In so doing, he will only cause broken hearts and broken lives.

Yet James gives Clifford the benefit of the doubt as to his *own* ability to follow such a rigorous scientific code:

> But even the distant reader must allow that Clifford's mental personality belonged to the highest possible type, to say no more. The union of the mathematician with the poet, fervor with measure, passion with correctness, this surely is the ideal. And if in these modern days we are to look for any prophet or savior who shall influence our feelings towards the universe as the founders and renewers of past religions have influenced the minds of our fathers, that prophet . . . must have what Clifford had in so extraordinary a degree – that lavishly generous confidence in the worthiness of average human nature to be told all the truth. . . . .[10]

One can still see the twinkle in James' eye.

I will not paraphrase Martin Heidegger by remarking that "Only a Clifford can save us now." But I do admit to an admiration of both the man and his essays, especially "The Ethics of Belief". While I find it hard to think that Clifford literally believed all he wrote in that essay, I nonetheless grant him his sincere wish that humans should be more rigorous in their use of their cognitive powers. Clifford wished to motivate all members of society to utilize their intellectual abilities to the highest degree and—aware of the growing doubts about traditional Christian beliefs that had helped to gird society up to that time—he felt a personal responsibility to use his own gifts to further the cause of rationalism. He demonstrated this through his public lectures, his attempts to organize international freethinkers, and most of all by his membership in the Metaphysical Society, an organization of some of the most powerful and influential thinkers of his time.

Given the flaws we have seen addressed so far, how might one best understand Clifford's evidentialism? I myself find it to be a type of "as if" thinking, to use the term coined by the German philosopher Hans Vaihinger (1852-1933) in his book *The Philosophy of "As If"* (1924). This work defended the notion of creative fictions—propositions that are known to be false but which nonetheless are the means to some definite end if treated as if they were true. In *The Philosophy of "As If"*, Vaihinger gives an evolutionary explanation for metaphysics—thus, like Clifford, he

---

[10] Ibid., 138-139.

attempts to apply the theory of evolution not only to biology but to philosophy as well. Human consciousness, Vaihinger argues, grew organically as the means by which our species adapted itself to its environment. But at some point in this evolution, thought broke free from its original aim and became an end in itself, which is to say humans became *self*-conscious, aware not only of their environment but of themselves as thinking beings. Vaihinger writes:

> . . . the emancipated thought sets itself problems which in themselves are senseless, for instance, questions as to the origins of the world, the formation of what we call matter, the beginning of motion, the meaning of the world and the purpose of life. If thought is regarded as a biological function, it is obvious that these are impossible problems for thought to solve, and quite beyond the natural boundaries which limit thought as such.[11]

Thus the birth of metaphysics, the quest for ultimate answers which we can never learn. An impasse occurs: the mind cannot achieve the knowledge that it seeks, and becomes frustrated. According to Vaihinger, false answers are then created in order to end this ceaseless and fruitless pursuit:

> In this light many thought-processes and thought constructs appear to be consciously false assumptions, which either contradict reality or are even contradictory in themselves, but which are intentionally thus formed in order to overcome difficulties of thought by this artificial deviation and reach the goal of thought by roundabout ways and bypaths . . . . The "As If" world, which is formed in this manner, the world of the "unreal" is just as important as the world of the so-called real or actual . . . indeed it is far more important for ethics and aesthetics.[12]

Religious beliefs, Vaihinger felt, serve a purpose by providing answers for unanswerable questions, to in a sense stop humans from thinking unproductively. Religious answers are thus nonsensical but, nonetheless, of vital importance. Without them, our minds would dwell endlessly on futile issues and not get to the business at hand, which is the survival of the species. It is a shame that Vaihinger was not a member of the Metaphysical Society—surely this unique interpretation would have helped to have kept the debate going for years!

---

[11] Hans Vaihinger, *The Philosophy of 'As If'*, translated by C. K. Ogden (New York: Harcourt, Brace, 1925), xliii.
[12] Ibid., xlvi-xlvii.

In the entry he wrote on Vaihinger for *The Encyclopedia of Philosophy,* SUNY-Buffalo philosopher Rollo Handy addresses the very different approaches toward pursuing the truth which Vaihinger and Clifford took: "Vaihinger's theory of fictions can be regarded as a denial of the view of W. K. Clifford and others that belief should always be proportionate to the evidence. Intellectually, practically, and morally we need false but expedient fictions to cope with the world."[13]

Yet ironically, Clifford's evidentialism itself seems to be a version of such a creative fiction. Even if Clifford did not actually believe that all people, regardless of their station, could live up to the ideal he set, he perhaps felt that by *assuming* they could do so one showed them respect and helped motivate them to fulfill whatever intellectual capacities they did in fact possess.

It is not so strange to suggest that Clifford adhered to an "as if" philosophy. Nicholas Rescher, in his 1985 book *Pascal's Wager* rightly observes that in practice Clifford was willing to put aside his own stringent evidentialist dictum:

> In actual fact Clifford did not adhere to this hyperbolic standard throughout his epistemology. Rejecting the prospect of certainty in the area of scientific knowledge, he took the line that man's scientific "knowledge" of nature rests on various principles that are not in the final analysis justified on cognitive grounds at all but must be accounted for in terms of natural selection. The principle of the uniformity of nature is a prime example, and "Nature is selecting for survival those individuals and races who act as if she were uniform; and hence the gradual spread of that belief over the civilized world."[14]

Contemporary critics of Clifford and his fellow empiricists, such as G. H. Ward and R. H. Hutton, made much of the metaphysical presuppositions of the agnostic members of the Metaphysical Society, and felt these to be the Achilles' heel of the entire empiricist challenge to theology and religion. Yet Clifford, unlike some of his fellow freethinkers, was willing to admit that an element of metaphysics grounded his worldview. But his was a *speculative* metaphysics, which could change with new evidence to the contrary, unlike the absolutist metaphysics of his

---

[13] Rollo Handy, "Vaihinger, Hans" in *The Encyclopedia of Philosophy,* volumes 7 and 8, edited by Paul Edwards (New York: MacMillan, 1967), 223.

[14] Nicholas Rescher, *Pascal's Wager* (Notre Dame, Ind.: University of Notre Dame Press, 1985), 144. The quote he gives is from Clifford's essay "Philosophy of the Pure Sciences"—Rescher erroneously attributes it to Clifford's book *The Common Sense of the Exact Sciences.*

theological opponents. Recall Ward's strictures against most Catholics examining the bases of their beliefs, for fear that this would bring about their eternal damnation. While Ward was willing to grant that a select few, such as himself, could enter the lion's den and argue with unbelievers, for the vast majority this would be a great moral danger.

Clifford freely admitted that his worldview was an evolving one. He was one of the first to try to apply Darwin's radical new theory to *all* aspects of the human condition. He might well have been intrigued by Vaihinger's speculations, but he would have seen them as exactly that. The "as if" is itself a creative fiction. Vaihinger himself held that, while useful constructs, such fictions should give way to real knowledge when it can be arrived at. And he further argued, much like Clifford, that it would be a great step forward in human development if the species as a whole became aware that religious beliefs *were* fictitious. Thus Clifford and Vaihinger were not as diametrically in opposition as Handy might suppose.

Clifford's evidentialism, if treated as a creative fiction, is closely akin to what his old adversary William James called "an overbelief." As I see it, the central irony of "The Ethics of Belief" is that it advocates a view for which no overwhelming evidence exists to support it.

2. Overbeliefs

On several occasions, William James took Clifford to task for his immoderate defense of evidentialism. He stated that it was wrong of Clifford to cast a stigma upon beliefs that have moved the world but which are not supported by overwhelming evidence. "What we complain of," James writes:

> . . . is that Clifford should have been willing . . . to use the conjuring spell of the name of Science, and to harp on Reverence for Truth as means whereby to force them on the minds of simple public listeners, and so still more unsettle what is already too perplexed. Splintered ends, broken threads, broken lights, and, at last, broken hearts and broken life! So ends this bright romance![15]

It is a supreme irony that Clifford's evidentialism is itself an example of what James referred to as an "overbelief". These are beliefs which go beyond the evidence, although they do not go against the evidence (an

---

[15] William James, *Collected Essays and Reviews* (New York: Longmans, Green and Col, 1920), 145.

important distinction often overlooked in discussions on James' own "Will to Believe").

Clifford asserts that it is immoral to hold any belief for which one lacks sufficient evidence. Yet, he himself goes beyond what the evidence seems to support regarding people's abilities to apportion beliefs to evidence. As seen in the first section, the entire question of whether it is possible to examine beliefs in the way Clifford proposes remains controversial. Where was the support he could offer to prove this assertion? It seems more like a profession of faith than a strictly scientific proposition.

Lorraine Code discusses James' own defense of an "as if" approach to religious belief:

> ... he states that there are areas in which we must make a choice of, and a commitment to, a certain kind of belief even though we can never know that our belief is true: we must think and act "as if." This argument applies quite straightforwardly to his view of religious belief, where he maintains we are forced to declare ourselves on one side or the other.[16]

But this can go beyond religious beliefs. Indeed, James felt that a good number of our everyday beliefs can be considered from this framework. He went so far as to claim that in morally judging a person, his or her ideals and overbeliefs are the most valuable and interesting things about them. The same can be said for nations and for historic epochs. All can be judged by their highest aspirations, more than by what they in fact achieved.

Code goes on to examine another central aspect of James' will to believe argument, namely that acting "as if" a belief is true can actually help to make it so. James has pointed out, for instance, that treating a stranger as if he were a friend could help to form a friendly relationship, whereas treating him as if he were an enemy would most likely bring about an adversarial relationship. Because, in this case, it is a stranger one is talking about, there is no telling evidence one way or another to guide one in making the decision as to whether he is a potential friend or enemy. Code writes:

> There is, in addition, an entire range of instances where acting "as if" can, in fact, bring about the desired state of affairs; where "faith in a fact can help create the fact," to use James's formulation. If I choose to believe that you like me and behave toward you on the assumption that you do, my acting in this way may quite possibly be instrumental in bringing about

---

[16] Code, 79.

precisely the kind of liking I believe exists. Again, in view of the good this attitude produces, it is not reasonable to accuse me of having violated James's epistemic commandment. Here, acting "as if" is a species of heuristic principle.[17]

Perhaps Clifford's evidentialism can be considered another type of such a heuristic principle. He acted as if all people could follow the formula so boldly asserted in "The Ethics of Belief", in the hopes that this would motivate them to follow more stringent habits of belief-formation.

In a sense, Clifford stresses the deleterious effects of overbeliefs in "The Ethics of Belief", while James stresses their beneficial effects in "The Will to Believe". Recall Clifford's strong words, that one must guard "the purity of his belief with a very fanaticism of jealous care, lest at any time it should rest on an unworthy object, and catch a stain which can never be wiped away."[18] Such language is akin to Barry Goldwater's alarming claim that "extremism in defense of liberty is no vice." It seems rather strange for a person who is arguing in favor of being open to new ideas to use words like "fanaticism" in so doing. One can see why James, referring to this passage, would claim that Clifford's advice is to keep one's mind in suspense forever, rather than risk believing lies.

Yet, while Clifford is seemingly advocating a sort of "underbelief"— like a general keeping his troops out of battle - James also points out that Clifford has his own overbelief: namely, the belief that humankind on the whole would be better off if its beliefs squared with the evidence. It is true that Clifford, at least in most of his popular writings, seems to accept without question that the attainment of truth would be beneficial to all humans, and that false beliefs are all harmful. Bertrand Russell (no admirer of James' pragmatism), shared Clifford's advocacy of truth-seeking, but nonetheless had reservations about whether such attainment would necessarily be the cause of happiness. Russell, more than Clifford, was willing to make a distinction between the duty to inquire and the resulting benefits of such inquiry.

But it is not true that Clifford was an epistemic ascetic. As he explicitly states in the section on "The Duty to Inquire" in "The Ethics of Belief", there are many cases in which we have a *duty* to act on probabilities, even when the evidence is not persuasive, "because it is precisely by such action, and by observation of its fruits, that evidence is got which may

---

[17] Ibid., 80.
[18] W. K. Clifford, "The Ethics of Belief" in *Lectures and Essays*, Vol. II (Macmillan, 1879), 267.

justify future belief."[19] Here Clifford sounds as if he had read James' "Will to Believe" and was agreeing with its central assertion! But he hastens to add that this is only permissible after one has already formed a habit of engaging in conscientious inquiry.

James, then, misrepresents Clifford in the sense that the latter never advocated a cautious epistemic course. He fully concurred that it is permissible to treat a proposition as if it were true, and then see what results follow. What Clifford opposed was the course of action Peirce had called "The Method of Tenacity"—continuing to believe even when the evidence goes against one, or shielding propositions from proper inquiry. What Clifford advocated was just the opposite: the Method of Open-Mindedness. For him, the openness to new ideas, coupled with an ever-present awareness of one's own fallibility, was the most defensible course to pursue.

Where James and Clifford part company is on the issue of "comforting" overbeliefs. Clifford fully granted that many of our most cherished beliefs – especially those relating to religion—provide a sense of comfort, and giving up these beliefs can be painful. Yet he points out that beliefs are not solely private matters. They affect society as a whole.

Perhaps Clifford's advice would be: treat your overbeliefs as tentative, and put them to the test. Don't shield them, and in fact actively look for evidence that might overthrow them. Usually, overbeliefs are treated not as hypotheses but as facts, and this is what leads to dogmas and bad habits of thought.

III. The Character of W. K. Clifford

1. Continuing Relevance

How relevant is Clifford's "The Ethics of Belief" to the present-day? While not mentioning Clifford himself, Stuart Sutherland, Professor of Psychology at the University of Sussex, argues in his 1994 book *Irrationality: Why We Don't Think Straight!* that the conditions which people like Clifford grappled with in the Victorian age are still pertinent. He writes, in a chapter entitled "Distorting the Evidence":

> ... I have demonstrated that beliefs – even current hypotheses that there is no reason to hold strongly – are remarkably resistant to change. I have also outlined four reasons, all of which have received experimental support. First, people consistently avoid exposing themselves to evidence that might

---

[19] Ibid., 268.

disprove their beliefs. Second, on receiving evidence against their beliefs, they often refuse to believe it. Third, the existence of a belief distorts people's interpretation of new evidence in such a way as to make it consistent with the belief. Fourth, people selectively remember items that are in line with their beliefs. To these four reasons one might add a fifth, the desire to protect one's self esteem....[20]

Many of the same debates which Clifford engaged in during the mid to late 1800s are still being debated in much the same language in the present-day. From Clifford's perspective, this would be unfortunate not only from the present perspective, but also from that of the evolution of the species as whole. As described in chapter two, Clifford can be considered one of the earliest proponents of evolutionary ethics, a controversial field which has many adherents at the beginning of the twenty-first century, as well as a forerunner of evolutionary epistemology. His relevance as a pioneer in these two fields needs to be noted, if not overstressed.

2. Evolutionary Ethics and Evolutionary Epistemology

In Clifford's view, the moral sense is something which all humans are born with. It needs to be cultivated through common struggle and through adherence to the truth. "Virtue is a habit", he wrote, "not a sentiment nor an *ism* . . . the spring of virtuous action is the social instinct, which is set to work by the practice of comradeship."[21]

Taking an evolutionary approach to knowledge, Clifford argued that theistic theories are no longer appropriate means for binding people together, as they are based upon outmoded hypotheses.

As discussed in chapter four, one can easily see a Nietzschean element in Clifford's writings. He, too, saw the death of God as an opportunity for a new ethics, one based not upon following the commandments of metaphysical beings, but rather on self-cultivation. Unlike Nietzsche, however, Clifford was not an elitist. He would not have accepted Nietzsche's ideal of the overman, nor Nietzsche's distinction between slave and master moralities. Clifford did not have contempt for what Nietzsche referred to as "the herd". Rather, he wished to encourage all people to rise to the level of their cognitive abilities. Clifford was a

---

[20] Stuart Sutherland, *Irrationality: Why We Don't Think Straight!* (New Brunswick, New Jersey: Rutgers University Press, 1994), 151-152.
[21] W. K. Clifford, *Lectures and Essays,* second edition (London: Macmillan, 1886), 389.

democrat in his politics, influenced strongly by the revolutionary Guiseppe Mazzini, and an advocate of social reform, influenced strongly by the utilitarian approach of Jeremy Bentham and John Stuart Mill.

It is interesting to compare Clifford's ethics of belief with that of David Hume, which was discussed in chapter one. John Passmore, in his essay "Hume and the Ethics of Belief", claims that Hume would have been skeptical of Clifford's evidentialism as it applies to the common man:

> The vulgar, he would then say, do not examine evidence; their beliefs are entirely the product of "education." It is not wrong for them to believe on insufficient grounds; that is how they are made. But the wise, if only as a result of experience, develop critical principles, "general rules," which enable them to proportion their belief to the evidence . . . the wise resist the influence of their education, they resist vivid but implausible stories, they weigh evidence. And if they do not do this they act wrongly.[22]

"In the jargon of our own days", Passmore adds, "Hume was an elitist."

Clifford would have none of this. His essays on ethics were written to exhort his intellectual contemporaries to break away from belief systems that could no longer be rationally supported and to encourage all people to cease relying upon superstitions and myths, no matter how comforting these might be. If his language was at times extreme and if his arguments were often uncharitable (an unpardonable sin for a logician), then this was perhaps due to his sense of urgency and his own excitement over what he saw as a new phase in the moral development of the human species.

As George Levine writes in his admiring essay about Clifford and his fellow scientific naturalists, entitled "Scientific Discourse as an Alternative to Faith": "Addressed to audiences who were, by all reports, enthralled, Clifford's lectures are designed to destabilize, to turn the world on his head, so the new possibilities, alternatives to traditional notions of faith and order, might come in. Clifford was the Oscar Wilde of the naturalists."[23]

Clifford not only hoped to combat the growth of nihilism which he felt might spring from the growing dissatisfaction with theologically-grounded ethics, but he also welcomed the challenge. He hoped to foster a new,

---

[22] John A. Passmore, "Hume and the Ethics of Belief" in *David Hume – Bicentennary Papers,* edited by G. P. Morice (Edinburgh: Edinburgh University Press, 1977), 89.

[23] George Levine, "Scientific Discourse as an Alternative to Faith" in *Victorian Faith in Crisis,* edited by Richard J. Hemlstadter and Bernard Lightman (Stanford, California: Stanford University Press, 1990), 257.

more scientifically-grounded ethics which could unify all humankind. This was surely a belief that went far beyond the evidence—an overbelief—but it did not go *against* the evidence. For the importance of public education as a means of raising the standards for an entire society was still a revolutionary idea in Clifford's time. Hailing from the middle class himself, he saw the need for providing the means of education to all members of society, not just the upper classes.

What Clifford recognized was that the old elite system of education was no longer appropriate for the times in which he was living. An industrialized and technological society was emerging, which relied heavily upon specialized knowledge. This was the reason he fought so strongly to free the academic world from the control of ecclesiastics, and why he was so vociferous in his denunciation of what he called "the priestcraft." As Van Harvey points out:

> He must have intuited that the growth in size of the intellectual classes was to be the single most striking feature of modern culture. They would become larger than ever before in history, both in absolute numbers and in proportion to the population as a whole. Moreover, these classes would live in a culture generated and sustained by academic institutions of all sorts. Consequently, the virtue of believing reasonably, which was once an ideal of an elite, becomes a virtue increasingly essential to a culture in which the crucial roles will be performed by engineers, doctors, journalists, lawyers, scientists, and educators of all sorts. The virtue of reasonableness is a part of this "form of life," to use Wittgenstein's phrase. It is an essential virtue for anyone that would participate in a rationalized civilization.[24]

In the modern industrialized society, Hume's elitism was no longer acceptable. For Clifford, the duty to examine one's beliefs is the same for the intellectual in the ivory tower as it is for the simple tradesman quaffing a beer in the alehouse.

It is true that Clifford's writings continue not only to illuminate, but also to outrage. In this, he is following in the age-old philosophical tradition of being a gadfly. We should consider the importance of those who get us to reexamine our beliefs through their use of polemics. As Code states:

> . . . too much emphasis upon prudence leads not only to timidity but to a picture of epistemic life as essentially cautious and conservative, more concerned with avoidance of error than with creativity and exploration of

---

[24] Harvey, 200.

new possibilities. There must be room, within the larger sphere where good knowers *live,* for the Socratic gadfly and for those who take outrageous stances to keep the epistemic community on its toes, to prevent it from settling into complacency or inertia. Nietzsche comes to mind in this regard, with his challenges both to moral and to epistemological patterns of thought . . . [25]

So too does Clifford. While William James might have unfairly criticized Clifford for advocating a policy of prudential timidity in belief-formation, it seems that the model to which he comes closest is the Nietzchean philosopher with a hammer, the "free spirit" whom Nietzsche himself upheld as an ideal. It is difficult, after reading "The Ethics of Belief" for the first time, to continue to think about one's own beliefs in quite the same way. One can only imagine the impact which Clifford himself must have made on his initial hearers that fateful day in 1876 when he first delivered this talk to the assembled dignitaries of the Metaphysical Society.

3. Clifford as Role Model

W. K. Clifford exemplified the Victorian virtues of hard work and self-cultivation. An overachiever, he impressed all who came in contact with him by his meticulous concern for details, his long hours of work, and his willingness to follow an argument to its logical conclusion, even when it was a conclusion he was not initially prepared to accept.

One must also keep in mind the context in which Clifford spoke. As Alan Willard Brown, in his history of the Society, notes: "The members of the Metaphysical Society were committed to rational discourse. Their attitude toward man and his universe, whether expressed in intuitional or empirical terms, demanded that all analysis of human problems be in a form communicable to one another."[26] He fully expected his own outrageous writings to be criticized.

Brown further notes:

> Certain it is that criticism of the evidence for Christian revelation has led to a far wider religious pluralism even among believers than would have been possible a hundred years ago. Thus, a general recognition of the private or limited "truth" in each of a number of different religions and sects has become even more characteristic of modern religious life than was

---

[25] Code, 55.
[26] Alan Willard Brown, *The Metaphysical Society* (New York: Columbia University Press, 1947), 290.

dreamed of in the seventeenth and eighteenth centuries by those who first propounded the principle in order to gain freedom for their own often highly dogmatic beliefs. But this accepted pluralism of faiths and dogmas also parallels the modern secularization of many aspects of life, especially education, with the result that even in their totality religious myths and beliefs can no longer be recognized as expressing a central social and moral consensus. This tendency was already clear in the seventies and constituted not only one of the major problems which the Metaphysical Society faced, but was, as we have seen, one of the causes of its failure to develop a common philosophical method.[27]

This was written in 1947. Perhaps William James' tongue-in-cheek call for a Cliffordian savior may have some merit after all. In the modern secularized world, who will help us to reach a central social or moral consensus?

William Kingdon Clifford throughout his short life demonstrated the virtues of intellectual integrity and the values of philosophical inquiry. His essay "The Ethics of Belief", for all its hyperbole, remains a testament to his optimistic hopes for both the epistemic and the ethical betterment of the human species. While he might have had no right, given his own terms, to believe in this betterment, looking at his life and his writings from a virtue approach gives a fresh perspective on the continuing importance of this deliberately outrageous thinker.

---

[27] Ibid., 280.

BIBLIOGRAPHY

Adler, Jonathan. *Belief's Own Ethics*. Cambridge, Massachusetts: The MIT Press, 2002.

Altick, Richard D. *Victorian People and Ideas: A Companion for the Modern Reader of Victorian Literature*. New York: W. W. Norton, 1973.

Alston, William P. *Epistemic Justification*. Ithaca, New York: Cornell University Press, 1989.

American Mathematical Society. *Geometry and Nature: In Memory of W. K. Clifford – A Conference on New Trends in Geometrical and Topological Methods*. Providence, Rhode Island: American Mathematical Society, 1997.

Ammerman, R. M. "Ethics and Belief." *Proceedings of the Aristotelian Society* 1964-1965: 257-266.

Anderson, Douglas. *Strands of System: The Philosophy of Charles Peirce*. West Lafayette, Indiana: Purdue University Press, 1995.

Andersson, Stefan. *In Quest of Certainty*. Stockholm, Sweden: Almqvist & Wiksell International, 1994.

Annan, Noel. *Leslie Stephen: The Godless Victorian*. New York: Random House, 1984.

Arnold, Matthew. *God and the Bible*. Ann Arbor: University of Michigan Press, 1970.

Audi, Robert. *Belief, Justification and Knowledge*. Belmont, California: Wadsworth, 1988.

Audi, Robert and William J. Wainwright, editors. *Rationality, Religious Belief, and Moral Commitment*. Ithaca, New York: Cornell University Press.

Bell, E. T. *The Development of Mathematics*. New York: McGraw-Hill, 1945.

Benn, Alfred William. *The History of English Rationalism in the Nineteenth Century*. 2 Volumes. New York: Russell & Russell, 1962.

Berman, David. *A History of Atheism in Britain: From Hobbes to Russell*. New York: Routledge, 1988.

Bird, Graham. *William James.* London and New York: Routledge and Kegan Paul, 1986.

Blackwell, Kenneth. *The Spinozistic Ethics of Bertrand Russell.* London: George Allen & Unwin, 1985.

Brent, Joseph. *Charles Sanders Peirce: A Life.* Bloomington, Indiana: Indiana University Press, 1993.

Brody, Baruch. *Readings in the Philosophy of Religion: An Analytic Approach,* second edition. Englewood Cliffs, New Jersey: Prentice-Hall, 1992.

Brown, Alan Willard. *The Metaphysical Society.* New York: Columbia University Press, 1947. London: Heinemann, 1977.

Budd, Susan. *Varieties of Unbelief: Atheists and Agnostics in English Society, 1850-1960.*

Chandler, James, Arnold I. Davidson, and Harry Harootunian, editors. *Questions of Evidence: Proof, Practice, and Persuasion Across the Disciplines.* Chicago: University of Chicago Press, 1994.

Chisholm, M. *Such Silver Currents: The Story of William and Lucy Clifford, 1845-1929.* Cambridge: Lutterworth Press, 2002.

Chisholm, Roderick. *Theory of Knowledge,* second edition. Englewood Cliffs, New Jersey: Prentice-Hall, Inc., 1966.

Clark, Kelly James. *Return to Reason.* Grand Rapids, Michigan: William B. Eerdmans, 1990.

Clay, Marjorie and Keith Lehrer, editors. *Knowledge and Skepticism.* Boulder, Colorado: Westview Press, 1989.

Clifford, W. K. *The Common Sense of the Exact Sciences.* New York: Alfred A. Knopf, 1946.

—. *The Ethics of Belief and Other Essays.* Amherst, New York: Prometheus Books, 1999.

—. *Lectures and Essays, Volumes I and II.* London: Macmillan, 1879.

Clifford, W. K. *Lectures and Essays,* second edition. London: Macmillan, 1886.

—. *Mathematical Papers.* London: Macmillan, 1882.

—. *Seeing and Thinking.* London: Macmillan, 1890.

Cockshut, A. O. J. *The Unbelievers.* London: Collins, 1964.

Code, Lorraine. *Epistemic Responsibility.* Hanover, New Hampshire: University Press of New England, 1987.

Cohen, Daniel J. *Equations from God: Pure Mathematics and Victorian Faith.* Baltimore: The Johns Hopkins University Press, 2007.

Conway, Moncure Daniel. *Autobiography: Memories and Experiences of Moncure Daniel Conway.* 2 volumes. Boston and New York: Houghton, Mifflin & Co., 1904.

Copleston, Frederick. *A History of Philosophy, Vol. VIII: Modern Philosophy*. New York: Image Books, 1994.

Croce, Paul Jerome. *Science and Religion in the Era of William James: Eclipse of Certainty, 1820-1880*. Chapel Hill: University of North Carolina Press, 1995.

Darwin, Charles. *The Autobiography of Charles Darwin*. New York: W. W. Norton, 1969.

Davis, Stephen T. "Wishful Thinking and 'The Will to Believe.'" *Transactions of the Charles S. Peirce Society*, Volume 8 (1972): 142-161.

Dole, Andrew and Andrew Chignell, editors. *God and the Ethics of Belief: New Essays in Philosophy of Religion*. New Yorkl; Cambridge University Press, 2005.

Doore, Gary L. "William James and the Ethics of Belief." *Philosophy*, Vol. 38: 353-364.

Double, Richard. *Metaphilosophy and Free Will*. New York: Oxford University Press, 1996.

Eves, H. *Mathematical Circles Squared*. London: Prindle, Weber and Schmidt, 1972.

Farber, Paul Lawrence. *The Temptation of Evolutionary Ethics*. Berkeley: University of California Press, 1994.

Feather, Norman T., editor. *Expectations and Actions*. Hillsdale, New Jersey: Lawrence Erlbaum Associates, 1982.

Feldman, Richard. "Subjective and Objective Justifications in Ethics and Epistemology," *The Monist*, Vol. 71 (1988): 405-419.

Feldman, Richard and Earl Conee. "Evidentialism." *Philosophical Studies*, Vol. 48 (1985): 15-34.

Firth, Roderick. "Chisholm and the Ethics of Belief." *Philosophical Review* (1959): 493-506.

Fisch, Max. *Peirce, Semeiotic, and Pragmatism*. Bloomington, Indiana: Indiana University Press, 1986.

Foley, Richard. *The Theory of Epistemic Rationality*. Cambridge: Harvard University Press, 1986.

Gale, Richard. *On the Nature and Existence of God*. New York: Cambridge University Press, 1993.

—. "Pragmatism and Mysticism: The Divided Self of William James." *Philosophical Perspectives 5, Philosophy of Religion,1991*: 245-265.

—. "William James and the Ethics of Belief. *American Philosophical Quarterly*, Vol. 17 (1980): 1-14.

Garver, Eugene. *For the Sake of Argument: Practical Reasoning, Character, and the Ethics of Belief.*. Chicago: University of Chicago Press, 2004.

Griffin, Nicholas. *Russell's Idealist Apprenticeship.* Oxford: Clarendon Press, 1991.

Haack, Susan. "'The Ethics of Belief' Reconsidered." *The Philosophy of Roderick Chisholm,* edited by Lewis Hahn. Chicago: Open Court, 1997: 129-144.

Handy, Rollo. "Vaihinger and the 'As If'." *Free Inquiry*, Vol. 15, No. 3:45-46.

—. "Vaihinger, Hans." *The Encyclopedia of Philosophy,* edited by Paul Edwards. New York: Macmillan, 1967.

Hare, Peter H. "William Kingdon Clifford." *Encyclopedia of Unbelief,* Gordon Stein, editor. Buffalo: Prometheus Books, 1985: 112-114.

Hare, Peter H. and Edward H. Madden. "William James, Dickinson Miller and C. J. Ducasse on the Ethics of Belief." *Transactions of the Charles S. Peirce Society*, Vol. 4 (1968): 243-252.

Harrison, Jonathan. "Some Reflections on the Ethics of Knowledge and Belief." *Religious Studies,* Vol. 1 (1987): 328-334.

Harvey, Van. "The Ethics of Belief Reconsidered." *The Ethics of Belief Debate,* edited by Gerald D. McCarthy. Atlanta: Scholars Press, 1986: 192-210.

Heil, John. "Doxastic Incontinence." *Mind,* Vol. 93 (1984): 56-70.

—. "Minds Divided." *Mind,* Vol. 98 (1989): 571-583.

Hemlstadter, Richard J. and Bernard Lightman, editors. *Victorian Faith in Crisis.* Stanford, California: Stanford University Press, 1990.

Hester, Marcus, editor. *Faith, Reason, and Skepticism.* Philadelphia: Temple University Press, 1992.

Hoitenga, Dewey J. *Faith and Reason From Plato to Plantinga: An Introduction to Reformed Epistemology.* Albany: State University of New York Press, 1991.

Hollinger, David. "James, Clifford, and the Scientific Conscience." *The Cambridge Companion to William James,* edited by Ruth Anna Putnam. New York: Cambridge University Press, 1997: 63-76.

Holyer, Robert. "Scepticism, Evidentialism and the Parity Argument: A Pascalian Perspective." *Religious Studies*, Vol. 25 (1989): 191-208

Houghton, Walter E. *The Victorian Frame of Mind, 1830-1870.* New Haven: Yale University Press, 1957.

Hudson, Yeager. *The Philosophy of Religion: Selected Readings.* Mountain View, California: Mayfield, 1991.

Hutton, R. H. *Aspects of Religious and Scientific Thought.* London: Macmillan and Co., Limited, 1899.
Huxley, Thomas Henry. *Agnosticism and Christianity and Other Essays.* Amherst, New York: Prometheus Books, 1992.
Irvine, William. *Apes, Angels, and Victorians: Darwin, Huxley, and Evolution.* New York: Time Incorporated, 1963.
James, William. *Will to Believe and Other Essays.* Cambridge: Harvard University Press, 1979.
—. *The Works of William James: Essays, Comments and Reviews.* Cambridge: Harvard University Press, 1987.
Jasper, David and T. R. Wright, editors. *The Critical Spirit and the Will to Believe: Essays in Nineteenth Century Literature and Religion.* London: Macmillan, 1989.
Kaufmann, Walter, editor. *Religion from Tolstoy to Camus.* New Brunswick, New Jersey: Transaction Publishers, 1994.
Kauber, Peter. "The Foundation of James' Ethics of Belief." *Ethics,* Vol. 4 (1974): 151-166.
Kauber, Peter and Peter H. Hare. "The Right and Duty to Will to Believe." *The Canadian Journal of Philosophy*, Vol. 4 (1974): 327-343.
Kaufmann, Walter. *Critique of Religion and Philosophy.* New York: Anchor Books, 1961.
—. *The Faith of a Heretic.* New York: Anchor Books, 1963.
—. *Religion from Tolstoy to Camus.* New Brunswick, New Jersey: Transaction Publishers, 1994.
Kennedy, Eugene. *Believing.* New York: Doubleday and Sons, 1977.
Kenny, Anthony. *Faith and Reason.* New York: Columbia University Press, 1983.
Kessler, Gary E., editor. *Voices of Wisdom: A Multicultural Philosophy Reader.* Belmont, California: Wadsworth, 1992.
Kornblith, Hilary. "Justified Belief and Epistemically Responsible Action." *Philosophical Review*, Vol. 93 (1984): 33-47.
Kvanvig, Jonathan. "The Evidentialist Objection." *American Philosophical Quarterly,* Vol. 20 (1983): 47-55.
Lehrer, Keith, editor. *Analysis and Metaphysics: Essays in Honor of R. M. Chisholm.* Dordrecht, Holland: D. Reidel, 1975.
Levi, Isaac. *The Fixation of Belief and Its Undoing.* Cambridge: Cambridge University Press, 1991.
Levine, George. "Scientific Discourse as an Alternative to Faith." *Victorian Faith in Crisis,* edited by Richard J. Helmstadter and Bernard Lightman. Stanford, California: Stanford University Press, 1990: 220-238.

Levinson, Henry Samuel. *The Religious Investigations of William James.* Chapel Hill: University of North Carolina Press, 1981.
Lewis, C. S. "On Obstinacy in Belief." *The World's Last Stand and Other Essays.* New York: Harcourt Brace Jovanovich, 1960.
Lightman, Bernard. *The Origins of Agnosticism: Victorian Unbelief and the Limits of Knowledge.* Baltimore: Johns Hopkins University Press, 1987.
Livingston, James C. *The Ethics of Belief: An Essay on the Victorian Religious Conscience.* Tallahassee: American Academy of Religion, 1974.
Mackie, J. L. *The Miracle of Theism: Arguments for and Against the Existence of God.* Oxford: Clarendon Press, 1986.
Madigan, Timothy J. "Ethics and Evidentialism: W. K. Clifford and 'The Ethics of Belief.'" *The Journal for the Critical Study of Religion, Ethics, and Society,* Volume 2, Number 1, Spring/Summer 1997: 9-18.
—. "Verily, He Died Too Young: A Comparison of Friedrich Nietzsche and W. K. Clifford." *The NewZealand Rationalist and Humanist,* Spring 1998: 2-7.
—. "The Virtues of 'The Ethics of Belief': W. K. Clifford's Continuing Relevance." *Ethical Record,* Vol. 101, No. 10, November 1996: 12-19.
Mallock, William H. *The New Republic: Or, Culture, Faith and Philosophy in an English Country House.* Gainesville: University of Florida Press, 1950.
Martin, Michael. *Atheism: A Philosophical Justification.* Philadelphia: Temple University Press, 1990.
—. *The Case Against Christianity.* Philadelphia: Temple University Press, 1991.
Martin, Mike W. *Self-Deception and Morality.* Lawrence, Kansas: University Press of Kansas, 1986.
Mavrodes, George, editor. *The Rationality of Belief in God.* Englewood Cliffs, New Jersey: Prentice-Hall, 1970.
McCarthy, Gerald D., editor. *The Ethics of Belief Debate.* Atlanta: Scholars Press, 1986.
McGrath, Alister. *The Twilight of Atheism.* New York: Doubleday, 2004.
Meiland, Jack. "What Ought We To Believe? Or, The Ethics of Belief Revisited." *American Philosophical Quarterly,* Vol. 17 (1980): 15-24.
Mill, John Stuart. *Theism.* New York: The Bobbs-Merrill Company, 1957.
Miller, Ed. L. *God and Reason: An Invitation to Philosophical Theology.* Englewood Cliffs, New Jersey: Prentice-Hall, 1995.

Miller, J. Hillis. *The Disappearance of God.* Cambridge: Cambridge University Press, 1963.
Misak, C. J. *Truth and the End of Inquiry.* Oxford: Clarendon Press, 1991.
Monk, Ray. *Bertrand Russell: The Spirit of Solitude.* London: Jonathan Cape, 1996.
Montmarquet, James A. *Epistemic Virtue and Doxastic Responsibility.* Lanham, Maryland: Rowman and Littlefield, 1993.
—. "Justification: Ethical and Epistemic." *Mind,* Vol. 96 (1987): 482-497.
Moser, Paul. *Empirical Justification.* Dordrecht, the Netherlands: D. Reidel, 1985.
—. *Knowledge and Evidence.* Cambridge: Cambridge University Press, 1989.
—. "Knowledge Without Evidence." *Philosophia*, Vol. 15: 109-116.
Muyskens, James L. *The Sufficiency of Hope: The Conceptual Foundation of Religion.* Philadelphia: Temple University Press, 1979.
Nathan, N. M. L. "Evidential Insatiability." *Analysis*, Vol. 47, No. 2, March 1987: 110-115.
Nathanson, James. "Nonevidential Reasons for Belief: A Jamesian View." *Philosophy and Phenomenological Research* (1982): 572-580.
Newman, James R. "William Kingdon Clifford." *Scientific American*, Vol. 188 (1953): 78-84.
Newton, C. A. da Costa and Steven French. "Belief, Contradiction and the Logic of Self-Deception." *American Philosophical Quarterly,* Vol. 27 (1990): 179-197.
Nickerson, Sylvia and Nicholas Griffin. "Russell, Clifford, Whitehead and Differential Geometry." *Russell: The Journal of the Bertrand Russell Society,* Vol. 28, No. 1, Summer 2008: 20-38.
Nietzsche, Friedrich. *Human, All Too Human: A Book for Free Spirits,* translated by Marion Faber. Lincoln, Nebraska: University of Nebraska Press, 1996.
—. *The Portable Nietzsche,* translated by Walter Kaufmann. New York: Penguin, 1968.
North, John D. "William Kingdon Clifford." *Dictionary of Scientific Biography*, Charles Coulston Gillespie, editor. New York:
Charles Scribner's Sons, 1971: 43-45.
O'Connell, Robert J. "'The Will to Believe' and James's 'Deontological Streak". *Transactions of the Charles S. Peirce Society,* Vol. XXVIII (1992): 781-831.
—. *William James on the Courage to Believe.* New York: Fordham University Press, 1984.

Oppenheimer, Janet. *The Other World: Spiritualism and Psychical Research in England, 1850-1914.* Cambridge, England: Cambridge University Press, 1985.

Parsons, Keith. *God and the Burden of Proof.* Buffalo: Prometheus Books, 1989.

Passmore, John. "Hume and the Ethics of Belief." *David Hume: Bicentenary Paper,* G. P. Morice, editor. Edinburgh: Edinburgh University Press, 1977: 46-58.

—. *Hume's Intentions,* third edition. London: Duckworth, 1980.

—. *A Hundred Years of Philosophy.* Baltimore: Penguin Books, 1968.

Pearson, Karl. *The Grammar of Science.* London: J. M. Dent & Sons, 1951.

Peirce, Charles. *Philosophical Writings of Peirce,* Justus Buchler, editor. New York: Dover, 1955.

Perry, Ralph Barton. *In The Spirit of William James.* Indianapolis: Indiana University Press, 1958.

Peterson, Houston. *Huxley: Prophet of Science.* London: Longmans, Green, 1932.

Peterson, Michael, William Hasker, Bruce Reichenbach and David Basinger, editors. *Reason and Religious Belief.* Oxford: Oxford University Press, 1991.

Plantinga, Alvin. "Rationality and Religious Belief." *Contemporary Philosophy of Religion,* Steven M. Cahn and David Schatz, editors. Oxford: Oxford University Press, 1982: 134-146.

—. "Self-Portrait." *Alvin Plantinga,* edited by James E. Tomerlin and Peter van Inwagen. Boston: D. Reidel, 1985.

—. *Warrant: The Current Debate.* Oxford: Oxford University Press, 1993.

—. *Warrant and Proper Function.* Oxford: Oxford University Press, 1993.

Pojman, Louis P., editor. *Introduction to Philosophy: Classical and Contemporary Readings.* Belmont, California: Wadsworth, 1991.

—. editor. *Philosophy: The Quest for Truth,* Second Edition. Belmont, California: Wadsworth Publishing Company, 1992.

—. *Religious Belief and the Will.* London: Routledge and Kegan Paul, 1986.

Pollock, Frederick. *Remembrances of an Ancient Victorian.* London: John Murray, 1933.

Price, H. H. *Belief.* London: George Allen & Unwin, 1969.

Pyle, Andrew, editor. *Agnosticism: Contemporary Responses to Spencer and Huxley.* Bristol, England: Thoemmes Press, 1995.

Pruyser, Paul. *Between Belief and Unbelief.* New York: Harper and Row, 1974.

Quinton, Anthony. "British Philosophy." *Encyclopedia of Philosophy*, edited by Paul Edwards. New York: Macmillan, 1967: 385-390.
—. *From Wodehouse to Wittgenstein*. New York: St Martin's Press, 1998.
Rescher, Nicholas. *Pascal's Wager*. Notre Dame, Indiana: University of Notre Dame Press, 1985.
Richards, R. L. "The Reception of a Mathematical Theory: Non-Euclidean Geometry in England, 1868-1883". *Natural Order: Historical Studies of Scientific Culture,* edited by Barry Barnes and Steven Shapin. London: Sage Publications, 1979: 140-154.
Rorty, Richard. "Religious Faith, Intellectual Responsibility, and Romance." *Cambridge Companion to William James,* edited by Ruth Anna Putnam. New York: Cambridge University Press, 1997: 78-89.
Ruse, Michael. "William Kingdon Clifford." *Oxford Companion to Philosophy,* edited by Ted Hondrich. Oxford: Oxford University Press, 1937: 136-137.
Russell, Bertrand. *Bertrand Russell on God and Religion*. Amherst, New York: Prometheus Books, 1986.
—. *Collected Papers of Bertrand Russell*. New York: Routledge, 1997.
—. *Ideas and Beliefs of the Victorians*. London: Sylvan Press, 1949.
—. *Why I Am Not a Christian and Other Essays*. New York: Simon and Schuster, 1957.
Ryan, Alan. *Bertrand Russell: A Political Life*. New York: Hill and Wang, 1988.
Schiller, F. C. S. *Problems of Belief.* London: Hodder and Stoughton, 1926.
Schlesinger, George. "Theism and Evidence." *International Journal of Philosophy and Religion,* Vol. 21: 179-184.
Shipka, Thomas and Arthur J. Minton, editors. *Philosophy: Paradox and Discovery,* fourth edition. New York: McGraw-Hill, 1996.
Simmons, Howard. "Nathan on Evidential Insatiability." *Analysis*, Vol. 48, January 1988: 57-59.
Smokler, Howard. "William Kingdon Clifford." *The Encyclopedia of Philosophy*, edited by Paul Edwards. New York: Macmillan, 1966: 123-125.
Sober, Elliot. *Core Questions in Philosophy*. New York: Macmillan, 1990.
Soffer, Reba. *Ethics and Society in England: The Revolution in the Social Sciences, 1870-1914*. Berkeley: University of California Press, 1978.
Solomon, Robert C. "God and Rationality." *The Canadian Journal of Philosophy,* Vol. 4 (1974): 283-292.
Somervell, D. C. *English Thought in the Nineteenth Century*. New York: David McKay, 1965.

Stephen, Leslie. "William Kingdon Clifford." *The Dictionary of National Biography,* Vol. IV. London: Oxford University Press, 1968: 538-541.

Stevenson, J. T. "On Doxastic Responsibility." *Analysis and Metaphysics,* Keith Lehrer, editor. Dordrecht, Holland: D. Reidel, 1975: 239-251.

Stewart, David, editor. *Exploring the Philosophy of Religion.* Englewood Cliffs, New Jersey: Prentice-Hall, 1992.

Stich, Stephen. *The Fragmentation of Reason.* Cambridge: MIT Press, 1991

Stocker, Michael. "Responsibility Especially for Beliefs." *Mind,* Vol. 91 (1982): 398-417.

Stump, Eleanor and Norman Kretzmann. "Theologically Unfashionable Philosophy." *Faith and Philosophy,* Vol. 7 (1990): 329-339.

Suckiel, Ellen Kappy. "Adequate Evidence and 'The Will to Believe'." *Transactions of the Charles S. Peirce Society,* Vol. 15 (1979): 322-339.

—. *Heaven's Champion: William James's Philosophy of Religion.* Notre Dame, Indiana; University of Notre Dame Press, 1996.

Sutherland, Stuart. *Irrationality: Why We Don't Think Straight!* New Brunswick, New Jersey: Rutgers University Press, 1994.

Taliaferro, Charles. *Evidence and Faith.* Cambridge: Cambridge University Press, 2005.

Tomberlin, James E., editor. *Philosophical Perspectives 5: Philosophy of Religion.* Atascadero, California: Ridgeview, 1991.

Turner, Frank Miller. *Between Science and Religion: The Reaction to Scientific Naturalism in Late Victorian England.* New Haven: Yale University Press, 1974.

Vaihinger, Hans. *The Philosophy of "As If": A System of the Theoretical, Practical and Religious Fictions of Mankind..*Translated by C. K. Ogden. New York: Harcourt, Brace & Company, 1925.

Van Inwagen, Peter. "Quam Dilecta." *God and the Philosophers.* New York: Oxford University Press, 1994.

Wainwright, William. "William James and Rationality of Religious Belief." *Religious Studies,* Vol. 7 (1991): 232-240.

Wernham, James C. S. *James's Will-to-Believe Doctrine: A Heretical View.* Montreal: McGill-Queen's University Press, 1987.

Wisdo, David. "The Fragility of Faith: Toward a Critique of Reformed Epistemology." *Religious Studies,* Vol. 24 (1988): 365-374.

Wilson, A.N. *God's Funeral.* New York: W. W. Norton & Company, 1999.

Wisdo, David. *The Life of Irony and the Ethics of Belief.* Albany: State University of New York Press, 1992.

—. "Self-Deception and the Ethics of Belief." *The Journal of Value Inquiry,* Vol. 25 (1991): 339-347.

Wittgenstein, Ludwig. *On Certainty.* New York: Harper and Row, 1969.

Wolterstorff, "The Migration of the Theistic Arguments: From Natural Theology to Evidentialist Apologetics." *Rationality, Religious Belief, and Moral Commitment: New Essays in thePhilosophy of Religion,* edited by Robert Audi and William J. Wainwright. Ithaca, New York: Cornell University Press, 1986: 35-46.

Wood, Allen W. *Unsettling Obligations: Essays on Reason, Reality and the Ethics of Belief.* Stanford: CSLI Publications, 2002.

Zagzebski, Linda, editor. *Rational Faith: Catholic Responses to Reformed Epistemology.* Notre Dame: University of Notre Dame Press, 1993.

—. *Virtues of the Mind.* New York: Cambridge University Press, 1996.

INDEX

A
agnosticism, 14, 17, 21-23, 62, 63, 66, 95-96
Anderson, Douglas, 111
Andersson, Stefan, 8
Apostles, 30
Arnold Matthew, 3, 41-42, 44, 85, 86, 94-95
"as-if" methodology, 1, 4-5, 67, 174-179
Audi, Robert, 149-152

B
Bacon, Francis, 10
Bain, James, 62-63
Balfour, Arthur James, 7, 34
Bell, E. T., 53, 55, 57
Bentham, Jeremy, 13, 34, 117, 171
Berman, David, 12, 76
Bird, Graham, 99, 101
Brown, Alan Willard, 18, 19, 85, 86, 90, 92, 185-186

C
Cambridge University, 29-30, 51
Catholic Church, 9, 19, 45, 46
Chisholm, Roderick, 144-145, 159, 168
Clifford, Lucy, 36, 43, 44, 46-50, 53, 93
Clifford, W. K.
  as freethought activist, 42-45
  "Body and Mind", 61, 71
  Common Sense of the Exact Sciences, 27, 52-54, 57-58, 120, 121, 124, 131
  death of, 48-49
  "Decline of Religious Belief, The", 114
  "Ethics of Religion, The", 25, 67, 94, 115
  evolutionary ethics and evolutionary epistemology and, 182-185
  illnesses of, 37-38, 43, 46-50
  interest in psychology, 35-36, 57-65
  mathematical contributions, 50-57
  Metaphysical Society member, 1, 7-9
  "Mr. Saunders" in *The New Republic,* 39-42
  "On Some of the Conditions of Mental Development", 31, 51, 61
  "On the Nature of Things-in-Themselves", 63, 67
  "On the Scientific Basis of Morality", 61, 67
  "Philosophy of the Pure Sciences, The", 56
  "Unseen Universe, The", 40, 71
  Victorian Crisis of Faith and, 9, 15, 30
Code, Lorraine, 4, 133, 161-163, 165, 172, 178-179
Coleridge, Samuel Taylor, 76
Congress of Liberal Thinkers, 44-45
Conway, Moncure, 34, 43, 46, 48, 64
Copleston, Frederick, S. J., 112-113

D
Darwin, Charles, 16-17, 24, 32, 57, 64, 68, 95, 117, 119, 178
Dewey, John, 96
Double, Richard, 4, 8, 133, 143-144

E
Edwards, Paul, 129
Einstein, Albert, 57-58
English Civil War, 10-11
"Ethics of Belief" essay, 1, 4, 7, 8-10, 27, 29, 50, 68, 69, 71, 73-84, 92, 105-109, 111, 113, 123, 128, 165, 169, 180
"Ethics of Belief" lecture, 21, 38, 43, 74
"Ethics of Belief" (Hume), 11-12, 183-184
evidentialism, 1, 3, 8, 10, 23, 74, 77, 151, 158, 165-166
evolution, 15, 30

F
Farber, Paul Lawrence, 117
Fisch, Max, 107
Fortnightly Review, 40

G
Gale, Richard, 4, 7-8, 106, 133, 152-153, 171
Galton, Francis, 17, 124
Gladstone, William, 7, 36, 119
Griffin, Nicholas, 125, 127
Grote Club, 32

H
Haack, Susan, 4, 133, 153-157, 165, 170
Haeckel, Ernst, 16
Handy, Rollo, 177
Harvey, Van, 167-168, 184
Highgate Cemetery, 48
Hollinger, David A., 105-106, 107, 111-112
Houghton, Walter F., 15, 23
Hume, David, 1, 11, 24, 78, 167, 183-184
Hutton, R. H., 3, 18, 90, 134, 167, 177
Huxley, T. H., 3, 7, 8, 16, 20-25, 32, 34, 38, 41-42, 43, 45, 47, 58, 91, 95

I
Irvine, William, 21

J
James, Henry, 36
James, William, 3, 8, 13-14, 27, 61, 64, 77, 78, 86, 96, 97-107, 110, 111, 135, 137-142, 154, 156-157, 165, 172, 174-175, 178-180, 181, 185, 186
Jowett, Benjamin, 38-39

K
Kant, Immanuel, 29, 57, 64, 66, 74, 117, 171
Kaufmann, Walter, 4, 133, 137-141, 146, 169
King's College, London, 28
Knowles, Sir James, 1, 18-19, 86

L
Levine, George, 8, 69, 183
Lewis, C.S., 4, 133-137, 142
Lightman, Bernard, 66-67, 76
Livingston, James C., 15, 24, 86, 89, 91, 96
Lobachevski, Nikolai, 2, 54, 56, 57
Locke, John, 1, 10, 11, 91

M
MacIntyre, Alasdair, 172, 173
Mackie, J. L., 4, 133, 141-143
Mallock, W. H., 38-42
Manning, Henry Edward Cardinal, 7, 18, 36, 119
Marshall, Alfred, 32
Martin, Michael, 4, 133, 144-145, 165
Martineau, James, 18
Maurice, F. D., 7
Mavrodes, George, 103-105
Maxwell, James Clerk, 30, 33
Mazzini, Guiseppe, 9
McCarthy, Gerald, 10-12
Metaphysical Society, 1, 7-9, 18-25, 34, 36-38, 43, 59, 62, 63, 66, 73,

79, 85-86, 93, 125, 167, 175, 185
Mill, John Stuart, 1, 12-14, 19, 25, 76, 117, 126, 171
Milton, John, 76
"mind-stuff", 59-60, 61, 65, 122
Monk, Ray, 126, 127
Morrell, Ottoline, 127

N
Newman, James R., 28, 29
Newman, John Henry Cardinal, 19, 85, 86, 92, 122
Nietzsche, Friedrich, 3, 76, 95, 112-120, 182, 185
North, John D., 30, 50

O
"overbeliefs", 178-181

P
Passmore, John, 11, 122, 183
Pearson, Karl, 3, 52-55, 120-124, 157
Peirce, Charles, 3, 107-112, 150, 160, 165, 166
Plantinga, Alvin, 4, 133, 147-152, 167
Pollock, Frederick, 2, 19, 27-28, 33, 38, 43, 49, 55, 56, 65, 119, 122
Popper, Karl, 158
Price, H. H., 168
Pritchard, Charles, 18
Pyle, Andrew, 25, 74

Q
Quine, W. V. O., 166
Quinton, Anthony, 4, 133, 157-161

R
Rescher, Nicholas, 177
Riemann, Bernhard, 2, 54, 56, 57
Robertson, G. Croom, 62-63
Romanes, George John, 95
Rorty, Richard, 4, 89, 133, 153-155
Ruse, Michael, 64, 68

Ruskin, John, 36, 38
Russell, Bertrand, 3, 54, 59, 80, 96, 124-131, 143, 149
Ryan, Alan, 130-131

S
Sidgwick, Henry, 32, 34
Smith, Barbara Herrnstein, 169-170
Smith, H. J. Stephen, 47, 51
Smokler, Howard, 57, 62
Society for Psychical Research, 34
Soffer, Reba N., 53, 62, 63-64, 70, 123, 124
Spencer, Herbert, 19, 23, 64, 67, 74, 82, 90
spiritualism, 34-35
Stanley, Arthur, 18
Stanley, Augusta, 19
Stephen, Fitzjames, 91-92, 93
Stephen, Leslie, 2, 3, 8, 43, 47-48, 52, 86, 91-94, 122
Suckiel, Ellen Kappy, 98
Sunday Lecture Society, 42
Sutherland, Stuart, 181-182

T
Taylor, Richard, 14
Tennyson, Alfred Lord, 7, 18, 36
Thirty-Nine Articles, 31-32
Turner, Frank Miller, 16, 95

U
University College, London, 3, 7, 33-34, 46-47, 53, 69, 120, 121

V
Vaihinger, Hans, 175-178
Van Inwagen, Peter, 4, 133, 145-147, 169
Victorian Crisis of Faith, 1, 9, 14-16, 30
Voltaire, 44, 79-80, 146

W
Ward, W. G., 3, 18, 20-21, 87-90, 92, 134, 147, 151, 167, 177, 178

Wernham, James C.S., 102-103, 105
Wisdo, David, 120
Wittgenstein, Ludwig, 148, 150, 166

Wolterstorff, Nicholas, 10

Z
Zeno's Paradox, 165